The Failure of Capitalist Production

THE FAILURE OF CAPITALIST PRODUCTION

Underlying Causes of the Great Recession

Andrew Kliman

PlutoPress
www.plutobooks.com

First published 2012 by Pluto Press
345 Archway Road, London N6 5AA

www.plutobooks.com

Distributed in the United States of America exclusively by
Palgrave Macmillan, a division of St. Martin's Press LLC,
175 Fifth Avenue, New York, NY 10010

British Library Cataloguing in Publication Data
A catalogue record for this book is available from the British Library

ISBN   978 0 7453 3240 6   Hardback
ISBN   978 0 7453 3239 0   Paperback

Library of Congress Cataloging in Publication Data applied for

10   9   8   7   6   5   4   3

Designed and produced for Pluto Press by Chase Publishing Services Ltd
Typeset from disk by Stanford DTP Services, Northampton, England
Simultaneously printed digitally by CPI Antony Rowe, Chippenham, UK and
Edwards Bros in the United States of America

*In memory of Ted Kliman (1929–2009)
and Chris Harman (1942–2009)*

For Jesse

For Anne

Contents

List of Tables

List of Figures

List of Abbreviations

AIG	American International Group
BEA	Bureau of Economic Analysis
BLS	Bureau of Labor Statistics
CBO	Congressional Budget Office
CPI-U	consumer price index for all urban consumers
CPI-U-RS	CPI Research Series Using Current Methods
CPI-W	consumer price index for urban wage earners and clerical workers
Fed	Federal Reserve System
GDP	Gross Domestic Product
IMF	International Monetary Fund
IPE&S	information-processing equipment and software
LIBOR	London Inter-Bank Offered Rate
LTFRP	law of the tendential fall in the rate of profit
MELT	monetary expression of labor-time
NIPA	National Income and Product Accounts
OECD	Organization for Economic Cooperation and Development
OPEC	Organization of Petroleum Exporting Countries
PCE	personal consumption expenditures
S&Ls	savings and loan associations
S&P	Standard and Poor's
TARP	Troubled Assets Relief Program
TSSI	temporal single-system interpretation

Acknowledgments

I thank everyone who provided expert advice on technical matters and everyone who offered comments on the papers, book reviews, talks, interviews, and draft manuscript that eventually turned into this book. I have benefited enormously from their feedback. It not only improved the book significantly but guided the direction of my research in crucial ways. I would like to thank each one by name, but unfortunately I cannot. Even were they not too numerous to list, they include many audience members and reviewers whose names I do not know. If you are among them, please know that the difference between what you originally read or heard and the ideas as they appear in the final text is a sign of my debt and gratitude to you.

I thank my departmental colleagues at Pace University, who have been very supportive of my research. I also thank the university's Dyson College of Arts and Sciences, which granted me released time to pursue my research on profitability trends and provided a research grant that enabled me to purchase a supersized computer monitor. The monitor has made the work of data analysis much less onerous and more productive.

None of the book is a republication of previously published works of mine, but I have drawn freely on those listed below. I thank the following publishers for allowing me to do so:

- The Commune, which published "The Economic Crisis: An interview with Andrew Kliman" as pamphlet no. 4, November 2008.
- The Institute for Social Sciences of Gyeongsang National University, which published "Masters of Words: A reply to Michel Husson on the character of the latest economic crisis," in *Marxism 21*, vol. 7, no. 2, Summer 2010.
- *International Socialism*, which published "A Crisis for the Centre of the System," in issue no. 120, October 2008, and "Pinning the Blame on the System," a review of Chris Harman's *Zombie Capitalism*, in issue no. 124, September 2009.
- Lexington Books, which published *Reclaiming Marx's "Capital": A refutation of the myth of inconsistency* in 2007.

- Marxist-Humanist Initiative, which published "The Persistent Fall in Profitability Underlying the Current Crisis: New temporalist evidence" in March 2010 and, in *With Sober Senses*, its online publication: "On the Roots of the Current Economic Crisis and Some Proposed Solutions," April 17, 2009; "How (Not) to Respond to the Economic Crisis," May 5, 2009; "Cherry Picking Peaks and Troughs," May 13, 2009; "Appearance and Essence: Neoliberalism, financialization, and the underlying crisis of capitalist production," May 17, 2010, and "Lies, Damned Lies, and Underconsumptionist Statistics," September 16, 2010.
- *Megafoni*, an online journal, which published Joel Kaitila, Lauri Lahikainen, and Jukka Peltokoski's interview, "'Kukaan ei tiedä, onko kriisi ohi'—Andrew Klimanin haastattelu," on November 23, 2009.
- Palgrave Macmillan, which published "Production and Economic Crisis: A temporal perspective," in Richard Westra and Alan Zuege (eds), *Value and the World Economy Today* in 2003.
- Razón y Revolución, which published Juan Kornblihtt's interview, "Entrevista al Economista Estadounidense Andrew Kliman," in *El Aromo* no. 50, July 2009.
- Taylor & Francis, which published "'The Destruction of Capital' and the Current Economic Crisis," in *Socialism & Democracy*, vol. 23, no. 2, July 2009.
- The Workers' Liberty website, which published Martin Thomas' interview, "Andrew Kliman—The level of debt is astronomical," on January 12, 2009.

Special thanks go to Anne for her invaluable editorial advice and careful copy-editing, and for her intellectual, professional, and personal support, without which neither this nor my prior book could have been written.

New York City
June 2011

1
Introduction

A tremendous amount has already been written on the financial crisis that erupted in 2007, the Panic of 2008, and the Great Recession to which they led. Many competent and insightful analyses of these events and the factors that triggered them are widely available elsewhere. Do we really need yet one more book on the subject? Probably not. This book therefore focuses more on the underlying conditions that set the stage for the crisis and recession, and less on the proximate causes of these events.

Now, explanations of crises and slumps that appeal to underlying conditions are frequently less than illuminating. To take one key example, the recent financial crisis is often attributed to greed.[1] Yet as a popular saying goes, blaming the crisis on greed is like blaming an airplane crash on gravity. Gravity is always there, but airplanes do not always crash. The underlying conditions that we want to know about are not permanent conditions like gravity, but specific, contingent conditions that made a crash more likely than otherwise, or more likely than usual.

I will therefore not say much about greed, either in general or as it has been shaped by capitalism. Nor will I say much about capitalism as such. I do not believe that capitalism is here to stay in the way that gravity is, but it has been around for hundreds of years, so blaming the crisis on capitalism as such does little to illuminate why a major crisis erupted a few years ago rather than in the 1960s. It is not incorrect to blame the recent crisis on the nature of capitalism—just as it is not incorrect to blame the crisis on greed. The problem is simply that these explanations are not satisfying; they do not tell us what we want to know.

The "failure of capitalist production" in this book's title is therefore a reference, not to capitalism in general, but to specific and unresolved problems within the capitalist system of value production since the 1970s. I will argue that the economy never fully recovered from the recessions of the mid-1970s and early 1980s. I will put forward an explanation of why it did not. I will argue that the persistently frail condition of capitalist production was among the causes of the financial crisis. And, most importantly, I will argue that it set the stage for the Great Recession and "the new normal," the state of not-quite-recession that we now endure. In light of the frailty of capitalist production, the recession and its consequences were waiting to happen.

Just as more lay behind the Great Depression than the stock market crash and the bubble that preceded it, more lies behind the Great Recession and "the new normal" than the financial crisis and home-price bubble of the 2000s. As Paul Krugman and Robin Wells (2010) noted in an essay published 15 months after the recession officially ended in the U.S.:

> … [there] hasn't been much of a recovery. If the fundamental problem lay with a crisis of confidence in the banking system, why hasn't a restoration of banking confidence brought a return to strong economic growth? The likely answer is that banks were only part of the problem.

There is also reason to doubt that the financial crisis by itself—in the absence of longer-term conditions that reduced the economy's ability to withstand shocks—would have triggered such a severe recession. The actual declines in production, employment, and income that took place, large as they were, are not true measures of the U.S. economy's inability to absorb the shock of the financial crisis. The true measures are the declines that would have taken place if the Treasury had not borrowed madly to prop up the economy. In the first two years that followed the collapse of Lehman Brothers, it borrowed an additional $3.9 trillion, which caused its total indebtedness to rise by more than 40 percent. The additional debt was equal to 13.5 percent of the $28.6 trillion of Gross Domestic Product (GDP) that was produced during these two years. Yet despite the enormous increase in debt and the additional spending and tax cuts financed by means of it, real GDP at the end of the two years remained less than at the pre-recession peak. In contrast, the Treasury's debt *declined* in the two years between mid-1929 and mid-1931, and by mid-1932 it was still only 15 percent greater than in mid-1929. It is likely that the latest recession would have been almost as bad as the Great Depression, maybe even worse, if the government had refrained from running up the public debt.

This book focuses on the United States, partly because much of it consists of a detailed analysis of data. The data that are available for other countries' economies are not as complete and often not as reliable as data for the U.S. economy. The other reason why I focus on the U.S. is that it was the epicenter of the latest crisis. It cannot be automatically assumed that the analysis of the U.S. case applies to other countries. But since the U.S. was the epicenter—since, in other words, the crisis erupted elsewhere because it first erupted in the U.S. and then spread—the relative lack of discussion of other economies does not reduce the adequacy of this book's analysis of the long-term economic difficulties underlying the crisis and slump.

MAIN THESIS

The rate of profit—that is, profit as a percentage of the amount of money invested—has a persistent tendency to fall. However, this tendency is reversed by what John Fullarton, Karl Marx, and others have called the "destruction of capital"—losses caused by declining values of financial and physical capital assets or the destruction of the physical assets themselves. Paradoxically, these processes also restore profitability and thereby set the stage for a new boom, such as the boom that followed the Great Depression and World War II.

During the global economic slumps of the mid-1970s and early 1980s, however, much less capital value was destroyed than had been destroyed during the Depression and the following World War. The difference is largely a consequence of economic policy. The amount of capital value that was destroyed during the Depression was far greater than advocates of laissez-faire policies had expected, and the persistence of severely depressed conditions led to significant radicalization of working people. Policymakers have not wanted this to happen again, so they now intervene with monetary and fiscal policies in order to prevent the full-scale destruction of capital value. This explains why subsequent downturns in the economy have not been nearly as severe as the Depression. But since so much less capital value was destroyed during the 1970s and early 1980s than was destroyed in the 1930s and early 1940s, the decline in the rate of profit was not reversed. And because it was not reversed, profitability remained at too low a level to sustain a new boom.

The chain of causation is easy to understand. The *generation* of profit is what makes possible the *investment* of profit. So, not surprisingly, the relative lack of profit led to a persistent decline in the rate of capital accumulation (new investment in productive assets as a percentage of the existing volume of capital). Sluggish investment has, in turn, resulted in sluggish growth of output and income.

All this led to ever more serious debt problems. Sluggish income growth made it more difficult for people to repay their debts. The decline in the rate of profit, together with reductions in corporate income tax rates that served to prop up corporations' after-tax rate of profit, led to greatly reduced tax revenue and mounting government budget deficits and debt. And the government has repeatedly attempted to manage the relative stagnation of the economy by pursuing policies that encourage excessive expansion of debt. These policies have artificially boosted profitability and economic growth, but in an unsustainable manner that has repeatedly led to burst bubbles and debt crises. The latest crisis was the most serious and acute of these.

*   *   *

Although the financial crisis is over, and the recession officially ended two years ago, the debt problems persist—within the European Union, they are now critical—as do massive unemployment and the severe slump in home prices. These problems seem to be the main factors that have kept the U.S. economy from growing rapidly since the end of the recession. For a long time, Americans were willing to increase their borrowing and reduce their saving, since they believed that increases in the prices of their houses and shares of stock were an adequate substitute for real cash savings. But those increases have vanished, and many people are worried about whether they will hold on to their jobs and homes, so they have begun to borrow less and save more. And because of continuing debt, unemployment, and housing-sector problems—and probably because of concerns that they will suffer additional losses on existing assets and ultimately have to report losses that they have not yet "recognized"—lenders are less willing to lend. The low level of borrowing/lending has caused spending and economic growth to be sluggish.

I certainly do not advocate full-scale destruction of capital value—or any other policies intended to make capitalism work better; it is not a system I favor. Yet the destruction of capital value would indeed be a solution to the systemic problems I have outlined—unless it led to revolution or the collapse of the system. A massive wave of business and personal bankruptcies, bank failures, and write-downs of losses would solve the debt overhang. New owners could take over businesses without assuming their debts and purchase them at fire-sale prices. This would raise the potential rate of profit, and it would therefore set the stage for a new boom.

If this does not happen, I believe that the economy will continue to be relatively stagnant and prone to crisis.

THE CONVENTIONAL LEFT ACCOUNT

This is not a book that I set out to write. At the start of 2009, I began the empirical research that eventually became the core of the book, but at the time I had a different, and very limited, objective in mind. However, I soon discovered things that impelled me to dig deeper and widen the scope of my research.

To understand the significance of what I gradually learned, one needs to be familiar with the conventional wisdom on the left regarding recent U.S. economic history and its relationship to the recent crisis and recession. What follows is a brief summary of the conventional account. (Later in the book, I will quote various authors and provide citations.)

According to conventional wisdom, the rate of profit fell from the start of the post-World War II boom through the downturns of the 1970s and early 1980s. But by that time, economic policy had become "neoliberal" (free-market), and this led to increased exploitation of workers. Consequently, U.S. workers are not being paid more, in real (inflation-adjusted) terms, than they were paid decades ago, and their share of income has fallen. The increase in exploitation led to a significant rebound in the rate of profit. Normally, this would have caused the rate of accumulation to rise as well, but this time it did not.

The conventional account blames the "financialization" of the economy for the failure of the rate of accumulation to rebound. It holds that financialization, another component of neoliberalism, has induced companies to invest a larger share of their profits in financial instruments, and a smaller share in the productive capital assets (factories, machinery, and so on) that make the "real" economy grow. As a result, economic growth has been weaker during the last several decades than it was in the first few decades that followed World War II, and this factor, along with additional borrowing that enabled working people to maintain their standard of living despite the drop in their share of income, has led to long-term debt problems. These debt problems, and other phenomena that also stem from financialization, are said to be the underlying causes of the latest economic crisis and slump.

This was not an interpretation of recent economic history that I found particularly appealing, and I knew that proponents of the conventional wisdom mis-measure the rate of profit. But I had no reason to believe that their measures were *overstating* the rise in profitability instead of understating it. Nor did I doubt that their other empirical claims were based on fact. Yet in the course of my research, I found that:

- U.S. corporations' rate of profit did not recover in a sustained manner after the early 1980s. Their before-tax rate of profit has been trendless since the early 1980s and a rate of profit based on a broader concept of profit, more akin to what Marx meant by "surplus-value," continued to decline.
- Neoliberalism and financialization have not caused U.S. corporations to invest a smaller share of their profit in production. Between 1981 and 2001, they devoted a larger share of their profit to productive investment than they did between 1947 and 1980 (and the post-2001 drop in this share is a statistical fluke). What accounts for the decline in the rate of accumulation is instead the decline in the rate of profit.
- U.S. workers are not being paid less in real terms than they were paid decades ago. Their real pay has risen. And their share of the nation's income has not fallen. It is higher now than it was in 1960, and it has been stable since 1970.

These findings do no damage to the claim that a long-term buildup of debt is an underlying cause of the recent crisis and subsequent problems. However, all of the other causal claims in the conventional leftist account fall to the ground.

The conventional wisdom implies that the latest economic crisis was an *irreducibly financial* one. Of course, a financial crisis triggered the recession, and phenomena specific to the financial sector (excessive leverage, risky mortgage lending, and so on) were among its important causes. But what I mean by "irreducibly financial" is that conventional wisdom on the left holds that the recent crisis and slump are ultimately rooted in the financialization of capitalism and macroeconomic difficulties resulting from financialization. The persistent frailty of capitalist *production* supposedly has nothing to do with these macroeconomic difficulties. Indeed, on this view, the capitalist system of production has not been frail at all, since the rate of profit, the key measure of its performance, recovered substantially after the early 1980s.

The political implications of this controversy are profound. If the long-term causes of the crisis and recession are irreducibly financial, we can prevent the recurrence of such crises by doing away with neoliberalism and "financialized capitalism." It is unnecessary to do away with the capitalist system of production—that is, production driven by the aim of ceaselessly expanding "value," or abstract wealth. Thus, what the crisis has put on the agenda is the need for policies such as financial regulation, activist ("Keynesian") fiscal and monetary policies, and perhaps financial-sector nationalization, rather than a change in the character of the socioeconomic system.[2]

If, on the other hand, a persistent fall in the rate of profit is an important (albeit indirect) cause of the crisis and recession, as this book argues, then these policy proposals are not solutions. At best, they will delay the next crisis. And artificial government stimulus that produces unsustainable growth threatens to make the next crisis worse when it comes. The economy will remain sluggish unless and until profitability is restored, or the character of the socioeconomic system changes.

HOW THIS BOOK DIFFERS

Quite a few books have put forward different leftist perspectives on the recent crisis and recession. Many of them focus, as have most other books on these topics, on the proximate causes of these events. This book differs from them, as I noted above, in that it focuses on the long-term, underlying conditions that enabled the financial crisis to trigger an especially deep and long recession, and one with persistent after-effects.

Yet a fair number of other books from the left also focus on the underlying causes. Some of them—such as Foster and Magdoff (2009), Harvey (2010), Duménil and Lévy (2011), and McNally (2011)—put forward some version of the conventional leftist account discussed above. And some, like the works by Foster-Magdoff and Harvey, also stress the supposed facts that workers' share of total income declined and that this led to a lack of demand that was covered over by rising debt. From such a perspective, the crisis appears not to be a crisis of capitalism, but a crisis of a specifically neoliberal and financialized *form* of capitalism. I do not think the facts are consonant with these views, and I trust that disinterested readers will find, at minimum, that this book's empirical analyses call such views into question.

On the other hand, some other books from the left have appeared that regard the crisis as a crisis of capitalism, and that take issue with the conventional account or parts of it—including Harman

(2009), Roberts (2009), Carchedi (2011), and Mattick (2011). To these can be added articles such as Desai and Freeman (2011), Onishi (2011), and Potts (2011). I do not agree with all of these works in all respects, but I am proud that this book can now be counted among them.

Except for the book by Duménil and Lévy, this book contains the most in-depth and comprehensive data analyses of any of the works I have cited above, as well as most other books on the topic. And among the works that take issue with the conventional leftist account, its treatment of the underlying causes of the Great Recession is arguably the most comprehensive.

To some degree, this book's differences with the conventional account reflect methodological and theoretical differences. Like most of its other critics cited above, I am a proponent of the temporal single-system interpretation (TSSI) of Marx's value theory. It has long been alleged that the value theory and the most important law based upon it—the law of the tendential fall in the rate of profit (LTFRP), the core of Marx's theory of capitalist economic crisis—are internally inconsistent and must therefore be corrected or rejected. However, TSSI research has demonstrated that the inconsistencies are not present in the original texts; they result from particular interpretations. When Marx is interpreted as the TSSI interprets him, the inconsistencies disappear (see, for example, Kliman 2007).

As Chapter 6 will discuss in more detail, the TSSI's ability to reclaim Marx's *Capital* from the myth of inconsistency impinges upon the controversy over the underlying causes of the Great Recession in the following way. In their supposed proofs that the LTFRP is internally inconsistent, his critics *replace* the temporally determined rate of profit to which his theory refers with an atemporal "rate of profit" (the current-cost or replacement-cost rate), and they then find that Marx's law does not survive this process of substitution. Those who have accepted these proofs have also accepted the manner in which the proofs mis-measure the rate of profit. Thus, when they found that the atemporal "rate of profit" trended upward after the early 1980s, they took this as conclusive evidence that capitalist production has been sound, and that the true underlying causes of the Great Recession are therefore neoliberalism, financialization, and heightened exploitation. Analysis of actual rates of profit leads to quite different conclusions.

However, I do not want to overstate the role of methodological and theoretical differences. Prior to analyzing the data, I had no prior belief that actual rates of profit had failed to rebound since the early 1980s, and I even wrote that "profitability has been propped up by means of a decline in real wages for most [U.S.] workers" (Kliman 2009: 51), which I believed to be an unambiguous fact. Methodology and theory greatly influence the kinds of questions one asks and the data one regards as significant, but they have no influence over the data themselves.

In other words, this book is an *empirical analysis*, not a theoretical work. Even my claim that the atemporal "rate of profit" is not a rate of profit in any normal sense of the term is an empirical claim. If it, and this book's other claims and findings, are "true for" those who find its conclusions appealing, they are no less "true for" those who do not. Not everything is a matter of perspective. If I can now say that a persistent decline in U.S. corporations' profitability is a significant underlying cause of the Great Recession, and that Marx's explanation of why the rate of profit tends to decline fits the facts remarkably well, it is because I have crunched and analyzed the numbers. I could not have said these things a few years ago.

The relationship between Brenner's (1998) analysis and mine is complex. We both conclude that capitalism's recovery from the slumps of the 1970s and early 1980s was far from robust, though I find his expression "long downturn" misleading and instead refer to "relative stagnation." And we both conclude that profitability problems were a source of the malaise. However, Brenner arrived at this conclusion partly by analyzing movements in the atemporal current-cost "rate of profit," while I do not. Since proponents of the conventional leftist account looked at the *very same* rate, and pointed to its upward trend as crucial evidence that neoliberalism had put capitalism back on an expansionary path, Brenner in effect argued that the glass was half-empty in order to counter the claim that it was half-full. (I argue that it is not a glass in any normal sense of the term.)

On a theoretical plane, Brenner roots falling profitability in technical change, but in other respects his falling-rate-of-profit theory has little in common with Marx's. Indeed, he embraces the supposed proofs that Marx was wrong to conclude that cost-reducing technical change can cause the rate of profit to fall (see Brenner 1998: 11–12, n1 and Kliman 2007: 6–7, 82–3, 113). To explain falling profitability, Brenner (1998: 24–5) appeals to additional factors: "reduced prices in the face of downwardly inflexible costs," insufficient demand, and overproduction due to imperfect information. He argues that the *combination* of these factors and cost-reducing technical change can cause the rate of profit to fall.

The reason why Brenner appeals to inflexible costs is that his theory is atemporal, and it is therefore unable to explain how cost- and price-reducing technical change can cause the rate of profit to fall when costs are flexible. (In an atemporal theory, if costs fall by the same percentage that prices fall, the rate of profit remains unchanged.) But Marx's LTFRP has no need for this hypothesis, or for Brenner's other additional factors. Even when costs are flexible, costs incurred *in the past* do not fall when prices fall *today*. Because it recognizes this temporal distinction, Marx's law can explain how technical change itself—in the absence of special additional factors—can cause the rate of profit to fall.[3]

Let me finally note another difference between this book and some others on the topic: it discusses and quotes others' arguments at some length, especially those with which it takes issue. It does so partly because the dialectical intellectual tradition to which I belong strongly emphasizes debate and critique, holding that these are the principal means by which knowledge develops. I regard the refutation of incorrect claims and arguments as one of this book's primary tasks. I am not trying to tell a story about what has gone wrong, for readers to accept if they find it appealing or reject if they do not. *I am trying to separate what has gone wrong from what has not.* I also discuss and quote others' arguments at some length because I consider it intellectually irresponsible to ignore contrasting views or characterize them without supplying the evidence and arguments needed to support the characterizations—common practices to which my work is frequently subjected.

One author I quote frequently is Marx. I do not do so in order to support my arguments, but in order to help establish what his ideas actually were, to help explicate these ideas, to avoid plagiarism, and, in a few cases, to express something that I cannot express equally well in my own words.

SYNOPSIS OF SUBSEQUENT CHAPTERS

The next chapter sets out the theoretical framework that underlies the empirical analyses that follow. It discusses key components of Marx's theory of crisis—the tendential fall in the rate of profit, the operation of credit markets, and the destruction of capital value through crises—and how they can help account for the latest crisis and Great Recession.

Chapter 3 contains a brief discussion of the formation and bursting of the home-price bubble in the U.S., and the Panic of 2008 that resulted. I then discuss how Federal Reserve (Fed) policy contributed to the formation of the bubble. I argue that the Fed wanted to prevent the United States from going the way of Japan. After Japan's real-estate and stock-market bubbles burst at the start of the 1990s, it suffered a "lost decade," and the Fed wanted to make sure that the bursting of the U.S. stock-market bubble of the 1990s did not have similar consequences. The latest crisis was therefore not caused *only* by problems in the financial and housing sectors. As far back as 2001, underlying weaknesses had brought the U.S. economy to the point where a stock-market crash could have led to long-term stagnation.

Chapter 4 examines a variety of global and U.S. economic data and argues that they indicate that the economy never fully recovered from the recession of the 1970s. Because the slowdown in economic growth, sluggishness in the labor market, increase in borrowing relative to income, and other problems began in the 1970s or earlier, prior to the rise of neoliberalism, they are not attributable to neoliberal policies.

The next three chapters discuss movements in the rate of profit and related issues. Chapter 5 shows that U.S. corporations' rate of profit did not rebound after the early 1980s. It also shows that the persistent fall in the rate of profit—rather than a shift from productive investment to portfolio investment—accounts for the persistent fall in the rate of accumulation.

Chapter 6 discusses why many radical economists dismiss Marx's law of the tendential fall in the rate of profit and contend that the rate of profit has risen. They compute "rates of profit" that value capital at its current cost (replacement cost); almost everyone else uses the term "rate of profit" to mean profit as a percentage of the actual amount of money invested in the past (net of depreciation). The current-cost "rate of profit" did indeed rebound after the early 1980s, but I argue that it is simply not a rate of profit in any meaningful sense. In particular, although proponents of the current-cost rate have recently defended its use on the grounds that it adjusts for inflation, I argue that it mis-measures the effect of inflation and that this mis-measurement is the predominant reason why it rose.

Chapter 7 looks at why the rate of profit fell. It shows that changes in the distribution of corporations' output between labor and non-labor income were minor, and it decomposes movements in the rate of profit in the standard manner of the Marxian-economics literature. I then show that an alternative decomposition analysis reveals that the rate of profit fell mainly because employment increased too slowly in relationship to the accumulation of capital. This result implies that Marx's falling-rate-of-profit theory fits the facts remarkably well. The chapter concludes with a discussion of depreciation due to obsolescence ("moral depreciation"). I show that the information-technology revolution has caused such depreciation to increase substantially and that this has significantly affected the measured rate of profit. The rates of profit discussed in Chapter 5 and prior sections of Chapter 7 would have fallen even more if I had employed Marx's concept of depreciation instead of the U.S. government's concept.

Chapter 8 examines underconsumptionist theory, which has become increasingly popular since the recent crisis. This chapter shows that, contrary to what underconsumptionist authors contend, U.S. workers are paid more now, in inflation-adjusted terms, than they were paid a few decades ago, and their share of the nation's income has not fallen. The rest of this chapter criticizes the underconsumptionist theory of crisis. In particular, I argue that the underconsumptionist theory presented in Baran and Sweezy's influential *Monopoly Capital* rests on an elemental logical error.

Chapter 9, which concludes the book, discusses what is to be undone. I argue that the U.S. government's response to the crisis constitutes a new manifestation of state-capitalism, and I critically examine policy proposals based on the belief that greater state regulation, control, or ownership can put capitalism on a stable path. I then discuss the political implications of underconsumptionism and critique its view that redistribution of income would stabilize capitalism. Finally, I take up the difficult question of whether a socialist alternative to capitalism is possible. Although I do not believe I have "the answer," I address the question because I believe that the collapse of the U.S.S.R. and the latest crisis have made the search for an answer our most important task.

2
Profitability, the Credit System, and the "Destruction of Capital"

This chapter sets out the theoretical framework that guided the empirical analyses of later chapters. It briefly outlines the lynchpins of Marx's theory of capitalist economic crisis—the tendential fall in the rate of profit (LTFRP); the operation of credit markets, and the destruction of capital value through crises—and discusses their applicability to the latest crisis and the Great Recession.

The first section discusses Marx's LTFRP and how it can help account for economic crises and slumps—even if the rate of profit rises in the period immediately preceding the crisis, as it did in the mid-2000s. I argue that Marx's theory regards a fall in the rate of profit as an *indirect* cause of crises, it leads to crises only in conjunction with financial market instability and instability caused by low (as distinct from falling) profitability.

The second section examines what Marx and others have called the "destruction of capital"—losses due to plummeting values of financial and physical capital assets as well as destruction of the physical assets themselves—that occurs during crises and slumps. Later in this book, I will argue that the economy failed to recover fully from the slumps of the 1970s and early 1980s, and that the incomplete recovery problem and policymakers' response to it set the stage for the latest crisis. In this chapter, I offer an explanation of why the recovery was incomplete: the amount of capital value destroyed during the mid-1970s and early 1980s was not enough to restore the rate of profit and thereby allow productive investment to proceed at a healthy pace. My discussion of the destruction of capital will also help clarify why the LTFRP predicts recurrent crises, not a long-term decline in the rate of profit throughout the history of capitalism.

THE FALLING RATE OF PROFIT AS AN INDIRECT CAUSE OF CRISES

As Chapter 5 will show, some measures of U.S. corporations' rate of profit indicate that it was basically trendless between 1982 and 2007, and profitability rose sharply in the years immediately preceding the latest crisis. It may therefore be thought that a falling rate of profit cannot have been a cause of the latest crisis and slump. It certainly was not a *proximate* cause, but I shall argue that it was a key *indirect* cause. The rate of profit was low at the start of the 1980s and it never recovered in a sustained fashion. This led to a marked decline in the rates of capital accumulation and economic growth.[1] Government policies kept this problem from getting out of hand, but also prolonged and exacerbated it. The Treasury borrowed more and more in order to prop up after-tax profits and paper over the economy's sluggishness. Interest rate reductions, government loan guarantees, the elimination of the capital gains tax on most sales of homes, and other measures fueled a massive build-up of mortgage debt. And the government repeatedly bailed out domestic and foreign creditors.

Such policies succeeded in propping up demand, keeping it from falling back to levels consistent with the production of new value and the rate of profit. But in between, there were increasingly severe debt crises and burst bubbles—the Third World debt crisis, the stock-market crash of 1987, the U.S. savings and loan crisis, the East Asian crisis, the burst dot-com bubble, and finally, the biggest debt crisis and burst bubble since the Great Depression. The more sophisticated and widespread credit markets are, the greater is the degree to which such "forced expansion" (Marx 1991a: 621) can take place—but also the greater the degree of ultimate contraction when the law of value eventually makes its presence felt. It is like a rubber band stretching and snapping back.

MARX'S LAW OF THE TENDENTIAL FALL IN THE RATE OF PROFIT

Marx held that as capitalist production develops, capitalists tend to adopt more productive, labor-saving techniques; that is, they turn increasingly to methods of production that replace workers with machines. On the basis of this tendency and his theory that value is determined by labor-time, he deduced the LTFRP (Marx 1991a, part 3). The law is that productivity increases under capitalism produce a tendency for the general rate of profit to fall: "The progressive tendency for the rate of profit to fall is thus simply *the expression, peculiar to the capitalist mode of production*, of the progressive development of the social productivity of labour" (Marx 1991a: 319, emphasis in original).

Why do productivity increases resulting from labor-saving technical change tend to *lower* the rate of profit? This idea seems preposterous to many people. For instance, Brenner (1998:11–12, n1) argues that the LTFRP "flies in the face of common sense" and that its falsity is "intuitively obvious." So what? Almost all modern physics also flies in the face of common sense, but its conclusions are not less correct on that account.[2]

The LTFRP "flies in the face of common sense" because it seems intuitively obvious to many people that a more productive capitalism is a more profitable capitalism. This intuition is reinforced by the fact that technologically advanced companies are more profitable than backward ones—an individual company does raise its rate of profit by adopting techniques of production that are more advanced than those of its competitors. However, to assume that this implies that the economy-wide rate of profit will also rise when productivity rises throughout the whole economy is a logical error, the fallacy of composition. Here are a couple of analogous cases: if you are in a stadium and you stand up, you can see better; but if everyone stands up at once, you will not all see better. If you get a master's degree, you will get a better job and make more money; but if everyone has a master's degree, you will not all get better jobs and make more money.

So let us set intuitions aside and examine the actual logic of the situation. When labor-saving technical changes are introduced, more of each dollar of advanced capital is invested in means of production, while less is used to hire workers. But according to Marx's theory that value is determined by labor-time, it is workers' living labor that adds all new value. Moreover, an average hour of labor "always yields the same amount of value, *independently of any variations in productivity*" (Marx 1990a: 137, emphasis added). Technical innovation therefore causes a fall in the amount of new value created per dollar of advanced capital. And if surplus-value (profit) is a constant share of new value, the amount of surplus-value created per dollar of advanced capital—in other words, the rate of profit—necessarily falls as well.

Of course, capitalist businesses do not know about or care about value or surplus-value as measured in terms of labor-time. They know about and care about money prices and money profits. So it may help to restate Marx's law in terms of price and profit. When productivity increases, more physical things and physical effects (services) are produced per labor-hour. According to Marx's theory, however, the increase in productivity does not cause more new value to be created. The same amount of value is "spread out" among more items, so the increase in productivity causes the values of individual items to decline. In other words, things can be produced more cheaply. *And because they can be produced more cheaply, their prices tend to fall.*[3] In a competitive environment, companies must lower the prices they charge when their costs of production decline. If they fail to do so, they risk a significant loss of market share or even bankruptcy when competitors cut their prices in response to reduced production costs.[4] Yet even monopolies that enjoy lower costs will generally tend to reduce their prices, because the reduction in costs allows the profit on each item to increase even if its price is lower, and the reduction in price allows them to sell more items.

The tendency for prices to fall as a result of technical innovation is recognized even by non-Marxists like Alan Greenspan (2000):

> [F]aster productivity growth keeps a lid on unit costs and prices. Firms hesitate to raise prices for fear that their competitors will be able, with lower costs from new investments, to wrest market share from them.

> Indeed, the increased availability of labor-displacing equipment and software, at declining prices and improving delivery times, is arguably at the root of the loss of business pricing power in recent years.

But the "loss of business pricing power" due to "labor-displacing equipment and software" is the crux of the LTFRP; Marx presented the law not only in term of value and surplus-value, but also in terms of price and profit (see esp. Marx 1991a: 332–8). Assume that the rate of surplus-value (rate of exploitation) is constant, and that physical output and physical capital grow at the same rate. These are fairly reasonable assumptions. Under these conditions, technical innovation will not produce a tendency for the rate of profit to fall if it does not also tend to depress prices; but if it does tend to depress prices, the rate of profit will indeed tend to fall.[5]

As I stressed above, Marx regarded a fall in the rate of profit as an *indirect* cause of crises. To be legitimate, an explanation in terms of indirect causes must give an account of how they operate, through intermediate links, to produce the phenomenon in question. In the remainder of this section, I focus on two intermediate links—low profitability and the credit system—that connect the fall in the rate of profit during the post-World War II period to the latest economic crisis and slump.

LOW PROFITABILITY

A fall in the rate of profit can have persistent effects. Even if the rate of profit does not continue to fall up to the moment of economic crisis, a prior fall can set the stage for such a crisis by producing a *low* average rate of profit. This is so even if the rate of profit is constant or rising in the period immediately preceding the crisis.

As Farjoun and Machover (1983: 163–6) pointed out, relatively few businesses will encounter serious trouble when the average rate of profit is relatively high. Even businesses whose rates of profit are well below average will be able to survive. However, if a fall in the rate of profit has led to an average rate of profit that is relatively low, many more of the low-profitability businesses will find themselves in serious trouble, because their rates of profit are now less than the minimum needed in order to survive. This is just as much the case when the average rate of profit has stabilized as when it continues to decline.

If relatively few businesses' rates of profit are far below average, while a greater percentage are only somewhat below average, then the percentage of unviable businesses increases at a rising rate as the average rate of profit declines. Assume, for instance, that rates of profit are normally distributed (as in a bell curve), that 6 percent is the minimum rate of profit a firm needs in order to survive, and that the average rate of profit falls by three percentage points. As Table 2.1 and Figure 2.1 show, this fall results in many more business failures when the average rate is initially low (15 percent) than when it is initially high (30 percent). If the relative dispersion of rates of profit is the same in the two cases, as the table and figure assume, then only 0.5 percent more businesses fail when the average rate falls from 30 percent to 27 percent. But 4.4 percent more businesses—eight-and-a-half times as many—fail when the average rate of profit falls from 15 percent to 12 percent.

Table 2.1 Non-Linear Effect of Falling Profitability on Business Failures

Average (mean) rate of profit	30.0%	27.0%	15.0%	12.0%
Standard deviation	15.0%	13.5%	7.5%	6.0%
Relative dispersion (coefficient of variation)	0.5	0.5	0.5	0.5
Unviable businesses (rates of profit < 6%)	5.5%	6.0%	11.5%	15.9%

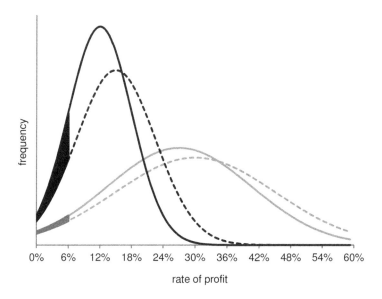

Figure 2.1   Distributions of Rates of Profit

Thus, short-term decline in profitability of similar amplitude have much more serious and widespread consequences when the average rate of profit is low than when it is high. Low profitability as such makes the economy less stable, more prone to crises and serious slumps. A fall in the average rate of profit will therefore have destabilizing effects that persist even if it stopped falling a long time ago.

Moreover, many phenomena that are sometimes regarded as effects of a *decline* in the rate of profit are actually effects of a *low* rate. For instance, when the rate of profit falls, the rate of accumulation of capital (productive investment) tends to fall as well. But this implies that if the rate of profit is low and fails to rebound, the rate of accumulation will also tend to be low and fail to rebound. (In Chapter 5, I will show that the rate of accumulation of U.S. corporations has tracked their rate of profit very closely.) A low rate of capital accumulation will in turn tend to result in low growth rates of employment, output, income, and demand for consumer goods and services. And when growth of income (profits, wages, tax income, and so on) is sluggish, it is more difficult for businesses, households, and governments to pay back their debts. This sets the stage for debt and financial crises down the road.

Another factor that can contribute to the problem is low interest rates. When the rate of capital accumulation is low, interest rates will tend to be low as well (all else being equal, the less businesses wish to borrow in order to fund productive investment, the more lenders have to reduce the interest rates they charge in order to induce them to borrow). But low interest rates make borrowing more attractive and cause bond, stock, and real-estate prices to rise, which encourages speculation in these asset markets and makes them more vulnerable to crisis.[6]

THE CREDIT SYSTEM

Another key intermediate link between falling profitability and economic crisis is finance. The credit market plays a crucial role in Marx's crisis theory, especially in Chapter 15 of *Capital*, Volume 3, which sketches out the relationship between the falling tendency of the rate of profit and economic crisis. Marx argues:

> If the credit system appears as the principal lever of overproduction and excessive speculation in commerce, this is simply because the reproduction process, which is elastic by nature, is now forced [once the credit system has developed] to its extreme limits; and this is because a great part of the social capital is applied by those who are not its owners, and who therefore proceed quite unlike owners who, when they function themselves, anxiously weigh the limits of their private capital. (Marx 1991a: 572)

A lot of ideas are packed into this sentence. The first half suggests that the credit system facilitates the formation of bubbles and thereby accentuates both booms and busts. It allows the economy to grow more rapidly for some time than is warranted by fundamental economic conditions such as profitability and the production of new value. But for this very reason, the eventual contraction is also more severe than it would otherwise be. Marx's use of the word "elastic" is apt.

The second half of the sentence deals with what is now called *moral hazard*—that is, failure to "anxiously weigh" whether your investment behavior is too risky, because you are not the one who will suffer the losses that result from excessive risk-taking. Moral hazard is frequently cited as a key factor that contributed to the latest crisis. Financial institutions that originated mortgage loans did not anxiously weigh the risks involved because they sold off the loans. Those who bought the loans in the form of mortgage-related securities bore the risks. Or they too failed to anxiously weigh the risks because the risks were borne by those who insured these securities. And those who lent to large financial institutions failed to anxiously weigh the risks because they suspected, correctly, that the government would regard the institutions as "too big to fail" and bail them out.[7]

I doubt that any of this would have surprised Marx. Indeed, he argues that moral hazard is *the* problem that makes the credit system "the principal lever of overproduction and excessive speculation." He also suggests that moral hazard is not a defect created by any particular financial system but an inevitable by-product of credit as such, since debtors inevitably take risks with creditors' funds, even when they do business directly, instead of through the intermediation of financial institutions. This suggests that regulation and the breaking up of too-big-to-fail institutions will not do away with moral hazard.

In any case, Marx's focus on the credit system makes clear that his crisis theory is not one in which a fall in the rate of profit causes a fall in the rate of accumulation, which then causes an economic crisis, in the manner of one billiard ball hitting a second one and the second one hitting a third. He does argue that "the rate of ... accumulation falls together with the rate of profit" (Marx 1991a: 349), but he does not hold that the fall in the rate of accumulation is a direct cause of an economic crisis. This is largely because he distinguishes between *crisis* (a rupture in the reproduction process of capital) and *stagnation* (slumps, recessions, depressions). The business cycle consists of "periods of moderate activity, prosperity, over-production, crisis and stagnation," or "periods of average activity, production at high pressure, crisis, and stagnation" (Marx 1990a: 580, 785). A fall in the rate of accumulation can directly cause a fall in the rate of growth of output, but the fall in the rate of accumulation must be mediated by other factors in order to result in a crisis.

Marx argued that a decline in the rate of profit leads indirectly to a crisis by encouraging speculation and overproduction. And because the fall in the rate of profit leads to a crisis only indirectly, it does not do so immediately:

> ... in view of the fact that the rate at which the total capital is valorized, i.e. the rate of profit, is the spur to capitalist production (in the same way as the valorization of capital is its sole purpose),

a fall in this rate slows down the formation of new independent capitals and thus appears as a threat to the development of the capitalist production process; it promotes overproduction, speculation and crises … . (Marx 1991a: 349–50[8])

If the rate of profit falls … we have swindling and general promotion of swindling, through desperate attempts in the way of new methods of production, new capital investments and new adventures, to secure some kind of extra profit, which will be independent of the general average [profit determined by the average rate of profit] and superior to it. (Ibid.: 367[9])

It is only when debts finally cannot be repaid that a crisis erupts, and the crisis then leads to stagnation:

The majority of these bills [of exchange] represent actual purchases and sales,[10] the ultimate basis of the entire crisis being the expansion of these far beyond the social need. On top of this, however, a tremendous number of these bills represent purely fraudulent deals, which now come to light and explode; as well as unsuccessful speculations conducted with borrowed capital; and finally commodity capitals [that is, businesses' inventories of finished products] that are either devalued or unsaleable, or returns that are never going to come in. (Ibid.: 621)

The chain of payment obligations at specific dates is broken in a hundred places, and this is still further intensified by an accompanying breakdown of the credit system, which had developed alongside capital. All this therefore leads to violent and acute crises, sudden forcible devaluations, an actual stagnation and disruption in the reproduction process, and hence to an actual decline in reproduction. (Ibid.: 363)

This account has a very modern ring. Capitalism has changed far less than many people—its critics as well as its supporters—want to think.

Several facts about the current crisis may at first glance seem to suggest that it did not result from the fall in the rate of profit. The crisis erupted well after much or all of the fall had occurred. Its main immediate cause was the bursting of an asset-price bubble. And it was immediately preceded by speculative frenzy and a huge rise in asset prices that led to a sharp (but temporary) increase in the rate of profit.[11]

As we have seen, however, Marx's theory holds precisely that a fall in the rate of profit leads to crises only indirectly and in a delayed manner. The fall leads first to increased speculation and the build-up of debt that cannot be repaid, and these are the immediate causes of crises. Thus, the timing of the current crisis and the sequence of events leading to it do not contradict the theory, but are fully consonant with it and lend support to it. Nothing anomalous has occurred that requires us to look elsewhere for explanations.

THE DESTRUCTION OF CAPITAL (VALUE)

The LTFRP implies that there is an ever-present tendency in capitalism for labor-saving technical innovation to lower the rate of profit. Yet Marx also argued that this tendency is interrupted and counteracted from time to time by "the destruction of capital through crises" (Marx 1989b: 127, emphasis omitted).

Part of what he was referring to is the destruction of physical capital assets. In an economic slump, physical capital is destroyed as machines and buildings lay idle, rust, and deteriorate. A tremendous amount of physical capital was also destroyed in World War II. But insofar as the theory of crisis is concerned, what matters is the destruction of capital in terms of *value*—the decline in the value of physical capital assets as well as the decline in the (fictitious) value of financial assets. Of course, when physical assets are destroyed, their value is destroyed as well, but the predominant factor that causes capital value to be destroyed is falling prices. As debts go unpaid, the prices of financial assets such as mortgage loans and mortgage-backed securities fall. Prices of equities also typically fall during recessions and depressions, and prices of produced commodities—both physical capital assets and consumer goods and services—have frequently fallen as well.

The decline in prices that took place during the Great Depression caused a massive amount of capital value to be destroyed. As measured by the GDP price index, prices of goods and services in the U.S. fell by 25 percent between 1929 and 1933. The prices of the fixed assets owned by U.S. corporations fell by 23 percent between the end of 1928 and the end of 1932. According to Irving Fisher (1933: 354, Chart V), the national wealth of the United States plummeted by 59 percent over the same period, mostly because of falling prices. And the Dow Jones Industrial Average fell by more than 89 percent between September 1929 and July 1932.

Yet the destruction of capital is not only a consequence of serious economic crises and the slumps they trigger. It is also a main cause of the booms that follow, because it is a crucial factor that helps to restore profitability.[12] Capitalists invest in equipment, hire workers, and produce only in order to make a profit. If the expected rate of profit isn't high enough, there won't be sufficient investment and hiring, so there won't be a boom. But by restoring profitability, the destruction of capital sets the stage for a new boom.[13]

Imagine, for instance, a business that can generate $3 million in profit annually. If the value of the capital invested in the business is $100 million, the owners' rate of profit is a mere 3 percent. Yet if, as a result of the destruction of capital value, new owners can acquire the business for only $10 million instead of $100 million, their rate of profit—the return they receive on *their* investment—is a healthy 30 percent. A tremendous incentive to invest, expand production, and employ more workers has been created. Notice that this is the case *even in the absence* of new markets or rising demand that would lead investors to expect greater profit.

Thus, the massive destruction of capital value that took place during the Great Depression and World War II set the stage for the boom that followed. At the start of the Depression, it is alleged, the destruction of capital—which was called "liquidationism"—was actually advocated by Andrew Mellon, President Hoover's Treasury Secretary. In his memoirs, Hoover (1952: 30) wrote:

> Mellon … felt that government must keep its hands off and let the slump liquidate itself. Mr. Mellon had only one formula: "Liquidate labor, liquidate stocks, liquidate the farmers, liquidate real estate." He held that even panic [in the financial system] was not altogether a bad thing. He said: "It will purge the rottenness out of the system … enterprising people will pick up the wrecks from less competent people."

Some conservative economists gave similar advice. According to Milton Friedman (1999):

> If you go back to the 1930s, which is a key point, here you had the Austrians sitting in London, [Friedrich] Hayek and Lionel Robbins, and saying you just have to let the bottom drop out of the world. You've just got to let it cure itself. You can't do anything about it. You will only make it worse.

However, it seems that the amount of capital value that needed to be destroyed in order to restore healthy rates of capital accumulation and economic growth was substantially more than liquidationists had expected. Both Hayek and Robbins later expressed regret at having recommended that activist policies not be used to counteract the deflation of the early 1930s (see White 2010: 112–13).

Policymakers in more recent times have understandably been afraid of another Great Depression, and another wave of radicalization of working people like that which the Depression of the 1930s triggered. This legacy of class struggle has helped shaped economic policy and performance during the last several decades. To prevent a repeat of the 1930s, policymakers have successfully used debt financing and debt guarantees to retard and head off the destruction of capital. The downturns of the mid-1970s and early 1980s, and even the latest downturn, were therefore nothing like the Great Depression. But since the destruction of capital restores profitability and thereby lays the foundation for the next boom, we have also not experienced anything like the boom that followed the Great Depression and World War II. On the contrary, *the economy never fully recovered from the slump of the 1970s.* (I will document this in detail in Chapter 4.)

Policymakers responded to the latest crisis and slump by once again papering over bad debt with more debt, and by using debt to stimulate the economy artificially—this time on a massive, unprecedented scale. In the first two years following the collapse of Lehman Brothers in mid-September 2008, the total debt of the U.S. Treasury increased by 40 percent, from $9.6 trillion to $13.5 trillion. The additional borrowing amounts to almost $12,500 per person. According to projections from the Obama administration—which are far more optimistic than those contained in a 2010 International Monetary Fund working paper (Celasun and Keim 2010)—the Treasury's debt will rise to $19.8 trillion by the end of fiscal year 2015, which means that it will have more than doubled in just seven years. The $10.1 trillion increase in the debt is equal to 9.0 percent of projected GDP throughout the 7-year period (and, to repeat, the administration's GDP projections are very optimistic).

If these measures succeed in extricating the economy from the effects of the Great Recession and the prospect of deflation, full-scale destruction of capital will once again have been averted. But for the foreseeable future, the U.S. will confront a debt burden that will be difficult to manage, at best, and probably slower economic growth as interest rates rise in response to the growing debt. Moreover, the huge increase in indebtedness suggests that the next debt crisis could be much worse than the latest one. If that proves to be the case, the next wave of panic to strike the financial markets will be even more severe and have more serious consequences.

DESTRUCTION OF CAPITAL VALUE AND THE LTFRP

The destruction of capital value through crises is a recurrent phenomenon. The restoration of profitability that this destruction brings about is therefore a recurrent phenomenon as well. Because of this, the rate of profit does not have a determinate secular trend throughout the entire history of capitalism, and efforts to deduce or predict such a trend are futile.

For instance, arguments that the rate of profit must trend downward in the long run, because technical progress leads to falling profit, overlook the fact that profit is only one determinant of the rate of profit. *An equally important determinant of the rate of profit is the capital value that is advanced, the magnitude of which depends largely upon how much capital value has been destroyed through crisis.* If capital value has been destroyed on a massive scale, the peak rate of profit in the boom that follows is likely to be *higher* than the prior peak. And if major slumps become increasingly frequent, the tendency for the rate of profit to fall between slumps has less and less time in which to operate, so it is likely that trough rates of profit *rise* over time.

The LTFRP therefore does not and cannot predict that the rate of profit will actually display a falling trend throughout the history of capitalism. And despite a common belief to the contrary, there seems to be no evidence that Marx predicted such a secular fall. On the contrary, he held that "[c]ounteracting influences [are] at work, checking *and cancelling* the effect of the general law," and that the LTFRP "has constantly to be overcome by way of crises" (Marx 1991a: 339, 367, emphasis added). Thus what Marx meant by the "tendency" of the rate of profit to fall was not an empirical trend, but what would occur if there were no destruction of capital value or other "counteracting influences" such as the tendency of the rate of surplus-value to rise.

The most likely source of the belief that Marx predicted a secular decline in the rate of profit is the fact that the classical economists to whom he was responding did indeed make this prediction. It is thus assumed that he and they were discussing the exact same issue. However, Marx explicitly repudiated this notion:

When Adam Smith explains the fall in the rate of profit [as stemming] from a superabundance of capital ... he is speaking of a *permanent* effect and this is wrong. As against this, the transitory superabundance of capital, overproduction and crises are something different. Permanent crises do not exist. (Marx 1989b: 128, starred note, emphasis in original)

That Marx regarded capitalism's economic crises as transitory, though unavoidable and recurrent, is also important to stress. The common belief that he predicted the collapse of capitalism, as a result of the LTFRP alone or in conjunction with other causes, is yet another belief for which evidence is lacking. Mandel, a prominent advocate of the view that Marx predicted a collapse of the system, acknowledged that no textual support for this claim can be found in his presentation of the LTFRP or elsewhere in Volume III of *Capital*. However, according to Mandel, "a number of passages ... from Volume 1" support the theory of collapse (1991: 79). Yet he cited only one such passage, the end of the penultimate chapter, and this passage says nothing about the system's collapse. Marx (1990a: 929–30) projects that the system's tendencies will result in social revolution ("The expropriators are expropriated"), and not because of any collapse, but because of the centralization of capital and growing revolt of the working class.[14]

The political implications of the LTFRP are therefore not fatalistic ones. But they are revolutionary. Theories that trace crises to low productivity, sluggish demand, the anarchy of the market, state intervention, high wages, low wages, and so on, suggest that capitalism's crisis tendencies can in principle be substantially lessened or eliminated by fixing the specific problem that is making the system perform poorly. But the LTFRP suggests that economic crises are inevitable under capitalism, because they are not caused by factors that are external to it, that is, factors that can be eliminated while keeping the system intact. As Marx (1973: 749–50, emphasis added) put it: "The violent destruction of capital *not by relations external to it*, but rather as a condition of its self-preservation, is ... advice ... to be gone and to give room to a higher state of social production."

According to his theory, the tendency of the rate of profit to fall and economic crises are instead rooted in a relationship that is "internal" to capital, the internal contradiction between physical production and the production of value that is built into the very functioning of capitalism: as physical productivity rises, commodities' values fall. As a result, their prices tend to fall, as does the rate of profit, and this leads ultimately to economic crises and the destruction of capital value.

Now, this contradiction and the crises to which it leads obviously exist only because products are commodities—that is, things that have *value* as well as having uses. But capital is nothing other than value that is invested in order to end up with more value, so the fact that products have value is part and parcel of capitalism as such, no matter what its forms of property and institutional structures may be.[15] Thus the contradiction within capitalism and the effects of the contradiction do not stem from any particular form of capitalism, and they cannot be overcome by replacing one particular form of the system with a different one. To overcome them, it is necessary to do away with capital, which requires, as we see, doing away with commodities and the production of commodities—in other words, with value and the production of value.[16]

3
Double, Double, Toil and Trouble: Dot-com Boom and Home-price Bubble

At first, the recent financial crisis was widely characterized as a "subprime mortgage crisis."[1] It is now generally recognized, however, that the increased rate of defaults on subprime loans was just one facet of a more general problem, the bursting of a home-price bubble in the U.S., and that this burst bubble was the main factor that triggered the crisis and Great Recession.

The first two sections of this chapter briefly discuss why the bubble formed and why it burst,[2] and how this eventually led to the Panic of 2008. The final section then looks more closely at the role of Fed policy as a factor that contributed to the formation and persistence of the bubble.

The so-called "dot-com" boom—the rapid rise in stock prices during the latter half of the 1990s that was fueled in part by the growth of the Internet and information technology—turned into a burst bubble in 2000. I shall argue that the Fed became gravely concerned that the U.S. might suffer a deflationary slump like the one that had recently led to Japan's "lost decade,"[3] and that it responded to this threat with an exceptionally "easy-money" policy that helped fuel yet another bubble. This shows that the latest crisis was not merely a consequence of financial-sector problems that developed later in the decade. It was also a consequence of economic weakness in the U.S. that extends back much further.

THE HOME-PRICE BUBBLE

A steep rise in home mortgage borrowing, which led to a steep rise in home prices, began in the latter half of the 1990s (see Figure 3.1).[4] One reason borrowing may have begun to skyrocket was that the latter half of the 1990s was the period of the dot-com bubble. A lot of money was being made in the stock market, some of which was then invested in residential and commercial real estate. Another factor that may have stimulated mortgage borrowing was a change in income-tax law. Prior to 1997, people who sold their homes at a price greater than the price at which they bought it were required to pay tax on the difference. But in that year Congress eliminated the tax on most of these capital gains; for a married couple filing a joint tax return, the first $500,000 is exempt. In 1999, the volume of mortgage borrowing was already 146 percent greater than in 1995 and 75 percent greater than in 1997. (Factors that caused the rise to continue will be discussed in the next section.)

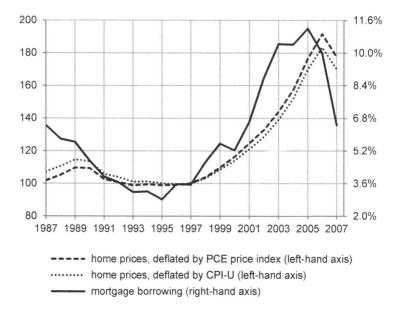

Figure 3.1   Mortgage Borrowing and Real Home Prices, U.S.
(mortgage borrowing as percentage of after-tax income; 1997 prices = 100)

The home-price bubble was not an isolated phenomenon. Commercial real-estate prices increased by roughly the same percentage, between the start of 2001 and late 2007, that home prices increased between the start of 2000 and mid-2006. And stock prices recovered quickly after crashing at the start of the decade. The S&P 500 index rose by 95 percent between early 2003 and late 2007, an average annual increase of over 20 percent.

Although households' demand for assets, both financial assets and tangible ones, increased rapidly, their liabilities increased rapidly as well. On average, increases in liabilities funded only 44 percent of households' newly acquired financial and tangible assets between 1952 and 1992—the rest were purchased out of people's actual incomes—and deviations from the average were modest (see Figure 3.2). But then came the dot-com "boom" of the 1990s and the "boom" of the 2000s, *both of which were inflated by an ever-growing mountain of debt*. By 1999, the ratio of new liabilities to newly acquired assets stood at 96 percent, which means that all but 4 percent of the additional assets were bought with borrowed money. And this situation persisted until the latest crisis erupted; from 1999 through 2006, the average ratio of new liabilities to newly acquired assets was 94 percent. Thus, while households in 1992 lent out (via deposits in banks, and so on) more than they borrowed by an amount equal to 2.9 percent of the nation's GDP, they increasingly turned into borrowers (see Figure 3.3). By 2005, their borrowing exceeded their lending by an amount equal to 2.9 percent of GDP.[5]

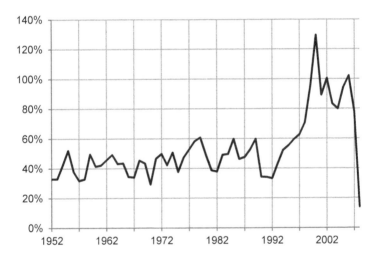

Figure 3.2   Relative Increases in Liabilities and Assets, U.S. Households
(increase in liabilities as percentage of newly-acquired assets)

But between 1995 and 2005, households' after-tax income increased only one-fourth as quickly as mortgage borrowing. This made it increasingly difficult for home purchasers to meet their mortgage payments. Income also grew far more slowly than home prices, a situation that would normally dampen demand for homes and bring their prices down. What happened in the 2000s, however, is that the shortfall in income was temporarily covered over with even more borrowed funds. Homes were bought with less money down and bigger mortgage loans, and homeowners who faced difficulty making their mortgage payments frequently took out additional loans in order to pay back the original ones. They were able to obtain these additional loans—as long as home prices kept rising—by using the increases in the "values" of their homes as collateral.

Figure 3.3   Net Lending or Borrowing by U.S. Households
(net lending (+) or borrowing (−) as percentage of GDP)

Yet in the long run, homes must be paid for out of income, and debts must be settled with income, not with more debt. So the boom in the housing market was unsustainable.

Sales of new and existing homes began to decline in the second half of 2005, and home prices began to decline about a year later. More and more recent home buyers were left with "negative equity"—mortgage balances that exceeded the current prices of their homes. They could therefore no longer pay their mortgage debt by going further into debt, and defaults on mortgage debt and foreclosures began to climb.

At first, the problem was identified as a subprime mortgage crisis, as if nothing more had gone wrong than that a lot of relatively poor people (disproportionately Blacks and Latinos), "who shouldn't have been given mortgage loans in the first place," found themselves unable to repay their debts. The real problem, however, was that home prices collapsed. Subprime borrowers were of course hit first and hit hardest by the collapse, but the problem was a general one.[6] As of June 2010, only about one-sixth of homes in foreclosure had been purchased by means of a subprime mortgage loan, while about three-fifths had been purchased by means of prime mortgage loans.[7]

Partly because the volume of bad mortgage debt was large, many financial institutions (and other entities) faced very serious cash-flow and solvency problems. But other factors also helped to make the crisis a severe one. It became a general and worldwide crisis, rather than just a crisis that mortgage lenders faced, because the mortgages were securitized: a wide variety of institutions purchased mortgage-backed securities (which are essentially shares of a pool of mortgages) and other securities whose prices depend on the flow of mortgage repayments.

On the other hand, the financial-sector crisis was as massive as it was partly because, despite the securitization of mortgage loans, some big institutions were heavily exposed to mortgage-debt default. In theory, securitization made mortgage lending safer; by selling off loans it originated instead of holding onto them, a lender reduced its exposure to default debt. In this case, however, banks securitized mortgages and then "tended to hold onto securitized assets" in order to exploit a regulatory loophole and thereby obtain greater leverage (Jablecki and Machaj 2009: 301 [abstract], emphasis omitted). By turning mortgage loans they owned into securities they owned, they were able to reduce the amount of capital they were required to set aside as a cushion against unexpected losses, and to lend out the funds they had freed up.

Another main reason why the crisis became so massive is that financial institutions were very highly leveraged. When things go well, leverage greatly magnifies the rate of return on investment (the profit or interest as a percentage of the money invested), because more of the money that is invested is borrowed, not one's own. But when things go poorly, leverage greatly magnifies the losses. For instance, if you invest $100 of your own money and your profit is $6 in year 1 but only $2 in year 2, then your rate of return falls from 6 percent to 2 percent. But if you invest $100 using $3 of your own money and $97 that you borrowed at 4 percent, then your rate of return is 70.7 percent in year 1 but –62.7 percent in year 2.[8] And your creditor (or the institution from which it bought insurance) is in trouble as well, since you owe it interest of $3.88 but can only pay back $2.

In retrospect, it may seem surprising that the run-up of home prices was not generally recognized at the time to be a bubble. But that is the case with every bubble, and bubbles are fairly common. In the 1990s, people allowed themselves to believe that stock prices would keep increasing indefinitely, because information technology, the Internet, and the emerging "dot-com" companies had created "the new economy," in which the stodgy old economic laws that governed capitalism in the past had been abolished.

Near the peak of the dot-com bubble, one physician told me that stock prices would continue to rise, because they have to rise if money keeps flowing into the stock market. As evidence that "the new economy" was no myth, another physician told me about a plumber whose stock portfolio had been doing so well that he was about to quit the plumbing business and become a full-time investor. And I had little success in shaking the confidence of some of my business students that the massive increases in stock prices were reasonable, even though profits had not risen commensurably, because the increases in stock prices were based on companies' "growth" (as measured by what, their stock prices?).

In the 2000s, it is possible that some financial institutions realized that the increases in home prices were unsustainable, but that they nonetheless sought to quickly reap lush profits and then protect themselves before the day of reckoning arrived.[9] In any case, there was a good reason—or what seemed at the time to be a good reason—why others failed to perceive that the boom times were unsustainable: home prices in the United States had apparently never fallen on a national level since the Great Depression.[10]

So it was "natural" to assume that home prices would keep rising or level off, or decline only slightly. If home prices had continued to go up, homeowners who had trouble making mortgage payments would have been able to get the additional funds they needed by borrowing against the increase in the value of their homes, and the crisis would have been averted. Even if home prices had leveled off or fallen only slightly, there probably would have been no crisis.

In light of the historical record, the credit-rating agencies assumed, as their *worst-case* scenario, that home prices would decline only modestly. It was because of this assumption that they gave high ratings to huge amounts of mortgage-related securities whose value was based partly on subprime and other higher-risk mortgage loans. These securities were later called "toxic"—very few investors were willing to touch them except at drastically reduced prices—but if the credit-rating agencies had been right about the worst-case scenario, investors who bought these securities would indeed have reaped a decent profit. But the credit-rating agencies were wrong, terribly wrong. Between mid-2006 and April 2009, home prices fell by one-third.

THE PANIC OF 2008: "THIS SUCKER COULD GO DOWN"

As mortgage-related losses mounted in 2007 and 2008, credit markets increasingly succumbed to a crisis of confidence—that is, mounting concern about whether moneys owed to creditors would in fact be repaid—and this tended to depress asset prices further. Players in the markets worried especially about the liquidity (access to cash) and financial health of other institutions with which they traded, and about how the governments of the U.S. and other countries would respond to the crisis. Worry turned to panic in September when the government let Lehman Brothers go bankrupt and the House of Representatives rejected a proposal to bail out the banking industry by means of the $700 billion Troubled Assets Relief Program (TARP).[11]

The government was brought to its knees—literally. On September 25, "the Treasury secretary, Henry M. Paulson Jr., literally bent down on one knee as he pleaded with Nancy Pelosi, the House Speaker, not to 'blow it up' by withdrawing her party's support" for TARP, and the President of the United States declared, "If money isn't loosened up, this sucker could go down" (Herszenhorn, Hulse, and Stolberg 2008).

These events turned the crisis of confidence into what Eric S. Rosengren, president of the Federal Reserve Bank of Boston, called a "liquidity lock": "extreme risk aversion by many investors and institutions, which makes short-term financing difficult to come by … even the most creditworthy firms … are finding it increasingly difficult to borrow other than overnight" (Rosengren 2008). Since even large and thriving companies borrow in order to conduct their day-to-day business—meet their payrolls, buy supplies, and extend credit to buyers—the slump in the "real" economy might have been much worse, qualitatively worse, than the slump we actually experienced if the liquidity lock had been allowed to persist.

Figure 3.4 helps to clarify what Rosengren meant by "extreme risk aversion." It measures the so-called "TED spread," which is the difference between the rate of interest that a bank can get by lending to another bank for three months (the three-month LIBOR in terms of U.S. dollars) and the rate of interest it can get by lending to the U.S. Treasury for three months. Lending to the Treasury is safer. The difference between these rates is a measure of the willingness or unwillingness to take on risk—the extra interest a bank demands before it will take on the extra risk of lending to another bank instead of lending to the U.S. government.

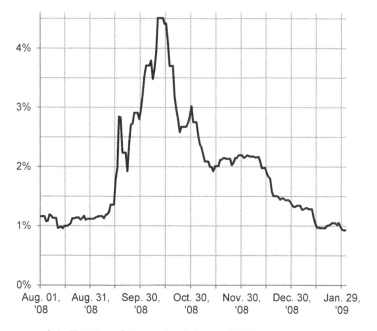

Figure 3.4   TED Spread, August 2008–January 2009

At the start of September 2008, the TED spread was slightly more than 1 percentage point, a bit less than its average rate between January and August (but about double its usual level). But on September 14, a bankrupt Merrill Lynch, once the world's largest securities firm, was bought by Bank of America for 39 percent of what it had been worth a year before. The next day, Lehman Brothers was allowed to collapse, and the U.S. government effectively nationalized the giant insurance company AIG the day after that. Lehman's collapse also triggered an acute crisis among money-market mutual funds; investors in these funds rushed to withdraw their money or found that they could not do so because the funds had declared moratoria on redemptions.

These events caused the TED spread to shoot up to 2.85 percentage points. It then temporarily declined, but it rose again to 2.80 points by September 29. On that day, Congress rejected the TARP bailout. Apparently in response to that rejection, the TED spread again shot up rapidly, and it continued to rise even after Congress reversed itself and TARP became law on October 3. By October 10, the spread stood at 4.51 points. It was only after the precise content of the TARP bailout, which had been in dispute, was clarified on October 14 that the TED spread began to subside.

At the time, many liberals and leftists told us that TARP was not needed, or that it was meant to provide windfall profits to the financial industry, or that the money could be spent differently—invested in infrastructure, used to protect homeowners against foreclosure, and so on. For instance, the historian Howard Zinn wrote:

> It is sad to see both major parties agree to spend $700 billion of taxpayer money to bail out huge financial institutions that are notable for two characteristics: incompetence and greed … A simple and powerful alternative would be to take that huge sum of money, $700 billion, and give it directly to the people who need it. Let the government declare a moratorium on foreclosures and help homeowners pay off their mortgages. Create a federal jobs program to guarantee work to people who want and need jobs. (Zinn 2008: 4–5)

But once one accepts the goal of saving the capitalist system, the only alternatives to TARP that remained were ones that differed from it only in the details. To save the system, the panic had to be quelled. "Confidence" had to be restored by means of government assurances that moneys owed to creditors would be repaid to them. And this required a bailout of the banking system. The measures that Zinn proposed were worth fighting for to help working people as the *recession* worsened. But they failed to address the *crisis of confidence*. Of course, one could say, "forget trying to restore confidence," but that is basically to say, "forget trying to save capitalism," and Zinn didn't say that.

And then there was the left-liberal economist Dean Baker (2008a), who was for the bailout before he was against it. On September

20, 2008, he characterized the liquidity lock and its possible consequences much in the manner that I characterized it above:

> There is a real risk that the banking system will freeze up, preventing ordinary business transactions, like meeting payrolls. This would quickly lead to an economic disaster with mass layoffs and plunging output.

> The Fed and Treasury are right to take steps to avert this disaster. … there is an urgency to put a bailout program in place.

But Baker (2008b) reversed course nine days later:

> The bail-out is a big victory for those who want to redistribute income upward. It takes money from school teachers and cab drivers and gives it to incredibly rich Wall Street bankers … This upward redistribution was done under the cover of crisis, just like the war in Iraq. But there is no serious crisis story. Yes the economy is in a recession that is getting worse, but the bail-out will not get us out of the recession, or even be much help in alleviating it.

Baker was correct that TARP would not do much to alleviate the recession. But it does not follow that its purpose was to make the rich richer, or that there was "no serious crisis story." Its purpose was to restore "confidence," in order to keep the financial system from melting down. That, and not the recession, was the crisis that TARP addressed.

Baker understood this point, of course, and he responded to it by arguing that the Fed could simply take over the major banks:

> In the event the banking system really did freeze up, then the Federal Reserve would step in and take over the major banks. (It had contingency plans for such a takeover in the 1980s, when the money centre banks were saddled with billions of dollars of bad developing country debt.)

> The banks would not be happy about a Fed takeover. The top executives would be out of their jobs, and the shareholders would likely lose their full investment. However, the rest of us would be able to carry on with our lives as we did before. (Ibid.)

Yet if the Fed were to take over the banks by buying them, the result would differ from TARP only in the details. The Fed would be bailing out the banks' creditors, and the bailout might cost just as much or more than TARP, depending on how extensive the nationalization was. The only other alternative is to take over the banks without compensation, as Baker suggested. If one wants to quell a crisis of "confidence" and get credit flowing again, this would not be a very wise move. Before banks, including nationalized banks, can make loans, they need to get the funds from people and institutions that lend to them and invest in them. I know that I wouldn't want to lend to or invest in any institution controlled by a government that is willing to expropriate without compensation.

Once again, of course, one can say, "forget trying to restore confidence and forget the sanctity of property rights"—in other words, "forget trying to save capitalism." But Baker didn't go there.

THE FED SAVES AMERICA FROM A JAPANESE-STYLE "LOST DECADE"

Paradoxically, the housing bubble formed and persisted, not because the U.S. economy was strong during the 2000s, but because it was weak. In particular, the weakness of the economy is what impelled the Fed to stimulate it artificially,[12] and its actions had the unintended consequence of contributing to the formation of, and prolonging, the home-price bubble.

In December 1996, Fed chairman Alan Greenspan (1996) asked, "But how do we know when irrational exuberance has unduly escalated asset values, which then become subject to unexpected and prolonged contractions as they have in Japan over the past decade?" The question was widely interpreted as a somewhat oracular warning that irrational exuberance had overtaken the U.S. stock market. But if the question was indeed a warning, it was one that wasn't heeded. Irrational exuberance continued. When Greenspan posed his question, the S&P 500 stock price index had risen by 64 percent during the previous two years (see Figure 3.5). By March 2000, the total rise was 237 percent, and the "technology-rich" NASDAQ composite index had risen by 577 percent.[13]

Yet corporations' after-tax rate of profit, which peaked at 13.0 percent in 1997, had fallen by more than one-third, to 8.3 percent in 2000.[14] Stock prices peaked in March 2000, stagnated for several months, and began to fall starting in September. By the end of the year, the S&P index had fallen by 13 percent, and the NASDAQ index had fallen by 42 percent, from their levels at the start of September. Industrial production, which had stopped growing after June, began to fall starting in October, at which time real GDP also stopped growing. Retail sales in December were also lower, in real (inflation-adjusted) terms, than in December 1999.

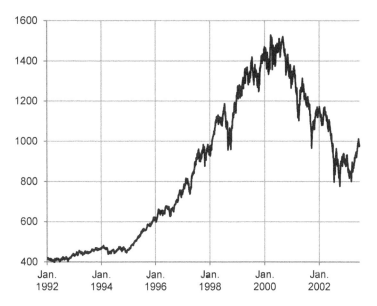

Figure 3.5 S&P 500 Index

Forward-looking indicators suggested that the U.S. economy would weaken further. In December 2000, the key leading indicator of housing construction—the number of building permits issued to build new homes—was 8 percent lower than a year earlier, and 11 percent below the December 1998 figure. The stock-market decline contributed to a fall in consumer confidence, particularly in December, when the University of Michigan's index of consumer sentiment, a leading indicator of consumer spending, fell by 8.6 percent. And by year's end, the three-month moving average level of businesses' orders for "core" capital goods, a key leading indicator of investment for future production, had declined for four months in a row and stood 4.7 percent below the peak level it had reached in August.

In an attempt to keep the decline from worsening, the Fed began to lower the federal funds (bank-to-bank) interest rate, its main policy tool. In a special conference-call meeting on January 3, 2001, the Federal Open Market Committee lowered its target for the federal funds rate by one-half percentage point, from 6.5 to 6 percent. The target federal funds rate was lowered by an additional half-point at the FOMC's regular meeting at the end of the month. During the next seven months, the Fed lowered the target rate five more times; by August, it stood at 3.5 percent.

Such monetary policy changes take time to work. In the meantime, the state of the economy worsened. Corporations' average after-tax rate of profit fell to 7.9 percent in 2001, only three-fifths of its 1997 level. The collapse of stock prices accelerated and continued until late 2002 or early 2003. When they hit bottom, the NASDAQ index stood at less than one-fourth of its peak level, and the S&P index had fallen by almost one-half. Real GDP failed to rebound in a sustained manner until December 2001, while industrial production continued to decline until the start of 2002. Employment began to decline in March 2001, the month in which the recession was later "officially" determined to have begun. The decline continued through August 2003, nearly two years after the recession "officially" came to an end in November 2001 (see Figure 3.6).[15]

In response to the terrorist attacks on September 11, the Fed reduced its target for the federal funds rate four more times during 2001. At the end of the year, the rate stood at 1.75 percent. *But the Fed continued to lower the federal funds rate long after the country recovered from 9/11 and long after the recession "officially" ended.* The target rate was reduced in late 2002 and again in mid-2003, to 1 percent. It remained at this level for another year.

Why did the Fed continue to bring down the federal funds rate and keep it down? It did so partly because employment was very slow to recover after the 2001 recession ended.

But it was also seeking to head off a longer-term threat that the weak economy had brought about—the prospect of deflation. In a speech delivered two weeks after the November 2002 reduction in the target federal funds rate, Ben Bernanke, at the time a member of the Fed's Board of Governors, noted that

> ... some have expressed concern that we may soon face a new problem—the danger of deflation, or falling prices. That this concern is not purely hypothetical is brought home to us whenever we read newspaper reports about Japan, where what seems to be a relatively moderate *deflation*—a decline in consumer prices of about 1 percent per year—has been associated with years of painfully slow growth, rising joblessness, and apparently intractable financial problems in the banking and corporate sectors. (Bernanke, 2002, emphasis in original)

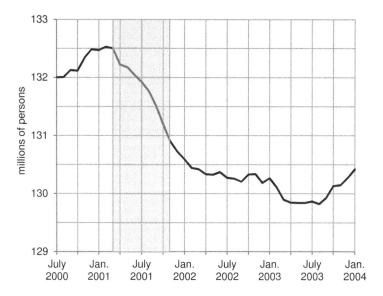

Figure 3.6   Nonfarm Payroll Employment, U.S.
(shaded area indicates recession)

Bernanke went on to assure his listeners that "for the foreseeable future, the chances of a serious deflation in the United States appear remote indeed." But he stressed that one thing that made the possibility of serious deflation remote was "*the determination of the Federal Reserve and other U.S. policymakers to act preemptively against deflationary pressures*" (Bernanke 2002, emphasis added). The official press release that announced the Fed's June 2003 reduction in the target federal funds rate referred guardedly to "the probability, though minor, of an unwelcome substantial fall in inflation," but in recent testimony before the Financial Crisis Inquiry Commission, Bernanke confirmed that fear of serious deflation was a main cause of the Fed's easy-money policy: "The Federal Open Market Committee brought short-term interest rates to a very low level during and following the 2001 recession, in response to persistent sluggishness in the labor market and what at the time was perceived as a potential risk of deflation" (Bernanke 2010).

Of course, the Fed has frequently acted to bring down short-term rates during recessions. But it seems that, in the early 2000s, the easy-money policy was much easier than usual. Gjerstad and Smith (2009: 271) characterize it as "exceptionally expansionary" and

John Taylor argues that "the actual interest-rate decisions fell well below what historical experience would suggest policy should be." After 2001, the Fed's actions "deviated from the regular way of conducting policy in order to address … a fear of deflation, as had occurred in Japan in the 1990s" (Taylor 2009: 342–3).

As Figure 3.7 shows, the real federal funds rate was negative throughout almost all of the three-and-a-half years between the start of 2002 and the middle of 2005.[16] This means that banks could borrow funds from other banks, lend them out, and then pay back less than they had borrowed, once inflation is taken into account. Only once before had this occurred over a sustained period—during and after the severe global economic crisis of the mid-1970s.

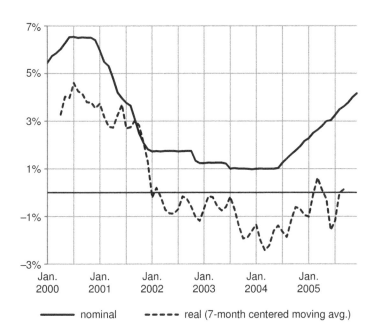

Figure 3.7   Nominal and Real Federal Funds Rates

Other interest rates, including interest rates on mortgage loans, fell in response to the reduction in the federal funds rate. And the lowering of mortgage rates boosted the volume of mortgage borrowing. Figure 3.8 shows the close relationship between the federal funds rate and mortgage borrowing (expressed as a percentage of after-tax income) one year later. Because the two series move in opposite directions, I have inverted the federal funds rate in order to make the close relationship more apparent. During the period shown in the graph, a one percentage point fall (or rise) resulted, on average, in a rise (or fall) of slightly more than one percentage point in the borrowing/income ratio, and changes in the federal funds rate account for two-thirds of the variation in the borrowing/income ratio.[17]

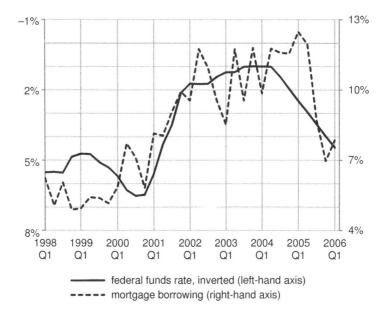

federal funds rate, inverted (left-hand axis)
- - - - - mortgage borrowing (right-hand axis)

Figure 3.8   Federal Funds Rate and Home Mortgage Borrowing
(mortgage borrowing figures are percentages of after-tax income one year after indicated quarter)

Correlation is of course not proof of causation, and other factors certainly stimulated demand for home mortgages. Earlier in this chapter, I discussed the role played by the near-elimination of the capital-gains tax on home resales, and I noted that rising stock prices in the late 1990s probably stimulated demand for homes at that time. But what about other factors?

The growth in subprime lending could not have been a major cause of the explosive increase in demand for mortgage loans, because subprime mortgages constituted only 8 percent or less of the total mortgages originated annually through 2003 (Federal Reserve Bank of San Francisco 2007: 8, Fig. 1). From 2004 through

2006, the subprime share was close to 20 percent, but mortgage borrowing had by that time stopped rising in relationship to income (see Figure 3.1).

Denying that "the 'easy money' policies of the Federal Reserve produced the U.S. housing bubble," Greenspan (2009) proposed an alternative explanation: "a surge in growth in China and a large number of other emerging market economies ... led to an excess of global intended savings relative to intended [productive] capital investment." The excess savings were used to purchase securities, which depressed long-term interest rates, including mortgage lending rates in the U.S. And according to Greenspan, it was the decline in mortgage rates, but not the decline in the federal funds rate, that produced the bubble. In testimony before the Financial Crisis Inquiry Commission, Bernanke (2010) repeated this claim and cited Europe as another source of significant financial inflows into the U.S. during the bubble years. (As additional causes of the bubble, he also pointed to the psychology that drives bubbles and riskier mortgage-lending practices.)

Taylor (2009: 345–6) has argued, however, that the lynchpin of this argument—the existence of a global savings glut—is a myth. Although savings exceeded productive capital investment elsewhere in the world, the opposite was true in the U.S., and to a similar degree. Since the two imbalances offset one another, there was no savings glut on a *global* level that could have caused interest rates to fall and mortgage borrowing to skyrocket.

The International Monetary Fund (IMF) data that Taylor produced to support his case are persuasive. As Figure 3.9—which employs the same dataset—shows, savings did not begin to exceed productive investment to a significant extent until 2005, while the bulk of the increase in U.S. home-mortgage borrowing took place before that time.[18] Between 1995 and 2004, a period in which worldwide savings either fell short of worldwide productive investment or exceeded it by a negligible amount ($28 billion in 1997 and $21 billion in 2004), the ratio of mortgage borrowing to after-tax income increased from 2.8 percent to 10.4 percent. And during the 2005–07 period, when savings did exceed productive investment to a non-trivial degree, the ratio of mortgage borrowing to after-tax income rose only modestly (to 11.2 percent in 2005) and then fell (to 10.0 percent in 2006 and 6.5 percent in 2007).

Yet the IMF data do not settle the matter definitively, since they pertain to *actual* savings and investment, while Greenspan refers to *intended* magnitudes. The data leave open the possibility that there

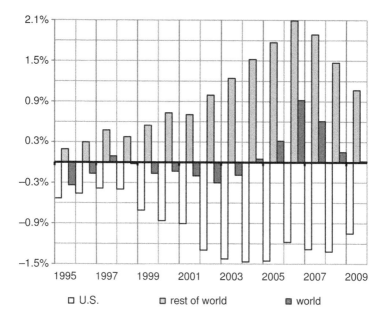

Figure 3.9   Excess Savings as Percentage of World GDP

was a savings glut in Greenspan's sense prior to 2005 that caused interest rates to fall, and that the fall in rates brought actual savings and productive investment into equilibrium.

However, Greenspan and Bernanke's rejection of the idea that Fed policy led to the housing bubble is problematic for other reasons as well. They reject this idea on the grounds that changes in the federal funds rate do not have much influence on the home mortgage market (Greenspan 2009, Bernanke 2010). But Figure 3.8, above, shows that the federal funds rate and mortgage borrowing *were* strongly associated during the years of the housing bubble.

Another problem is that, even if we accept that the Fed's easy-money policy did not cause home prices to rise, a sufficiently tight policy would almost certainly have caused the rise to stop. As Stiglitz has noted:

> The Fed had enough control, at least in the short run, to have raised interest rates in spite of China's willingness to lend to America at a relatively low interest rate. Indeed, the Fed did just that in the middle of the decade, which contributed—predictably—to the popping of the housing bubble. (Stiglitz 2009: 334)

My point is *not* that the Fed is to blame for the housing bubble, and it is *not* that everything would have been fine if only it had pursued a tighter monetary policy. When the "new economy" bubble burst, the U.S. economy was left in a weakened state, and it is this situation that is ultimately to blame for the housing bubble. In other words, the Fed's easy-money policy was not something it chose freely. As I discussed above, burst bubbles in Japan's real-estate and stock markets had resulted in deflation and "the lost decade," so ongoing deflation in the U.S. was a distinct threat at the start of the 2000s.

Thus, as Bernanke recently stressed, "*stopp[ing] the bubble at an earlier stage by more aggressive interest rate increases ... was not a practical policy option*" (2010, emphasis added). If the Fed had stopped the bubble, losses on mortgage-related securities would have been much smaller, and so the panic that gripped the financial sector in late 2008 might have been averted. But given the weakness of the U.S. economy after the collapse of the stock-market bubble, the recession, and the September 11 terrorist attacks—and given the uncertainty resulting from the attacks, the war in Afghanistan, and then the war in Iraq—tight monetary policy may well have caused the economy to descend into the Great Recession at the start of the decade rather than at the end. Or the economy might have sunk into a prolonged period of stagnation, as the Japanese economy did after the bursting of its real-estate and stock market bubbles.

Stiglitz, who wishes to blame the Fed (and many others) for the crisis, has responded to statements like Bernanke's by arguing that

> Apologists for the Fed sometimes ... [say] that they had no choice: Raising interest rates would have killed the bubble, but also would have killed the economy. But the Fed has more tools than just the interest rate. There were, for example, a number of regulatory actions that would have dampened the bubble ... It could have reduced maximum loan-to-value ratios as the likelihood of a bubble increased; it could have lowered the maximum house payment-to-income ratios allowed. If it believed that it did not have the requisite tools, it could have gone to Congress and requested them. (Stiglitz 2009: 336)

And then what? A central bank can pursue an expansionary monetary policy, or a contractionary monetary policy, but not both at once. It is conceivable, though unlikely, that the strategy recommended by Stiglitz would have dampened the total volume of borrowing in the economy and thereby ended the bubble. But by doing so, it might well have caused the Great Recession to come sooner rather than later, or the U.S. may have descended into its own lost decade.

Stiglitz also seems to have forgotten that *the bubble was not confined to the housing market*. As I noted earlier, stock prices and commercial real-estate prices shot up rapidly as well. This is important, because Stiglitz's strategy would most likely have altered the *composition* of borrowing without reducing its overall level, since interest rates would have remained low. Thus, the regulatory changes he recommends would have resulted in less borrowing to buy homes, but more borrowing to buy stocks and commercial real estate. Thus, the bubbles in these markets would have been even bigger, and it is not obvious that the bursting of these bubbles would have had consequences less serious than the consequences of the burst bubble in the housing market.[19]

After all, the bursting of the stock-price bubble of the 1990s was no small matter. As I have argued in this chapter, it triggered conditions so serious that the Fed felt compelled to take actions that contributed to and prolonged the home-price bubble. Our current economic troubles are in large part the delayed consequences of the dot-com bubble and the ultimately unsuccessful efforts to contain the damage once it burst (as well as deeper structural problems).

4
The 1970s—Not the 1980s—as Turning Point

WHAT IS AT STAKE?

This chapter examines data on a variety of economic trends of the last several decades. These have been decades of slow economic growth and financial crises in the U.S. and throughout the world. In the U.S., we have also experienced very large increases in the debt burdens of government and households, weak employment conditions and a sluggish growth of pay, rising inequality, and the deterioration of public infrastructure.

The evidence indicates that these trends all began with the economic crisis and slump of the mid-1970s, or, in some cases, even earlier. Thus, the evidence lends support to a key thesis of this book: because there was no real bust in the mid-1970s and early 1980s—no destruction of capital value resulting from the slumps of that period that was large enough to restore profitability—there was also no real boom thereafter. Episodes such as the dot-com bubble of the 1990s and the housing-bubble-driven expansion of the 2000s notwithstanding, the economy never fully recovered from the slump of the 1970s.

Together with the evidence discussed in the next chapter—on the persistence of the fall in profitability and the persistent decline in the rate of accumulation to which it led—the evidence presented here indicates that the turning point was the 1970s, because that decade was the start of a *long period of relative stagnation*. It thus calls into question a common view on the left—or at least what was a common view prior to the outbreak of the latest economic crisis—that the turning point was the early 1980s, because a *new expansionary phase* of capitalism began at that time. According to proponents of this latter view, the restructuring of capitalism along free-market or "neoliberal" lines that began in the early 1980s ushered in a new expansion by increasing the exploitation of the workforce and thereby restoring the rate of profit.

Elements of the common (or formerly common) view were first articulated before use of the term "neoliberalism" became prevalent. Stressing that a new boom does not necessarily bring about improvements in economic conditions for the average person, Henwood (1994) wrote:

> As I said four years ago, it's wrong to tune your rhetoric to crisis—either the permanent crisis favored by some lefties, or the inevitability of a real bone-cruncher just around the corner, predicted as imminent by others ... In a world of free trade, tight money, and fiscal orthodoxy, GDP can grow indefinitely—generously assuming no ecological flameout—but it can still feel pretty awful.

Some years later, Anwar Shaikh (1999) responded to a question by writing, "So, are we ultimately on a long wave upturn? On balance, I think so. Other advanced countries are beginning to move in the U.S. and U.K. direction, and lamenting it does not change the facts." A short while later, in *Capital Resurgent: Roots of the neoliberal revolution*, Gérard Duménil and Dominique Lévy wrote:

> "Neoliberalism" is the term now used to describe the transformations capitalism underwent at the turning point of the 1970s and 1980s ... [There was] a change whose principal trait was restoring many of the most violent features of capitalism, making for a resurgent, unprettified capitalism.
>
> [T]he profit rate reached a low at the beginning of the 1980s and has since been increasing. (Duménil and Lévy 2004: 1, 28)

And even after the collapse of Lehman Brothers, Michel Husson (2008) argued similarly:

> After the generalised recessions of 1974–5 and 1980–82, a new phase opened in the functioning of capitalism, one which one could for convenience call neo-liberal. The beginning of the 1980s was a real turning point. A fundamental tendency towards increasing the rate of exploitation was unleashed, and that has led to a continuous rise in the rate of profit.

In general, proponents of this view did not argue that the performance of the economy "under neoliberalism" was particularly strong. Yet, since they held that free-market policies succeeded in restoring the rate of profit, and that this *could* have resulted in much stronger economic performance, they attributed the relative stagnation to neoliberal policies rather than to underlying and unresolved problems in the functioning of the capitalist mode of *production*. Duménil and Lévy, for example, asked,

> Why was the restoration of the rate of profit not coupled with a parallel resumption of growth …? The key to this enigma may be found in the monetary and financial mechanisms … the continuing poor performance of the American and European economies [… is] actually the effect of the specific dynamics of neoliberalism. One can, therefore, assert that the structural crisis is over and blame neoliberalism … . (Duménil and Lévy 2004: 65)

The evidence I will present in this chapter shows that this argument is at variance with the facts, at least in the case of the U.S. The slowdown in economic growth, and the various other economic difficulties we will look at, *pre-date "neoliberalism" and therefore cannot be properly attributed to it.* They began when economic policy was "Keynesian," during the presidency of Richard ("I am now a Keynesian in economics") Nixon,[1] who resigned in August 1974. These economic difficulties are therefore not effects of changes in policy and ideology, but their cause. "Neoliberalism" and "financialized capitalism"—a related buzzword we hear these days—are the tail, not the dog that wags it. The characterization of a period of capitalist development as "neoliberal" is therefore not grounded in facts as much as in a strong tendency toward *political determinism*—the notion that the economic laws of capitalism can be fundamentally modified by political will and power. This tendency made its way into Marxist thought in various ways, such as through the Frankfurt School, structuralism and post-structuralism, and the *Regulation* school in France and the Social Structure of Accumulation school in the U.S. One might have expected that the failure of Keynesian policies in the face of the economic crisis of the mid-1970s, and the failures of social democracy and Stalinism, would have provoked a turn away from political determinism. Yet such a turn did not occur, and the popularity of this tendency seems to have increased in the wake of the latest economic crisis.[2]

While "neoliberalism" can be a helpful term when used to refer to the dominant politics and ideology of a particular period, the evidence that I will present below has led me to conclude that it is not a useful concept for explaining the trajectory of the economy over the last several decades. What I find much more useful is an idea of Marx's that political determinists have frequently dismissed: politics and ideology are based upon and conditioned by the relations of *production* that are the real foundation of society. This idea was centrally important to his *Critique of the Gotha Program* (Marx 1989a) and his critiques of related efforts to provide "political" solutions to socioeconomic problems. In light of the limited explanatory power of the concept of neoliberalism and the failures of political determinism, I think this idea is worthy of renewed consideration.

WORLD ECONOMIC GROWTH

This book focuses on the U.S. economy because, as I noted in Chapter 1, the U.S. was the epicenter of the latest crisis, and because the data that are available for other countries are not as complete and often not as reliable. A look at the world economy is nonetheless useful here, because it helps make clear that the relative stagnation of the economy since the mid-1970s is a global phenomenon. The U.S. case is not atypical and, in fact, the slowdown that took place in the U.S. was somewhat less drastic than in most other advanced industrialized countries and elsewhere in the world.

Figure 4.1 presents the average annual growth rate of real GDP per capita in the world as a whole. The estimates based on World Bank data, which begin with 1960, measure GDP in constant (inflation-adjusted) U.S. dollars, while the estimates based on the database compiled by the late Angus Maddison, which provides annual figures since 1950, measure GDP in constant international (Geary-Khamis) dollars.[3] Both series show that the growth rate of the world's real per capita GDP was fairly stable until 1973, and that it then fell abruptly and sharply, by about one-half. Both series also show that no substantial recovery in the growth rate took place during the remainder of the twentieth century. Note that the abrupt fall took place between 1973 and 1980—before the neoliberal period began.

For the period since 2000, the World Bank figures indicate that growth of real GDP per capita accelerated only minimally, while Maddison's figures suggest that the growth rate returned to pre-1973 levels after 2000. The main reason why these results differ is that the World Bank's estimate of the size of the Chinese economy is much smaller than Maddison's (even though the World Bank's

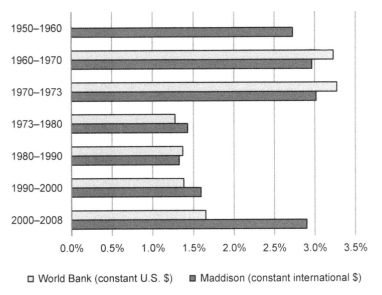

Figure 4.1   Growth of World GDP Per Capita
(average annual growth rate)

annual growth-rate estimates for China are almost always larger).
According to the World Bank, China's real GDP in 2008 was 56
percent that of the U.S., while Maddison's estimate was 94 percent.
Once China is excluded, as Figure 4.2 shows, the two series are very
similar, and both suggest that annual growth of GDP per capita fell
by more than half after 1973.

Table 4.1 presents the growth rates of real GDP per capita in
the eight largest advanced industrialized countries (ranked in order
of real GDP in 2008), and in the different regions of the world.
It shows that the slowdown in growth was a very widespread
phenomenon. After 1973, the growth rate fell by more than half
in Japan, Europe (including eastern Europe and the (ex-)U.S.S.R.),
Latin America and the Caribbean, and Africa. The slowdown in
growth we experienced in the U.S. was a good deal smaller, and
it was also somewhat smaller than the average slowdown in the
world as a whole.

Asia constitutes the main exception to the generalization
that growth rates fell markedly. This is wholly due to the rapid
acceleration of growth in China and India in recent years. In the
rest of Asia, the average annual growth rate of real GDP per capita

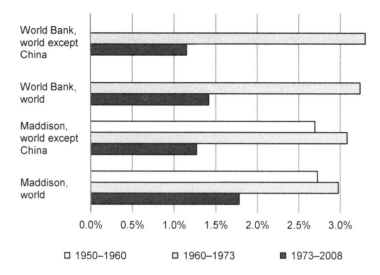

Figure 4.2   Impact of China on Growth of GDP Per Capita
(average annual growth rates)

Table 4.1   Growth Rates of Real GDP Per Capita (Maddison data)

	1950–73 (percent)	1973–2008 (percent)	Post-1973 as % of pre-1973
United States	2.4	1.8	74
Japan	7.8	2.0	25
Germany	4.9	1.6	32
United Kingdom	2.4	1.9	81
France	3.9	1.6	40
Italy	4.8	1.8	37
Canada	2.8	1.7	62
Spain	5.4	2.7	50
Western Europe	4.0	1.8	46
Western offshoots *	2.4	1.8	74
Eastern Europe	3.7	1.5	41
(ex-)U.S.S.R.	3.3	0.8	23
Latin America and Caribbean	2.6	1.2	49
Asia	3.8	3.4	89
Africa	1.9	0.7	37
World	**2.9**	**1.8**	**62**

* the United States, Canada, Australia, and New Zealand

since 1973, 2.0 percent, is only 41 percent of the rate between 1950 and 1973, 4.8 percent; the magnitude of the decline is similar to that which occurred in western Europe and Latin America.

U.S. ECONOMIC GROWTH

Turning to the U.S., we find that other measures of economic growth also indicate clearly that an abrupt slowdown began in the mid-1970s and persisted thereafter. I used the estimates of potential real GDP published by the Congressional Budget Office (CBO) to compute the gap between potential and actual real GDP.[4] On average, actual GDP exceeded potential GDP by 1.2 percent from 1950 through 1973, while it fell short of potential GDP by 0.6 percent between 1974 and 2008. Figure 4.3, which looks at the percentage gap between actual and potential GDP for different cycles, indicates that the averages are not misleading in this case. Actual GDP exceeded potential GDP in all but one of the cycles prior to the mid-1970s, while it was less than potential GDP in all but one of the cycles that followed.[5] Moreover, the percentage gaps during the two exceptional cycles were rather small.

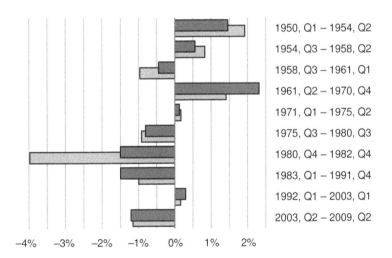

Figure 4.3   Gap between Actual and Potential Real GDP, U.S.
(percentage difference of actual from potential)

Figure 4.4 looks at the growth of the Federal Reserve's index of industrial production. It shows the percentage by which industrial production grew in the ten years prior to the indicated date. The growth rate fell sharply during the recession of the mid-1970s and never bounced back (except temporarily, during the dot-com bubble). The ten-year growth rate averaged 57 percent between 1957 and 1973, but plummeted to 30 percent, barely more than half of the earlier average, between 1975 and 2008. Even when the growth rate of the latter period peaked in 2000, it was less than the average growth rate between 1957 and 1973. If we use the inauguration of Ronald Reagan in January 1981 to mark the start of neoliberal policy in the U.S., we find that 80 percent of the total decline in the average growth of industrial production had already occurred prior to the start of neoliberalism.

Figure 4.4   Growth Rate of Industrial Production, U.S.
(percentage change during prior decade)

I used the index of industrial production and the Federal Reserve's capacity utilization rate series to compute the annual growth rate of the country's industrial capacity—the stock of means of production in the manufacturing, mining, and utilities industries (see Figure 4.5). Since the capacity utilization series begins with 1967, it is not possible to draw conclusions about the early part of the post-World War II period. But it is clear that growth of industrial capacity has slowed down markedly since the late 1960s, except during the investment boom that accompanied the dot-com bubble of the 1990s. Almost all the decline betwcen 1968 and the start of the latest recession occurred before the "neoliberalization" of the U.S. economy began. When Reagan took office, the growth rate of industrial capacity was already less than half of what it had been in early 1968.[6]

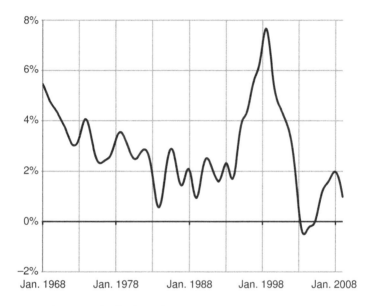

Figure 4.5   Growth of Industrial Capacity, U.S.
(annual percentage change)

GLOBAL FINANCIAL INSTABILITY

Table 4.2 is based on data reported in Tables 6.3 and 6.4 of Reinhart and Rogoff (2009: 95–6). Their study looked at 66 countries whose combined share of world GDP in 1990 was 89 percent. Between 1946 and 2005, 36 of these countries either defaulted on the debt they owed foreign entities or had their debt restructured—that is, they did not repay their debt, or they missed payments, or they negotiated repayment under easier conditions than those to which they originally agreed. (Because some countries defaulted or had their debts restructured multiple times, the total number of defaults and restructuring was much more than 36.) Prior to 1976, there were few defaults or restructurings, but the number skyrocketed between 1976 and 1985, mostly because of the Third World debt crisis of the early 1980s. Even after that crisis was resolved, defaults and restructurings continued to occur more frequently than in the early post-World War II period. For instance, in the ten-year period between 1996 and 2005, there were as many defaults on and restructurings of debt as there had been during the first 30 years after the war.

Table 4.2   Sovereign Debt Defaults and Restructurings, 1946–2005

Years	1946–55	1956–65	1966–75	1976–85	1986–95	1996–2005
Defaults and restructurings	1	8	7	35	20	16

Although the Third World debt crisis did not erupt until the early 1980s, the roots of the crisis extend back to the 1970s. The price of oil skyrocketed in the 1970s, and this impelled many countries to borrow heavily from U.S. banks. Yet the rate of GDP growth in these countries generally fell at the same time, which made it harder for them to manage their debts. Warnings that a crisis might lie ahead were issued as early as 1975, when the U.S. "Congress held hearings … and expressed concern about the excessive concentration of Third World loans and its related threat to the capital position of U.S. banks" (Federal Deposit Insurance Corporation 1997: 198). Two years later, a staff report from the Senate Subcommittee on Foreign Relations stated that "the stability of the U.S. banking system and by extension the international financial system may be jeopardized by the massive balance of payments lending that has been done by commercial banks since the oil price hike" (U.S. Senate Committee on Foreign Relations 1977: 5).

Another study by Reinhart and Rogoff (2008) used the same database to analyze the incidence of banking crises in various countries. In order to capture the fact that such crises are more significant when they occur in large economies, the authors weighted the number of crises by countries' shares of world GDP. In the first few years after World War II, the weighted percentage of countries that experienced a banking crisis was 5 percent or less, and from 1951 through 1973, it was close to zero. However, it then shot up sharply throughout the remainder of the 1970s, peaking at 10 percent in 1979. After falling briefly to about 5 percent between 1981 and 1983, the weighted percentage of countries that experienced a banking crisis skyrocketed to 26 percent by 1986. Between 1985 and 1999, the percentage fluctuated between 20 and 30 percent, and equaled 25 percent on average. The number of banking crises then plummeted to very low levels—until the latest global financial crisis, of course (see Reinhart and Rogoff 2008, Fig. 1).

The major banking crises that occurred from the mid-1980s through the 1990s include the following. First, the savings and loan crisis in the U.S. broke out in the mid-1980s. It was followed by a severe banking crisis in the Nordic countries in the late 1980s and early 1990s, and a banking crisis in Japan that erupted shortly thereafter, when massive bubbles in that country's stock and real-estate markets burst. Banks in some East European countries ran into trouble about the same time, as a result of the collapse of the Soviet bloc. And then there were renewed debt crises in the Third World: Mexico and Argentina experienced banking crises in the mid-1990s and, beginning in 1997, a currency crisis that began in Thailand rapidly spread, leading to banking crises in seven East Asian and South-east Asia countries, and banking crises in Russia and elsewhere.

Reinhart and Rogoff seem to suggest that a feature of neoliberalism, financial liberalization, is largely responsible for the increase in banking crises: "since the early 1970s, financial and international capital account liberalization—reduction and removal of barriers to investment inside and outside a country—have taken root worldwide. So, too, have banking crises." When they move from the general to the specific, however, a different picture emerges, one in which financial liberalization is much more of an effect than a cause:

> After a long hiatus, the share of countries with banking difficulties first began to expand in the 1970s. The break-up of the Bretton Woods system of fixed exchange rates, together with a sharp spike in oil prices, catalyzed a prolonged global recession, resulting in financial sector difficulties in a number of advanced economies. In the early 1980s, a collapse in global commodity prices, combined with high and volatile interest rates in the United States, contributed to a spate of banking and sovereign debt crises in emerging economies, most famously in Latin America and then Africa … .
>
> The United States experienced its own banking crisis, rooted in the savings and loan industry, beginning in 1984 … . (Reinhart and Rogoff 2009: 206)

What Reinhart and Rogoff call the "break-up" of the Bretton Woods system was in fact a *collapse*. In other words, the system did not end because of any preference for floating exchange rates, but because the U.S. government abrogated, and was forced to abrogate, its commitment to give foreign countries gold in exchange for the dollars they held. By the late 1960s, accelerating inflation in the U.S. and the country's balance-of-payments deficits had made it clear that the key assumption of the Bretton Woods system— that the dollar is "as good as gold"—was no longer true. This led to depletion of U.S. gold reserves and related problems, impelling Nixon to announce in 1971 that the U.S. would no longer abide by the Bretton Woods agreement.

I do not mean to deny that a floating exchange-rate regime makes banking crises more likely. My point is rather that the collapse of the Bretton Woods fixed-exchange rate regime should be understood as a consequence of financial instability rather than as its cause.

As for the other phenomena that Reinhart and Rogoff cite, the sharp spike in oil prices was mostly a consequence of the same phenomenon that caused the Bretton Woods system to collapse— the rapid depreciation of the dollar relative to gold in the late 1960s and early 1970s. Although the Arab–Israeli war of 1973 was the immediate event that caused OPEC, the international oil cartel, to cut production, the consequent rise in the price of oil served to accomplish OPEC's longer-term objective: reversal of the decline in revenues in terms of gold. The main causes of the Third World debt crisis were, as I noted above, the rise in the price of oil and a slowdown in GDP growth, which likewise cannot be attributed to financial liberalization. While the collapse of commodity prices in the early 1980s may have been the straw that broke the camel's back, the foundation for the debt crisis had been laid several years earlier.

I will discuss the savings and loan crisis in the U.S. in some detail in Chapter 9. Here let me simply note two things. First, the crisis began because of the accelerating inflation in the 1970s— for which the rise in the price of oil, not financial liberalization, is mostly responsible. Second, *strict government controls* on the interest rates that savings and loans could charge borrowers and pay depositors pushed much of the industry to the brink of insolvency. The subsequent deregulation of the industry was a (failed) attempt to avert the impending crisis.

RISING DEBT BURDENS IN THE U.S.

The "debt ratio," that is, debt as a percentage of the debtor's income, is a frequently used measure of the burden of debt—how difficult it is for the debtor to repay the principal and interest. The idea behind this measure is that a person who has twice as much outstanding debt as another, but three times as much income, can more easily repay his or her debt even though it is larger in absolute terms.

Since the GDP is the income of a country as a whole, its debt ratio is debt as a percentage of GDP. As Figure 4.6 shows, the debt ratio of the entire U.S. economy (excluding the financial sector) was stable from 1947 through 1981.[7] In the next decade, however, it shot up from less than 150 percent to more than 200 percent. Between 1991 and 2000, the debt ratio was again stable, but it jumped from 205 percent to 274 percent between 2000 and 2009.

When the post-World War II period began, the ratio of Treasury debt to GDP exceeded 100 percent, because the U.S. government had borrowed massively to fight the war. The Treasury's debt ratio then fell continually through 1974, after which it leveled off. However,

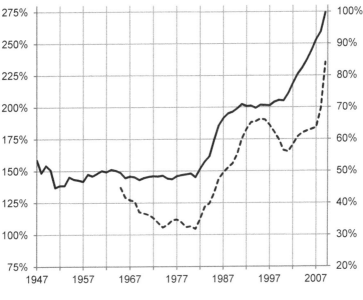

total debt, all domestic nonfinancial sectors (left-hand axis)
Treasury debt, gross, at end of fiscal year (right-hand axis)

Figure 4.6 Outstanding Debt as Percentage of GDP, U.S.

as Figure 4.6 shows, it rose very rapidly after 1981, as did the total economy's debt ratio. Except for a brief reversal that occurred during the dot-com bubble, the rise has been continuous. The increase in the Treasury's debt ratio during and after the Great Recession, which has been caused by depressed tax revenues as well as new tax cuts and "stimulus" spending, has been particularly rapid.

Here, finally, we seem to have phenomena that might properly be attributed to neoliberalism, since the timing, at least, appears right. Debt as a percentage of GDP did not begin to rise, either on the governmental level or in the economy as a whole, until Ronald Reagan became president. However, this appearance is very misleading. The long-term rise in the debt burden actually began in the 1970s, although it was temporarily masked by the rapid acceleration of inflation in that decade.

As Table 4.3 indicates, total debt and the Treasury debt both grew much more rapidly between 1973 and 1981 than they had before. The debt ratios nonetheless remained stable during this period, because the growth of (nominal) GDP also accelerated to a similar degree. However, more than three-fourths of the growth in GDP was due to inflation; the growth rate of real (inflation-adjusted) GDP fell substantially between 1973 and 1981.[8] If the rate of inflation had not increased, the debt ratios would have risen very rapidly during this period, by about 4 or 5 percent per year, on average.

Table 4.3 Debt and GDP, U.S. (average annual percentage growth rates)

| | Outstanding nominal debt | | GDP | | Debt growth minus nominal GDP growth | |
	Total, domestic nonfinancial	U.S. Treasury	Nominal	Real	Total, domestic nonfinancial	U.S. Treasury
1947–73	6.3%	2.3%	6.7%	3.9%	−0.3%	−4.4%
1973–81	10.1%	9.5%	10.2%	2.5%	−0.1%	−0.7%
1981–2007	7.9%	8.4%	5.8%	3.0%	2.1%	2.7%

In 1981, the total debt was equal to 145 percent of GDP. In 2007, it equaled 253 percent of GDP. However, if real GDP had increased after 1973 at the same rate that it increased, on average, between 1947 and 1973, the total debt in 2007 would have equaled only 180 percent of GDP.[9] Thus, the debt ratio, which actually increased by 108 percentage points between 1981 and 2007, would have increased by only 35 points. This implies that more than two-thirds of the increase was due to the slowdown in real GDP growth after 1973.

It is appropriate to measure the debt burden in nominal terms, since it is nominal debt, not real debt, which must be repaid. When inflation decelerated in the 1980s and thereafter, those who borrowed at fixed interest rates during the 1970s did not enjoy a reduction in the debt they owed! Yet ratios of debt to nominal GDP can be misleading statistics when the question is "when did the debt burden begin to rise?" Because increases and decreases in the rate of inflation affect debt and GDP to different degrees, they temporarily distort long-term trends in the ratios. When the rate of inflation rises, for instance, this causes nominal GDP to rise more rapidly in relationship to real GDP, but it does not cause existing debt to rise. Only new debt—current borrowing—is affected, and the debt ratio therefore falls temporarily. The opposite occurs when inflation decelerates.

To deal with this problem, it is helpful to set existing debt aside, and look just at the relationship between new net borrowing—that is, the *change* in debt—and GDP, both of which are affected by inflation to an equal degree. As Figure 4.7 shows, net borrowing

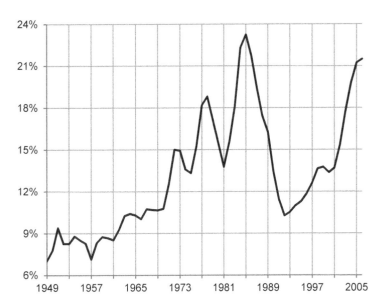

Figure 4.7   Change in Debt, All U.S. Domestic Nonfinancial Sectors
(as percentages of GDP; 3-yr centered moving average of annual percentage changes)

rose much more rapidly than GDP in the 1970s and early 1980s; the ratio of net borrowing to GDP more than doubled between 1970 and 1985. It then returned to its earlier level over the next several years, but only temporarily. From the early 1990s until 2007, the borrowing/GDP ratio kept rising, until it was once again double what it had been at the start of the 1970s.

Borrowing/GDP ratios of households and the Treasury are shown in Figure 4.8.[10] Household borrowing has fluctuated markedly, because of volatility in the housing market, but it rose rapidly as a share of GDP during the 1970s and its average level has risen since the early 1970s. The borrowing/GDP ratio of households averaged 3.3 percent between 1947 and 1970, rising to 4.7 percent between 1971 and 2001 and to 8.4 percent between 2002 and 2007. The recent rise in household borrowing was due mainly to rapid growth in home-mortgage borrowing, the causes of which were discussed

Figure 4.8 Changes in Debt of U.S. Treasury and Households
(as percentages of GDP; 3-yr centered moving averages of annual percentage changes)

in Chapter 3. Funds borrowed by the Treasury doubled as a share of GDP between 1970 and 1981, and more than doubled between 1981 and 1992. (The 1981 budget was adopted before Reagan was elected, during the final year of the Carter administration.) Between 1992 and 2000, the Treasury's borrowing/GDP ratio then gradually returned to its prior level, but it rose rapidly thereafter, to an average of 4.5 percent between 2002 and 2006.

All of the increase in the ratio of Treasury debt to GDP since 1970 is attributable to the falling profitability of U.S. corporations and to reductions in corporate income tax rates. As the income tax that corporations paid declined, much of the effect of falling profitability was shifted from corporations to the public at large. Although individual income tax revenue received by the federal government increased as a share of GDP after 1967, corporate income tax revenue fell dramatically (see Figure 4.9). The latter fell partly because of a relative decline in corporations' before-tax profits and partly because of reduced corporate tax rates. On average, before-tax profits equaled 11.6 percent of GDP between 1947 and 1969. Between 1970 and 2007, the average fell by almost

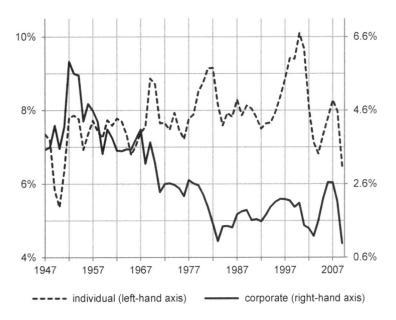

Figure 4.9   Individual and Corporate Income Taxes, U.S.
(tax receipts as percentages of GDP)

one-fourth, to 8.8 percent. And while the average effective tax rate on before-tax profits between 1947 and 1969 was 36.8 percent, it was reduced by more than one-third, to 23.5 percent, between 1970 and 2007.[11]

To measure the effect of these declines on the ratio of Treasury debt to GDP since 1970, I estimated what the ratio would have been if corporate tax revenue had not fallen as a share of GDP after 1967. (The 1967 share was slightly less than the average share between 1947 and 1967.) To obtain this hypothetical value, I first computed lost revenue by subtracting the actual corporate tax revenue figures from the hypothetical non-falling-share-of-GDP figures. I then reduced the level of Treasury debt in each year by the cumulative loss in revenue up to that point, and divided the difference by the year's GDP. The results of this exercise are shown in Figure 4.10. While the actual ratio of Treasury debt to GDP increased by 71 percent between 1970 and 2007, it would have *declined* by 19 percent if corporate income taxes had not fallen as a share of GDP. As of 2007, moreover, the debt/GDP ratio would have been 11 percent less than the minimum level it actually reached in 1981.

The point of this exercise was simply to assess the extent to which lost corporate tax revenue led to the government's rising debt

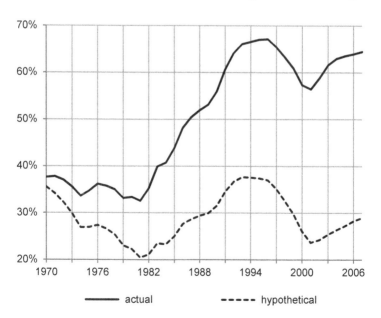

Figure 4.10   U.S. Treasury Debt as Percentage of GDP, Actual vs. Hypothetical

burden. I am not suggesting that the rise in the ratio of Treasury debt to GDP would *really* have been prevented by policies that kept corporate income taxes constant as a share of GDP. In 2001, such policies would have reduced corporations' average after-tax rate of profit, which was actually 7.9 percent, to a Depression-level 3.3 percent. It is thus very likely that such policies would have led—in the best case—to a drastic drop in the growth of productive investment spending and much slower GDP growth, and that the slowdown in GDP growth would have caused the debt/GDP ratio to rise instead of fall.

U.S. LABOR-MARKET CONDITIONS

Indicators of labor-market conditions likewise make clear that the recession of the mid-1970s was the turning point in recent U.S. economic history. I used the Congressional Budget Office's (CBO's) estimates of the potential labor force to compute the gap between it and the actual labor force. Since the *actual* labor force includes both employed and unemployed workers, the gap between the potential and actual labor forces is not a measure of unemployment. It instead measures the extent to which workers have dropped out of the labor force because of poor labor-market conditions. The gap is the difference between the numbers of people who are *potentially* available and *actually* available for work, where "available for work" means either working or actively searching for work.[12]

Between 1949 and 1973, the actual labor force was, on average, 0.13 percent greater than the potential one.[13] But between 1974 and 2008, the opposite was the case; on average, the actual labor force fell short of the potential one by 0.17 percent. Figure 4.11, which shows the percentage gap between the actual and potential labor forces for five-year periods since 1949, indicates that the average figures for 1949–73 and for 1974–2008 are fairly representative of these periods taken as a whole. The actual labor force exceeded the potential labor force in all but one of the five-year periods through 1973, while the potential labor force exceeded the actual labor force in all but one of the five-year periods thereafter.

Between 1974 and 1979, the actual labor force fell short of the potential labor force by 0.17 percent. This is the same percentage by which it fell short throughout the 1974–2008 period as a whole. This suggests that the deterioration of labor-market conditions after 1973 was immediate and persistent; it cannot properly be attributed to the rise of neoliberalism since the 1980s.

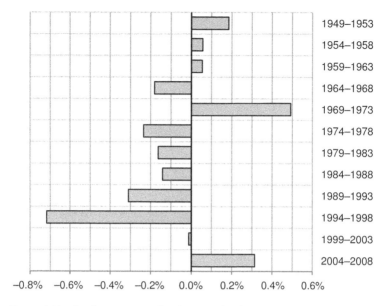

Figure 4.11   Gap between Actual and Potential Labor Force, U.S.
(percentage difference of actual from potential)

Figure 4.12 looks at the average (mean) duration of unemployment—the average number of weeks that currently unemployed workers (those without jobs who actively searched for work within the past month) have been unemployed.[14] Between 1948 and 1974, the duration figure was 11.2 weeks on average, and it fell slightly over time. But between 1975 and 2007—that is, even before the latest recession—the duration figure rose to 15.4 weeks on average, an increase of almost 40 percent, and it rose markedly throughout this period.

In January 1981, when Reagan became president, the average duration of unemployment was 14.3 weeks, the same as the trend value. This was 3.3 weeks greater than the trend value in 1974, and the trend value in 2007 was 6.0 weeks greater than in 1974. So if we use trend values to measure the long-run rise in the duration of unemployment, in order to avoid cherry picking of the data, we can say that more than half of the long-run rise in the duration of unemployment between 1974 and 2007 had already occurred prior to the "neoliberalization" of the U.S. economy.

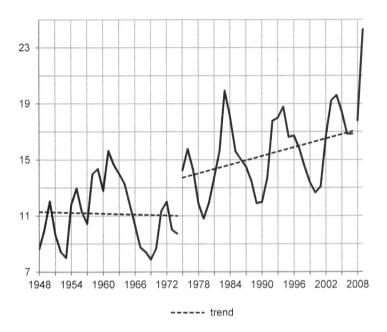

------ trend

Figure 4.12   Average Duration of Unemployment, U.S.
(mean number of weeks)

Figure 4.13 shows the growth of employees' pay—total
compensation per hour—after adjustment for inflation. In one case,
nominal compensation is adjusted for changes in the consumer
price index (CPI-U); in the other, it is adjusted for changes in the
GDP price index.[15] The dotted curves in Figure 4.13 show what
compensation would have been if it had grown in accordance with
its trend between 1948 and 1973. Although the different methods
of adjustment for inflation produce rather different trends in
compensation, that difference is not particularly important here,
where our focus is on the *changes* in the trends during the post-World
War II period and the timing of these changes.

Both compensation measures indicate that actual compensation
remained very close to the 1948–73 trend level throughout that
whole period, but that growth of compensation fell ever-further
behind that trend beginning in 1974. As I will discuss in Chapters
7 and 8, the decline in the growth of compensation was due entirely
to a decline in the growth of GDP and related measures of total

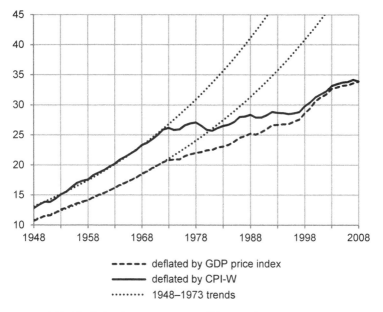

Figure 4.13   Real Hourly Compensation of U.S. Employees
(in constant 2008 dollars)

income and output, not to a decline in the share of income and
output that employees received.

By 2008, hourly compensation was far less than what it would
have been if the trend between 1948 and 1974 had persisted—36
percent less when we use the GDP price index to remove the effect of
inflation, or 53 percent less when we use the consumer price index.
But already by 1980, before Reagan took office, hourly compensation
was 11 percent below, or 21 percent below, its prior trend value.
Thus, 30 to 40 percent of the total decline in compensation relative
to the prior trend occurred during the first 20 percent of the period
following 1973, which implies that compensation growth slowed
down more rapidly in the 1970s than it did later. Hence the sharp
decline in the growth of compensation persisted under neoliberalism
but was not created by it.

INEQUALITY IN THE U.S.

Figure 4.14 shows movements in the degree of income inequality
among U.S. households between 1947 and 1992. It uses the

Gini coefficient to measure inequality; when the coefficient rises, inequality is greater. The graph ends in 1992 because the U.S. Census Bureau's figures for 1993 and later years are not comparable with those of earlier years.[16] Incomes were most equal in 1968, but inequality then increased, more or less continually. The trend toward greater inequality therefore began long before neoliberalism, and even before the recession of 1973–75.

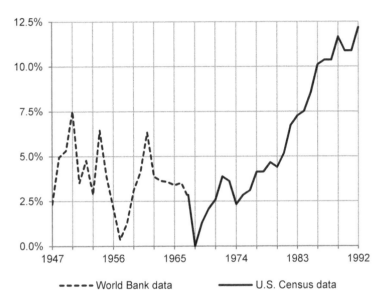

Figure 4.14 Changes in Income Inequality among U.S. Households
(percentage differences between Gini coefficients of indicated years and 1968)

The share of total income that the poorest 40 percent of households received fell by 1.1 percentage points between 1968 and 1981, and by 1.0 point between 1981 and 1992. The share received by the poorest 60 percent of households—the poorest 40 percent plus the middle 20 percent—fell by 2.0 percentage points between 1968 and 1981, and 1.9 points between 1981 and 1992.[17] Thus, the declines in the income shares of the poorest 40 percent and 60 percent through 1981, the year in which Reagan became president, were greater than the declines that occurred during the next 11 years.

Rising inequality in the U.S. is often attributed to neoliberalism, as if it alone were responsible for the rise. Yet as Figure 4.14 shows, the trend toward greater inequality began when economic policy was still Keynesian.

PUBLIC INFRASTRUCTURE IN THE U.S.

Government investment in infrastructure is an important indicator of the quality of life. Since overall economic conditions affect governments' ability to tax and borrow in order to fund infrastructure investment, such investment is also an indicator of the relative strength or weakness of the economy. The deterioration of public infrastructure in the U.S. has become a major concern in recent years, especially after 13 people were killed and 145 were injured when an eight-lane bridge in Minneapolis collapsed during rush hour in August 2007. Here I will be concerned to identify when the deterioration began.

Figure 4.15 shows the rate of growth in the net stock of state and local structures, alone and combined with the net stock of the federal government's nonmilitary structures, over the five years preceding the dates indicated.[18] At both the federal level and the

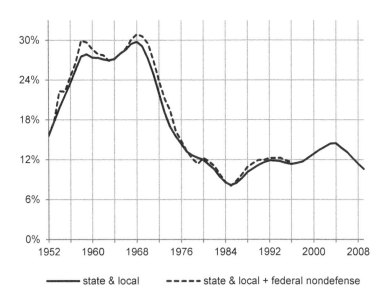

Figure 4.15   Growth of Government Structures, U.S.
(percentage change during prior 5 yrs)

state and local levels, about four-fifths of these "structures" consist of highways, streets, transit systems, and airfields; educational and health-care facilities; sewage, water supply, and public utilities facilities, and "conservation and development" structures. The net (post-depreciation) stock of structures is therefore a good proxy for public infrastructure.

As Figure 4.15 indicates, the growth in the net stock of public-sector structures plummeted drastically after 1968, for almost two decades. A very modest rebound then took place between the mid-1980s and mid-2000s, but the most recent trend is downward.[19]

Now, it is possible in principle that the decline of the country's infrastructure is attributable to neoliberalism, even though the decline began well before the neoliberal era. Assume that the very rapid growth in infrastructure spending through 1968 provided the country with so much excess capacity that little growth in the stock of structures was needed until the early 1980s. If that assumption were correct, then the sharp decline in the growth of structures from 1969 to 1980 would not have posed an imminent threat to the country's infrastructure, and we could blame neoliberalism for a problem that developed only thereafter.

However, what actually happened seems to be much different. According to Weiner (1999: 156), "Concern for the nation's deteriorating infrastructure prompted Congress to enact the Public Works Improvement Act of 1984" that created a group to assess the magnitude of the problem and make recommendations. In its final report of February 1988, the group stated:

> … this country's great public works inheritance … is in danger …

> At present, most major categories of public works in the United States are performing at only passable levels …

> Overall investment in public works has *slowed down in the last two decades in relation to the demands of growth and environmental concerns.* We have worn through the cushion of excess capacity built into earlier investments. In effect, we are now drawing down past investments without making commensurate investments of our own. (National Council on Public Works Improvement 1988: 1, emphasis added)

It would thus be very difficult to argue that neoliberal policies are exclusively or primarily responsible for the danger that this report describes. Deterioration of U.S. public infrastructure began sometime earlier, under Keynesian administrations.

CONCLUSION

The other trends that have been reviewed in this chapter also began prior to the rise of neoliberalism. Inequality began to increase even before the 1970s. Rising debt burdens in the U.S. have their origins in increases in borrowing that began to outpace GDP growth at the start of the 1970s. Debt and banking crises first accelerated as a result of the collapse of the Bretton Woods system at the start of the 1970s, and the rising rates of inflation and falling growth of GDP during that decade. And various measures of economic growth and labor-market conditions indicate clearly that relative stagnation began with the recession of the mid-1970s and that the economy never fully recovered thereafter. When this evidence is considered together with evidence of falling rates of profit and accumulation that we will consider next, it is clear that the turning point in recent U.S. economic history was the 1970s, not an imagined, but nonexistent, long-run boom that started in the 1980s "under neoliberalism."

For decades, the relative stagnation was kept under control largely by throwing debt and more debt at the problem. This "solution" also created some short-term artificial booms, especially in the 1990s and again in the 2000s. So you could think that a genuine boom was underway—if you refused to "tune your rhetoric to crisis" (Henwood 1994) and therefore refused to recognize that the "booms" were just the flip side of the ongoing series of debt crises and burst bubbles, by-products of the same artificial "solution."

Yet even those who argued that neoliberalism had put capitalism on a new and stable expansionary path had to belatedly change the tune of their rhetoric once the U.S. housing-market bubble burst and the world economy sank into the Great Recession. For instance, Duménil and Lévy recently acknowledged that

> ... when our book *Capital Resurgent: Roots of the Neoliberal Revolution* was published by Harvard University Press [in 2004, the neoliberal] strategy appeared successful ... The contemporary crisis is an outcome of the contradictions inherent in that strategy. The crisis revealed the strategy's unsustainable character. (Duménil and Lévy 2011: 1)

Of course, it is easy to revise conclusions in light of new events. It is more difficult, but just as necessary, to uncover the methodological and theoretical deficiencies that produced wrong conclusions in the first place, as I hope to do in the next three chapters.

5
Falling Rates of Profit and Accumulation

Note: The U.S. Department of Commerce's Bureau of Economic Analysis (BEA) is the main source of the data discussed in Chapters 5–7. Profit data come from the BEA's National Income and Product Accounts (NIPA) tables; investment, depreciation, and advanced capital ("net stock") data come from the BEA's Fixed Asset tables. Both sets of tables can be accessed from the BEA's homepage, www.bea.gov.

THE MOST OBVIOUS EXPLANATION

I argued in Chapter 4 that relative economic stagnation in the U.S. set the stage for the debt buildup of the last several decades and the latest crisis and recession. But what caused the relative stagnation? The most obvious explanation, and therefore the explanation that would seem most plausible, is that:

(1) the rate of profit fell and, because capital value was not destroyed to an extent sufficient to restore profitability, the rate of profit failed to rebound significantly following the economic slumps of the mid-1970s and early 1980s;

(2) the persistent fall in the rate of profit produced a persistent fall in the rate of capital accumulation;[1] and

(3) the fall in the rate of accumulation led in turn to sluggish growth of per capita GDP, corporations' output, and their compensation of employees, to rising debt burdens, and so on.

I will argue in this chapter that the above explanation is not only the most obvious one, but that it is *correct* as well.

   Points (1) and (2) are quite controversial, since many leftist economists contend that the rate of profit did rebound after the early 1980s and they therefore deny that persistent profitability problems were an underlying cause of the Great Recession. They instead regard the latest crisis and recession as *irreducibly* financial—that is, as phenomena caused by the "financialization" of capitalism and macroeconomic difficulties to which it led (and by the more immediate financial-sector problems that triggered the crisis). In contrast, point (3) is not particularly controversial; those who regard the crisis as irreducibly financial largely agree with it (see, for example, Duménil and Lévy 2004, Husson 2008, Stockhammer 2009). My defense of the obvious and plausible explanation will therefore focus on points (1) and (2).

In order to avoid burdening the main text of this chapter with long methodological digressions and detailed documentation of my data sources and computations, I discuss these matters mostly in an appendix at the end of the chapter. The points on methodology explain why I think that my findings cannot properly be dismissed on the grounds that my rate-of-profit measures are not all-purpose indexes of the "health" of the economy or "the Marxian" rate of profit, and why I focus on the profitability of the corporate sector rather than that of the U.S. economy as a whole.

RATE-OF-PROFIT TRENDS

My profit and rate-of-profit data pertain to the entire corporate sector of the U.S. economy; they thus include the profits of financial corporations as well as nonfinancial ones. Later in this section, I shall discuss the profitability of U.S. multinational corporations' foreign investment, but unless otherwise indicated, my analysis pertains to what the BEA calls "domestic" corporations. (Because the two sets of data are not strictly comparable, they need to be discussed separately.) The domestic data include foreign-based corporations' profits from their U.S. operations and their fixed assets located in the U.S., but exclude U.S.-based corporations' profits from abroad and their fixed assets located abroad. My references to "U.S. corporations" should therefore be understood in a geographical sense, not as references to the "nationality" of the corporations.

Figure 5.1 depicts movements in two measures of U.S. corporations' rate of profit. Both have the same denominator—fixed assets (fixed capital) valued at historical cost—but they measure profit in two different ways. One measure of profit is before-tax profit. The other, which I will call "property income,"[2] is a much broader measure of profit that is much closer to what Marx meant by "surplus-value." It counts as profit all of the output (net value added) of corporations that their employees do not receive. In addition to the before-tax profits of corporations, it includes the moneys spent to make interest payments and transfer payments (fines, court settlements, gift contributions, and so on), to pay sales and property taxes, and other minor items.

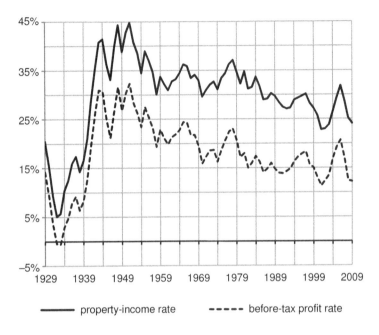

Figure 5.1   Rates of Profit, U.S. Corporations
(profits as percentages of historical cost of fixed assets)

On the whole, movements in these two rates of profit have been quite similar. Both rates plummeted sharply during the early years of the Great Depression, after which they rebounded substantially, most likely because of the massive destruction of capital value that had taken place. By 1939, the property-income rate of profit had regained 74 percent of the ground it lost after 1929, while the before-tax rate had regained 60 percent.

The rates of profit skyrocketed during World War II. However, the rebound in profitability was not solely a wartime phenomenon. Nor was it driven solely by demand—government borrowing to fight the war, foreign purchases of military equipment, and the "pent-up demand" that was supposedly unleashed when the war ended. It is doubtful that pent-up demand explains much of anything, since real

GDP fell after the war—largely because of an 81 percent decline in national defense spending between 1944 and 1947—and did not return to its 1945 level until mid-1950. And strong demand during the war cannot account for the fact that the rates of profit remained quite high *through the mid-1950s.*

What a purely demand-side explanation ignores is the tremendous boost to profitability provided by the destruction of capital value during the Depression and war. During the 14 years between the start of 1931 and the start of 1945, U.S. corporations' advanced capital increased by 3 percent. To understand the magnitude of destruction that this implies, the 3 percent increase can be contrasted to the 164 percent increase in GDP during the same period, and the 192 percent increase in corporations' advanced capital during the following 14 years. If advanced capital had not fallen in relationship to GDP between the start of 1930 and the start of 1947, its level at the start of 1947 would have been more than twice as great as it actually was, which means that rates of profit would have been less than half of what they actually were—that is, roughly at the same levels as those to which they fell during the next 60 years. And if that situation had persisted through the mid-1950s, *there would have been no postwar boom in profitability. It is doubtful whether there would have been a postwar boom at all.*

As it was, a long decline in profitability began in the latter half of the 1950s. It is true that the two rates of profit were basically trendless—neither rising nor falling on average—during the 1960s and 1970s, but that was largely because of accelerating inflation, as we will see below. Especially in the 1970s, the increase in the rate of inflation tended to boost nominal profitability and counteract the fall in the rates of profit that would otherwise have taken place. Once Federal Reserve policy drove up interest rates and the double-dip recession of the early 1980s occurred, the rates of profit, especially the before-tax profit rate, fell substantially.

In the period between 1982 and the latest crisis, neither rate of profit experienced a sustained recovery. The property-income rate of profit continued to fall; the only significant exception to the general trend was the sharp but brief rise in profitability produced by the asset-price bubble that preceded the crisis. The before-tax rate of profit was also a good deal lower in the trough year of 2001 than in the 1982 trough. Between 1982 and 2001, the property-income rate of profit fell by 26.9 percent (not percentage points), and the before-tax rate of profit fell by almost as much, 26.3 percent.

On the other hand, while the property-income rate of profit trended downward between 1982 and 2007, the before-tax rate of profit trended upward to a slight extent—by 0.04 percentage points per year—during the same period. The main reason why the trajectories of the two rates of profit differed is that interest rates fell, which allowed corporations to reduce their interest payments. The sales, property, and similar taxes that corporations pay also fell as a share of property income. Thus, if we count all non-labor income (property income) as profit, we can say that the rate of profit trended downward during this period, but that corporations were able to keep a larger share of the relatively shrinking pool of profit for themselves as the share that they turned over to their creditors and tax authorities declined.

The sharp fall in the rates of profit that occurred at the end of the 2000s is also evidence that neither rate of profit recovered in a sustained manner. Given the severity of the Great Recession, it may be wondered why the rates of profit did not fall even more sharply. The answer is that the BEA does not treat losses due to bad debt, funds set aside to cover losses on loans, or reduced asset prices as factors that reduce profit. In contrast, corporate financial accountants do generally subtract these items from profit. The rates of profit would have fallen further in the late 2000s, probably much further, if the BEA did not exclude these items from its profit estimates. Between the second quarter of 2007 and the fourth quarter of 2008, after-tax profits of all corporations as measured by the BEA fell from $1003 billion to $283 billion, while the "as reported" operating earnings of the five hundred corporations that make up the S&P 500 fell from $194 billion to –$202 billion.[3]

PROFITABILITY OF U.S. FOREIGN INVESTMENT

The trends discussed above pertain to "domestic" corporations only. If the rate of profit that U.S. multinational corporations obtained from their foreign operations had risen, the evidence that the domestic rate of profit fell and failed to recover might not be very significant. However, the rate of profit on foreign investment also fell and failed to recover. To be sure, the share of profits that U.S. multinationals receive from their foreign operations has risen markedly. Yet their fixed assets located abroad have risen even more markedly as a share of their total fixed assets.

To measure the profitability of U.S. multinationals' foreign investment, I computed their income from direct investment abroad as a percentage of their direct investment abroad.[4] The pre-2006 incomes figures measure profits after payment of U.S. and foreign withholding taxes, while the figures for subsequent years measure profits before payment of these taxes. In cases in which a foreign company is only partly U.S.-owned, the BEA estimates the U.S. owners' income by assuming that their share of the company's income is equal to their share of the company's equity.

Figure 5.2 shows the movements in this rate of profit since 1982, the first year for which data are available, and compares them to the before- and after-tax rates of profit of domestic corporations. On the whole, the movements in all three series are similar. But while the domestic rates were basically trendless from 1982 through 2007, the rate of profit on foreign investment trended downward by 0.13 percentage points per year. It also fell somewhat more sharply than the domestic rates between the 1982 and 2001 troughs. The after-tax domestic rate of profit was 3.1 percentage points (28 percent) lower in 2001 than in 1982, and the before-tax domestic rate was 3.7 points (25 percent) lower, while the rate of profit on foreign investment was 4.4 points (37 percent) lower.

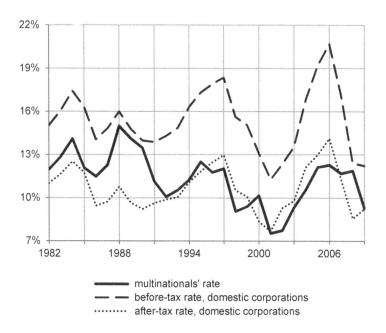

———— multinationals' rate
— — before-tax rate, domestic corporations
·········· after-tax rate, domestic corporations

Figure 5.2   U.S. Multinationals' Rate of Profit on Foreign Direct Investment (all rates are profits as percentages of the historical cost of fixed assets)

Thus, even though my analysis of declining profitability elsewhere in this book relies on data for domestic corporations only, the above comparisons suggest that this is not a serious limitation. It does not cause us to overstate, and may cause us to understate, the magnitude of the fall in the U.S. corporations' rate of profit since 1982.

The decline in the rate of profit on foreign investment was an extremely broad-based phenomenon. Between 1982 and 2007, 86 percent of all U.S.-owned foreign capital was invested in 20 countries. U.S. *multinationals' rate of profit trended downward in 18 of these countries.*[5] Since very few of them were less-developed countries, it does not appear that rising wages in the Third World account for the downward trend. And since the downward trend was so broad-based, it also does not appear that other area-specific factors can account for it. On the contrary, the generalized decline in the profitability of U.S. multinationals suggests that rates of profit may well have fallen throughout most of the world during this period.

CIRCULATING CAPITAL

The denominators of my rate-of-profit measures include only fixed capital (fixed assets). They exclude circulating capital—compensation paid to employees, and expenditures for inventories of raw materials and the like—because information on the turnover of circulating capital is not available.

To see why turnover information matters, consider a worker who is paid $500 every week. Her annual pay is $26,000, but it would be wrong to say that $26,000 is advanced in order to hire her for a year. Imagine that the company that employs her advances $500 at the start of some week, but it recovers the whole $500 by the end of the week when it sells the products she produces. It can then hire her at the start of the next week by advancing the *same* $500. If it recovers this advance by the end of the week, it can hire her for a third week with the *same* $500 advance. And so on. Thus only $500, not $26,000, is advanced during the year in order to hire her. But if we know only the annual wage figure, $26,000—that is, if we do not know that the capital that is advanced "turns over" 52 times a year—there is no way to know how much capital is advanced in order to hire the worker for a year. And the same problem prevents us from saying how much capital is advanced for raw materials and other inventories.

Nonetheless, some researchers have chosen to include inventories as part of advanced capital. The ratio of property income (or some closely related measure of profit) to the sum of fixed assets and inventories is sometimes regarded as the "Marxian" rate of profit, that is, as a close proxy for what Marx meant by the ratio of surplus-value to advanced capital. However, inclusion of inventories in the denominator of the rate of profit is problematic, not only because of the turnover problem, but also because some inventory expenditures are not advances of capital.

In national accounts, inventories include not only stocks of raw materials, semi-finished goods, and "work-in-progress" (partially completed goods and services), but also stocks of finished goods that have not been sold.[6] The last item is clearly not part of what Marx meant by advanced capital. In terms of what he called the circuit of capital, M – C ... P ... C' – M', the capital advanced before production (M – C) did not include expenditures on unsold finished goods; these expenditures are instead part of C'.

In any case, inclusion of inventories in the denominator of the rate of profit does not significantly affect the results. As Figure 5.3 makes clear, the extent to which the before-tax rate of profit falls

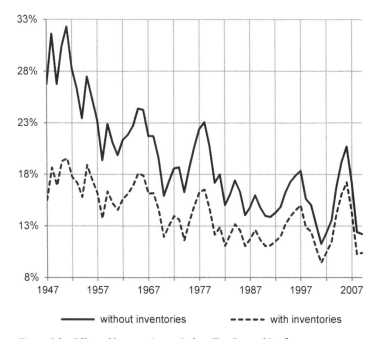

Figure 5.3   Effect of Inventories on Before-Tax Rate of Profit

is less when inventories are included, but it remains true that the rate of profit falls through 1982 and that no sustained rebound occurs thereafter. And as Table 5.1 shows, it remains true that the property-income rate of profit also fell during the first part of the postwar period and continued to fall after 1982. Thus, the conclusion that the rate of profit of U.S. corporations failed to experience a sustained recovery after the early 1980s is robust; it does not depend on the selection of any particular numerator or denominator.

Table 5.1   Rates of Profit, U.S. Corporations, Selected Trough Years

	Before-tax rate		Property-income rate	
	Without inventories	*With inventories*	*Without inventories*	*With inventories*
Percentage-pt. change				
1949–2001	–15.5	–7.5	–16.0	–5.5
1949–61	–6.9	–2.4	–7.9	–1.9
1961–82	–4.8	–3.5	0.3	0.3
1982–2001	–3.7	–1.6	–8.4	–3.9
Percentage change				
1949–2001	–57.8%	–44.2%	–41.3%	–22.2%
1949–61	–25.7%	–14.0%	–20.3%	–7.7%
1961–82	–24.4%	–23.9%	0.8%	1.5%
1982–2001	–24.9%	–14.7%	–26.9%	–16.9%

ADJUSTING FOR INFLATION

This conclusion is also robust in the sense that it holds true even after rates of profit are adjusted for inflation and for changes in the relationship between money and labor-time.[7] As we shall see, although such adjustments have a significant effect on the *level* of the rate of profit, they have little effect on its *trend* since the early 1980s. This finding is extremely important. As I will discuss below and in the next chapter, evidence of a persistent fall in historical-cost rates of profit has been dismissed on the grounds that historical-cost measures are distorted by inflation and therefore meaningless. But since such distortion has been negligible, the evidence cannot be properly dismissed.

According to the concept of inflation with which we are most familiar, inflation occurs if there is an increase in the money price of a given set of physical items. However, Marx employed a different concept of inflation, according to which inflation occurs if there is an increase in the money price of a set of items that has a given cost in terms of labor-time.[8]

To adjust for inflation in the first sense, I deflated (divided) each year's profit and net investment in fixed assets by that year's GDP price index. To adjust for inflation in the latter sense, I deflated the same variables by a proxy for the monetary expression of labor-time (MELT). The MELT is the amount of new value, measured in money terms, that is created by an hour of labor. Thus, a 10 percent rise in the MELT signifies that commodities' prices have risen by 10 percent, on average, in relationship to their values as measured in terms of labor-time. (For further discussion of the MELT and its application, see Kliman 2007: 25–6, 127–32, and Chapters 9 and 10.) Although both procedures give us variables that are adjusted for inflation, in order to avoid confusion I will call variables that result from the first procedure "inflation-adjusted" and variables that result from the second procedure "MELT-adjusted."

Figures 5.4 and 5.5 show the trajectories of the inflation- and MELT-adjusted rates of profit and, for comparison, the unadjusted rates of profit, during the post-World War II period. In general, the adjustments do not significantly affect trends in the rates of profit

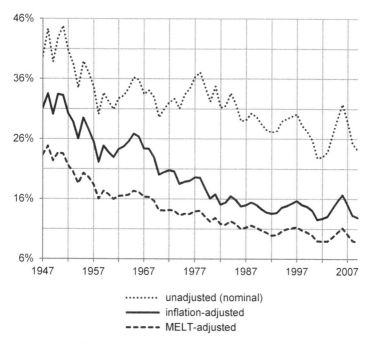

Figure 5.4   Inflation-Adjusted Property-Income Rates of Profit

even though they result in rates of profit that are much lower than the unadjusted rates. The period of rapidly accelerating inflation, the 1970s, is the key exception to this generalization. The nominal (unadjusted) rates of profit rose substantially between 1970 and 1979, but three of the four deflated rates fell. (The remaining deflated rate—the MELT-adjusted before-tax profit rate—rose by 3 percent, while its nominal counterpart rose by 30 percent.)

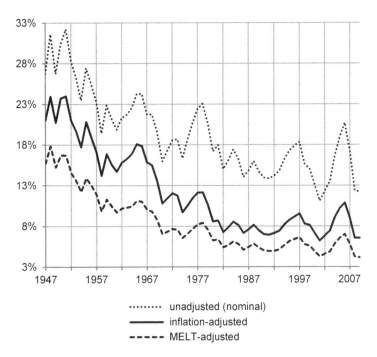

Figure 5.5   Inflation-Adjusted Before-Tax Profit Rates

Since 1982, on the other hand, the trajectories of the inflation- and MELT-adjusted rates of profit have been very similar to one another and to the trajectories of the unadjusted rates of profit, as Figure 5.6 shows. This reflects the fact that, throughout this period, the rate of inflation of the general price level and the rate of inflation of the MELT were both roughly constant in relationship to the growth rate of net investment.[9]

The conclusion that no sustained recovery of the rate of profit occurred after 1982 therefore remains valid even after we adjust for changes in prices and the MELT. Not only the nominal rates,

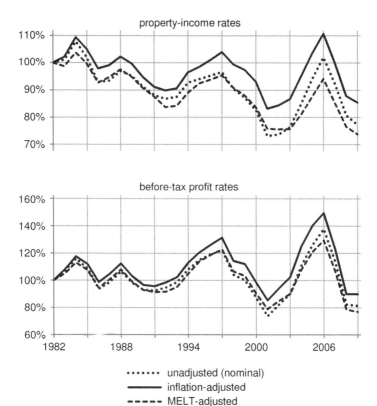

Figure 5.6   Adjusted and Unadjusted Rates of Profit
(percentages of 1982 rates, U.S. corporations)

but also all four adjusted rates of profit, fell between the troughs of 1982 and 2001. The percentage fall in the MELT-adjusted rates of profit was almost as great as the fall in the nominal rates, while the percentage fall in the inflation-adjusted rates was about three-fifths as great. Both adjusted property-income rates of profit trended downward between 1982 and 2007, while the adjusted before-tax profit rates trended upward to a slight extent.

These results were challenged by Michel Husson (2009), a proponent of the view that the rate of profit rebounded significantly after 1982 as a result of neoliberal policies that increased the rate of exploitation. He claimed that my inflation-adjustment procedure produces inflation- and MELT-adjusted rates of profit that are "systematic[ally] biased" in a downward direction, that is, that they fall further and further below rates of profit that are adjusted for inflation in a "correct" manner.

As we will see, this claim is incorrect, and Husson's objection turns out to have little practical significance for the key question under discussion: was there a sustained recovery of the rate of profit after the early 1980s? Its practical significance is minimal because there is only a very slight difference between the trends in my deflated rates of profit and the trends that result when depreciation figures are deflated in a manner like the one Husson proposed.

His objection has to do with how I adjust net investment figures. Net investment is the difference between gross investment and depreciation. Since the depreciation figures I use value depreciation at historical cost, when I deflate a particular year's net investment by the GDP price index or MELT of that year, I in effect use the same deflator to deflate both gross investment and historical-cost depreciation. However, Husson argued, it is incorrect to deflate the current year's historical-cost depreciation by the *current* year's GDP price index or MELT, since the fixed assets that are depreciating were bought in *earlier* years at different prices, not at the prices of the current year.

The correct procedure, he maintained, is to deflate depreciation by "something like" the price index or MELT of the year in which fixed assets of average age were purchased. Husson evidently wrote "something like" because the ideal procedure he had in mind was to deflate the depreciation figure for each fixed asset by the price index or MELT of the year in which that fixed asset was purchased. The procedure he recommended should yield "something like" the same result. Yet it is unclear how close the approximation would be, especially because the U.S. government's depreciation estimates are not straight-line, and because different years' contributions to total depreciation are unequal.

Consequently, in Kliman (2010a), I implemented the spirit of Husson's proposal in a slightly different way.[10] His essential point was that expenses incurred in any year should be deflated by the price index (or MELT) of the same year. I produced new inflation-adjusted figures that fulfill this requirement by using current-cost depreciation data instead of the historical-cost depreciation data I used originally. Since current-cost depreciation figures use *current* prices to measure the depreciation of fixed assets purchased in the past, and my revised procedure deflates these depreciation figures by the *current* GDP price index or MELT, it overcomes Husson's objection to my original deflation procedure.

Use of the current-cost depreciation figures yields estimates that are "something like" the ones that would result by deflating each historical-cost depreciation figure by the price index or MELT of the year in which the associated investment was made. Indeed, if the index of fixed asset prices were to change by the same percentage that the GDP price index or MELT changes, the results would be identical.[11]

Figure 5.7 shows how—and how little—the revised deflation procedure affects the trends in the deflated property-income rates of profit. *The revised procedure, just like my original one, leads to the conclusions that no sustainable rebound in inflation- or MELT-adjusted rates of profit took place after the early 1980s, and that the deflated rates of profit trended downward during this period.* Differences between the trends in the original and revised

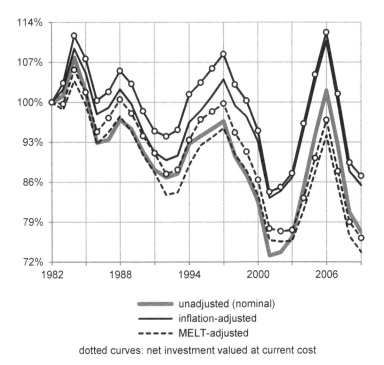

Figure 5.7   Effect of Alternative Adjustments on Rates of Profit
(property-income rates, U.S. corporations, as percentages of 1982 rates)

rates of profit were quite small throughout the whole period, and they narrowed considerably in the late 1990s and early 2000s. This shows that, contrary to what Husson claimed, my original procedure does *not* produce deflated rates of profit that fall further and further below rates of profit that result from the kind of inflation-adjustment procedure he proposes.

Husson (2010) subsequently responded to these arguments in *International Viewpoint* (an official publication of the Fourth International political grouping):

> ... what has been the evolution of the rate of profit since the early 1980s ...? ... the main controversy concerns the mode of valorisation of [that is, the method of valuing] capital: either at current prices—as done by most contributions—or at historic cost which is, according to Andrew Kliman ... the only correct method. I have discussed this position in a text called *Les coûts historiques d'Andrew Kliman* ... The response by Kliman (*Masters of words*, 2010[a]) does not seem to me to change the terms of the debate on this point nor to fundamentally challenge the arguments I have advanced. In truth, this choice (historic cost or current prices) does not have enormous empirical implications. The true difference resides in the corrections subsequently made by Kliman to measure the rate of profit in value which lead to tendentially falling rates of profit over the last 50 years.

What Husson means by "corrections ... to measure the rate of profit in value" is my procedure for adjusting the rate of profit to eliminate the effect of changes in the MELT. He writes that the "true difference" between my empirical results and his stems from this procedure, rather than from the fact that I value advanced capital at its historical cost while he values it at its current cost. However, Figures 5.6 and 5.7—and similar graphs contained in the response to which he refers—clearly show that deflation of the nominal variables by the MELT has extremely little effect. During the period in question, the trends in the nominal rates of profit (with capital valued at historical cost) and the MELT-adjusted rates of profit are almost identical.[12]

THE FALLING RATE OF ACCUMULATION

The rate of accumulation is the ratio of net investment to advanced capital. Since the rate of profit is the ratio of profit to advanced capital, the rate of accumulation is equal by definition to the ratio of net investment to profit times the rate of profit.[13] The rate of profit is therefore a key determinant of the rate of accumulation. If all profit were invested, the rate of accumulation would equal the rate of profit, so the rate of profit is essentially the maximum rate of accumulation. Moreover, if the fraction of profit that is used for (productive) investment is roughly constant over time, the rate of accumulation will rise and fall by roughly the same percentage that the rate of profit rises or falls. It is therefore reasonable to expect that the rate of accumulation will track the rate of profit.

Those who deny that a persistent fall in the rate of profit lies at the root of the Great Recession therefore face a serious problem. To measure profitability, they use the current-cost "rate of profit," which did indeed rebound after the early 1980s. Yet if the rate of profit experienced a sustained recovery during the quarter-century that preceded the financial crisis, how can we explain the extremely curious fact that the rate of accumulation (and thus GDP growth, compensation of employees, and so on) failed to recover along with it?

The most obvious—and, *prima facie*, the most plausible— explanation is the one I shall put forward in the next chapter: the current-cost "rate of profit" is actually not a rate of profit at all. In particular, it does not regulate businesses' investment behavior. Thus, it is not surprising that the rate of accumulation has declined even as the current-cost "rate of profit" has risen.

Instead of embracing this obvious and plausible explanation, those who reject the idea that falling profitability was an indirect cause of the Great Recession have hypothesized that a distinctly neoliberal "regime of accumulation" emerged in the early 1980s (Husson 2008, Stockhammer 2009). They argue that the rate of accumulation fell, not because of a lack of profit, but because the new neoliberal regime of accumulation was one in which profit was diverted away from productive investment and into financial markets. And they thus contend that the latest crisis of capitalism is an irreducibly financial one, rather than a crisis rooted in underlying profitability problems.

For instance, Duménil and Lévy wrote that

… the continuing poor performance of the American and European economies with respect to capital accumulation [is] actually the effect of the specific dynamics of neoliberalism. One can, therefore, assert that the structural crisis is over and blame neoliberalism for poor accumulation rates. (Duménil and Lévy 2004: 65)

Similarly, Husson (2008) argued that

> [the] decrease of the wage-share has allowed a spectacular recovery of the average rate of profit from the mid 1980s.
>
> But ... the rate of accumulation has continued to fluctuate around a level lower than that before the crisis. In other words, the drain on wages has not been used to invest more.
>
> ... The growing mass of surplus value which has not been accumulated has [to] mainly be distributed in the form of financial revenues, and that is where the source of the process of financialisation is to be found. The difference between the rate of profit and the rate of investment is a good indicator of the degree of financialisation.

If it were true that the rate of productive accumulation has failed to respond, throughout an entire quarter-century of capitalism, to a substantial rise in the rate of profit, it would be extremely peculiar. As Husson (2008) acknowledged, such a disconnect between the rates of profit and accumulation is "more or less unprecedented in the history of capitalism."

But it isn't true. At least, it isn't true of the last quarter-century of U.S. capitalism. As Figure 5.8 shows, the rate of accumulation of U.S. corporations has indeed tracked the rate of profit quite closely during the last *four decades*, in the sense that both rates fell and in the sense that movements in the rate of profit almost always preceded movements in the rate of accumulation by one or more years.[14] The property-income rate of profit peaked at 37.1 percent in 1978 and fell to 22.8 percent in 2001, while the rate of accumulation fell from a peak of 13.3 percent in 1979 to a pre-crisis trough of 2.8 percent in 2003.

This relationship is no fluke. During the period shown in Figure 5.8, variations in the rate of profit account for 83 percent of the variations in the rate of accumulation of the following year (that is, the R^2 is 0.83), and the p-value is less than 1/900 trillion. This means that, if there were *actually* no relationship between the rates of profit and accumulation, there would be less than one chance in 900 trillion that the *observed* relationship between them would be as strong as the one we observe here.

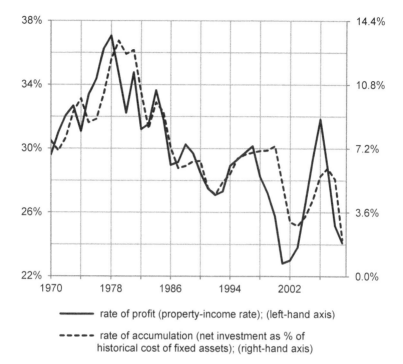

rate of profit (property-income rate); (left-hand axis)

rate of accumulation (net investment as % of
historical cost of fixed assets); (right-hand axis)

Figure 5.8   The Rate of Profit and the Rate of Accumulation

The evidence also fails to support the claim that a distinctive
"regime of accumulation" emerged under neoliberalism that
induced companies to purchase financial instruments with their
profit, instead of using the profit to acquire additional productive
assets. As Figure 5.9 indicates, U.S. corporations' net investment
in fixed productive assets constituted a slightly *larger* percentage of
their profit during the 1981–2001 period than it did between 1947
and 1980, and this result holds true for all four measures of profit
that the graph considers.[15] The share of profit that was invested in
production did plummet drastically after 2001, but since it did not
decline during the first 21 years of the neoliberal era, the post-2001
decline cannot be attributed to a distinctively neoliberal "regime
of accumulation."

The cause of the post-2001 decline was instead the lag with which
corporations responded to the rapid rise in profits during the bubble
years that preceded the latest crisis. (This lag is not surprising;
major investment projects often take a good deal of time to plan

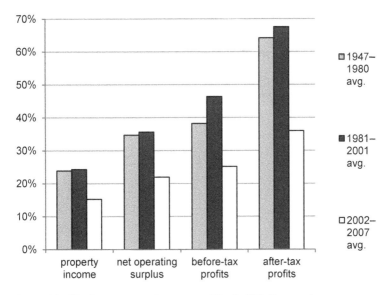

Figure 5.9 Net Investment as Percentage of Profit, U.S. Corporations

and fund.) After-tax profits jumped by 35 percent between 2001 (a trough-rate-of-profit year) and 2003, but net investment declined by 41 percent during the same period, as corporations continued to carry out investment decisions—or non-investment decisions—they made while the rate of profit was falling sharply.

Between 2003 and 2007, on the other hand, productive investment increased far more rapidly than did profit, as corporations' investment decisions finally caught up with the bubble. After-tax profit increased by 35 percent during that period, while net investment shot up by 151 percent. In fact, *while corporations' after-tax profit increased by $222 billion during those four years, their net investment increased by far more than that amount, $280 billion. They were investing all of the additional profit they made, and then some.* This is certainly not the kind of behavior that would occur under a distinctive "regime of accumulation" in which portfolio investment increasingly takes the place of productive investment. Yet because productive investment continued to fall during 2002 and 2003 while profit was rebounding, the average share of profit that was invested during the 2002–07 period was much lower than normal.

The economists who claim that the neoliberal era is characterized by a diversion of profit from productive investment into financial markets point to the fact that the share of profit invested in fixed assets has declined markedly since the early 1980s (see, for example, Stockhammer 2009: 9–11; Husson 2010). As Figure 5.10 shows, this is indeed a fact, but an extremely misleading one. What happened is that the before-tax rate of profit plummeted sharply between 1978 and 1982 (see Figure 5.5), but the rate of accumulation at first declined much more modestly, owing to the lag with which corporations respond to changes in profitability. As a result, the percentage of after-tax profit that was invested in additional fixed assets at the start of the 1980s was abnormally high—119 percent in 1980, 104 percent in 1981, and 94 percent in 1982.

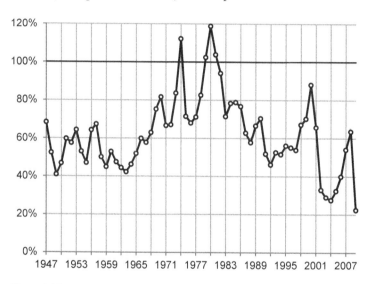

Figure 5.10   Net Investment as Percentage of After-Tax Profit, U.S. Corporations

In other words, *U.S. corporations were investing more after-tax profit than the after-tax profit they actually had*. Since dividends continued to be paid, this meant that corporations were depleting the funds set aside to replace and maintain their physical capital. This situation was obviously unsustainable, so the share of profit that was accumulated fell markedly beginning in 1983. But the important point is that it fell back to *normal* levels. Between 1983 and 2001, net investment equaled 64 percent of after-tax profit, on average, which was well above the average level between 1947 and 1972 (57 percent) and somewhat above the average level between 1947 and 1978 (61 percent).[16]

The data therefore fail to support the notion that "finance" has become uncoupled from the "real" economy. No neoliberal shift away from productive investment in favor of portfolio investment took place. The *entire* fall in the rate of accumulation is therefore attributable to the fall in the rate of profit.

APPENDIX: METHODOLOGY, DATA, AND COMPUTATIONS

No Single Rate of Profit

I have made no attempt to construct a measure of "the correct" rate of profit. I believe that there are many different legitimate ways of measuring rates of profit,[17] and that none serves as an all-purpose measure. The most relevant rate of profit to consider always depends upon the particular question being addressed.

Here are some examples of what I mean. If we are concerned with companies' investment behavior, we should look at measures of profitability that they know and care about, not "underlying" ones, and we should ideally look at anticipated rates of profit rather than actually realized rates. However, if we are concerned (as I am here) to assess historical trends in profitability, we should refer to actually realized rates of profit. If we wish to inquire (as I will do in Chapter 6) about the relationship between rates of profit and stock-market rates of return, or the rate of profit as a determinant of investment decisions, a rate of profit based on a "narrow" definition of profit such as after-tax profits may be appropriate. On the other hand, if we wish to inquire into the effect of class-based changes in income distribution on the rate of profit (as I will also do, in Chapter 7), a rate of profit based on a broad definition of profit, such as my property income measure, is called for. If we wish to *explain* fluctuations in observed rates of profit, then theory-based measures of the rate of profit, such as a rate of profit that adjusts for changes in the MELT, and/or a rate that adjusts for changes in the price level, may play a significant role in the analysis. And if we wish to explain phenomena such as crises and slumps, theory-based measures of the rate of profit may well be more appropriate than more directly observable ones.

Because there is no all-purpose measure of "the" rate of profit, it is not legitimate to reject a particular measure on the grounds that it fails to fulfill an all-purpose role. For instance, the ratio of nominal profits to advanced capital measures the actually realized nominal rate of return on capital investment. It is not an all-purpose index of "the health of the economy," or of how well capitalists are currently doing. Yet it is not *meant* to be either of these things, and it is therefore not legitimate to reject it because it fails to serve these functions.

One reason why the nominal rate of profit is not an all-purpose index of how well capitalists are doing is that, while inflation raises the nominal rate of profit, it also erodes the real wealth of investors and hurts those businesses whose nominal costs happen to increase more rapidly than their sales revenues. This does not mean that the nominal rate of profit is somehow an "incorrect" measure of profitability: it correctly measures what it is intended to measure. What it does mean is that rates of profit generally, and the nominal rate in particular, are not the only things that matter. An analysis of "the health of the economy," or of how well capitalists are doing, needs to look at a variety of factors and perhaps employ other measures of profitability—such as rates of profit adjusted for changes in the MELT and/or the price level—in *addition* to the nominal rate, in order to address questions other than ones about movements in the actually realized nominal rate of return on capital investment.

The key reason why the nominal rate of profit matters is that businesses do not use their profits only in order to buy goods and services. If that were the only use of profits, it wouldn't matter how much nominal profit they bring in. All that would matter is the quantity of goods and services that the profit can buy, that is, inflation-adjusted profit. But businesses also use—and need—profit in order to repay their debts and pay taxes, and so the level of nominal profit is important. If a business must repay $10.5 million this year, $11 million in profits when the rate of inflation is 10 percent is *not* equivalent to $10 million in profits in a zero-inflation environment. The difference between them might well be the difference between solvency and bankruptcy, or solvency and being taken over by the government.

"The Marxian" Rate of Profit?

I have also made no attempt to construct "the Marxian" rate of profit. One reason why I have not done so is that there is no such animal. Marx employed several different rates of profit in his economic writings. With regard to units of measurement, his theoretical discussions generally refer to a rate of profit measured in terms of labor-time or adjusted for changes in the MELT. But when analyzing empirical data, he also discussed the nominal rate of profit (Marx 1989b: 93–4). He sometimes used the surplus-value *created* in the numerator of the rate of profit, while at other times he used the profit actually *received* (these two things are equal in the aggregate, according to his theory, but not at the firm or industry level). And in addition to a rate of profit in which the numerator includes all parts of surplus-value (industrial profit, interest, rental income, and so on), he also referred to a rate with only industrial profit in the numerator (Marx 1991a, Chapter 15).

Another reason why I have not attempted to construct the Marxian rate of profit is that the data that would be needed to estimate it with any precision are not available. Marx's LTFRP pertains to the total social capital, which in our day is the capital of the world economy as a whole, not that of any one nation or region. But reliable profitability data for the world economy do not exist. There is also a sizable discrepancy between surplus-value as defined by Marx and profit as defined by the BEA, my main source of data. This is because depreciation due to obsolescence ("moral depreciation") does not reduce surplus-value but does reduce profit as defined by the BEA. And because advanced capital figures are net of depreciation, they too are seriously affected by this problem. Yet data that would allow one to reliably correct for the moral depreciation problem are not available.[18]

In addition, the rates of profit to which Marx's theory refers differ from the rates that some researchers have christened "the Marxian" rate. This is because the "Marxian" rates include only fixed assets (fixed capital), or sometimes fixed assets and inventories, in their measures of advanced capital, while Marx included such items as wage payments, stocks of money, and purchases of land and financial instruments, and he excluded some inventories.

Another reason why I have not tried to construct the Marxian rate of profit is that the task of theory is to account for *observed* phenomena. Thus the purpose of a study of profitability should be to account for movements in what businesses and investors mean when they talk about the rate of profit or rate of return, rather than to account for movements in a theoretical construct. The latter is of interest only insofar as it helps to explain the former.

I think that some theoretical profitability constructs do help significantly to explain real-world phenomena. However—and this is my final reason for eschewing efforts to construct the Marxian rate of profit—such constructs are not *determinants* of real-world phenomena; they play a role in analysis but not a causal role in the real world. It is thus strictly speaking wrong to say that a rise or fall in the Marxian rate of profit (or "value rate of profit," and so on) caused a rise or fall in the observed rate. I think that this hypostatization is the source of the persistent, misguided search for the holy-grail rate of profit, the Marxian rate that is supposedly the underlying cause of observed phenomena. The actual causes of changes in the observed rate of profit are processes resulting from human actions, such as technical innovation. Movements in theoretical profitability constructs and their subcomponents (the rate of surplus value, the value composition of capital) are *effects* of these processes. Thus what theorists should do, and what I attempt to do in this book is explain observed phenomena in terms of the processes affecting them.

As long as hypostatizations are not thought to be real entities, it does no harm to say that a theoretical construct rather than a process "caused" a phenomenon—for instance that "a rise in the technical composition of capital," rather than the process of technical innovation, "caused" the rate of profit to fall. But there is no *need* to say this, and thus there is no *need* to construct the Marxian rate of profit or to argue over which rate is the Marxian one. The analysis can be conducted in terms of the processes actually doing the causing. An explanation in which the causal processes are those of Marx's theory is a Marxian explanation, even if it makes no reference to the Marxian rate of profit. Apropos of this, I note that Marx never estimated a Marxian rate of profit and that he was able to explain movements in profitability and economic crises and slumps quite well without one.

Why Focus on the Corporate Sector?

I restricted my study to corporations, rather than the entire U.S. economy, for two reasons. One is that corporate businesses are the dominant part of the private sector. The other is that I believe that inclusion of data for partnerships and sole proprietors can lead to seriously misleading conclusions if we are concerned, as I am here, to analyze *capitalist* production in the U.S.

Between 1968 and 2007, the corporate share of the national income produced by domestic businesses was roughly constant, 77 percent on average.[19] The corporate share of the business sector's fixed assets (valued at current cost) was similar, 76 percent on average, and between 1995 and 2007, it averaged 77 percent.[20] By these measures, then, somewhat more than three-fourths of the private business sector is corporate.

Although the above percentages are quite large, they nonetheless significantly underestimate corporations' role in U.S. *capitalist* production, and it is capitalist production with which we must be concerned when we talk about profits and rates of profit. Between 1970 and 2005, corporations received between 83 percent and 90 percent of the total receipts (revenues) of businesses.[21] The absolute numbers are even more revealing. In 2000, for instance, the average "net income" of businesses that filed federal tax returns was $12,000 in the case of nonfarm proprietorships, $131,000 in the case of partnerships, and $184,000 in the case of corporations.

Now, from what economists call a functional perspective in contrast to a legal perspective, the majority of the "net income" of noncorporate businesses consists of payments made to the owners as compensation for their work. It is not *property* income (profit, interest, or rental income). Although figures for the property income received by noncorporate businesses are not reported, they can be estimated by assuming that all corporate net income consisted of profit and other property income, and that the ratio of property income to total receipts was the same for corporations and noncorporate businesses. On the basis of these assumptions, I estimate that the average property income of businesses that filed federal tax returns for 2000 was about $3,000 in the case of nonfarm proprietorships, $53,000 in the case of partnerships, and $184,000 in the case of corporations. And if we assume that the average number of partners per partnership was the same in 2000 as it was in 2005, the average property income per partner was about $9,000.

It thus seems that the majority of partnerships, and certainly the overwhelming majority of sole proprietorships, do not generate enough property income to allow their owners to live without working. They work (in these businesses or elsewhere) out of necessity, not by choice.[22]

Although the proprietorships and partnerships that do not really function capitalistically are typically very small, they are also numerous, and together they have an effect on the aggregate figures. The size of this effect is difficult to estimate. As a rough, somewhat conservative guess, I would say that the corporate share of the receipts and property income (and probably also the output and fixed assets) of those private-sector businesses that do function capitalistically has been about 90 percent since the late 1960s.

This is one factor that suggests that it is reasonable to restrict analysis to the corporate sector. A second is that figures for noncorporate businesses that operate on a capitalist basis would have to be estimated, and the estimates would depend heavily on several questionable assumptions. In particular, I would have to make the very dubious assumption that trends in the capitalistic and noncapitalistic components of the noncorporate sector have been similar. I much prefer that data be presented "straight up" whenever possible, without being subjected to elaborate manipulations and guess-work, so that readers can easily replicate the results. A third factor is that those noncorporate businesses which *are* operated capitalistically have probably experienced trends (in profitability, investment, employee compensation, and so on) similar to those in the corporate sector. If that is so, the trends reported here for the corporate sector are applicable to them as well.

Data and Computations

All measures of profit, net investment, and advanced capital are based partly on estimates of depreciation. In this chapter and elsewhere, my measures are based on depreciation figures valued at historical cost, unless I explicitly indicate otherwise. Historical-cost depreciation is the difference between gross investment in fixed assets and net investment in fixed assets, valued at historical cost, and the latter is the change in the net stock of fixed assets, also valued at historical cost, between the start and end of the year. Corporations' gross investment is reported in the BEA's Fixed Asset Table 6.7, line 2. Data on the net stock of their fixed assets, valued at historical cost, is reported in Fixed Asset Table 6.3, line 2.

The BEA's figures for the net stock of fixed assets are for the end of the year. Since my rates of profit divide the profit of a year by the capital (net stock of fixed assets) advanced at the *start* of the year, my net stock figures in a particular year are the BEA's net stock figures for the year before.

What I call "property income" is net value added minus compensation of employees. Data on corporations' compensation of their employees is reported in the BEA's NIPA Table 1.14, line 4. The net value added by corporations (valued at historical cost) is their gross value added, reported in NIPA Table 1.14, line 1, minus the historical-cost depreciation of their fixed assets.

Corporations' net operating surplus is their property income minus the "taxes on production and imports less subsidies" they pay: the latter is reported in NIPA Table 1.14, line 7. Their before-tax profit is their net operating surplus minus their "net interest and miscellaneous payments," reported in NIPA Table 1.14, line 9, and the "current transfer payments" they make, reported in NIPA Table 1.14, line 10. Their after-tax profit is their before-tax profit minus "taxes on corporate income," reported in NIPA Table 1.14, line 12.

Two of the series shown in Figure 5.8 are based on current-cost estimates of net investment, and the findings reported in notes 15 and 16 are based on current-cost estimates of both profit and net investment. The various current-cost measures of profit are computed in the same way as their historical-cost counterparts, except that net value added, valued at current cost, is gross investment minus the depreciation of corporations' fixed assets as valued at current cost, which is reported in Fixed Asset Table 6.4, line 2. Net investment valued at current cost is gross investment minus the depreciation of corporations' fixed assets as valued at current cost.

Corporations' inventories are not reported by the BEA. I estimated them by assuming that the ratio of inventories to fixed assets is the same for corporate and noncorporate businesses. The estimated inventories are (i) the inventories of private businesses, valued at current cost, reported in NIPA Tables 5.7.5A and B, line 1, times (ii) corporations' share of the net stock of private businesses' fixed assets, also valued at current cost. Each year's figure for (i) is the average of the quarterly figures reported by the BEA. The data used to compute (ii) are reported in Fixed Asset Table 6.1, line 2 (corporate), line 5 (noncorporate), line 8 (nonprofit institutions) and line 9 (households); (ii) is line 2 divided by the fixed assets of all businesses (line 2 plus line 5 minus lines 8 and 9). The BEA does not report inventories for 1946 and earlier years.

My inflation- and MELT-adjusted rates of profit are based on the fact that the historical cost of fixed assets, the denominator of my main measures of the nominal rate of profit, is their historical cost at the start of the "initial year" plus the running total of all net investments in fixed assets, valued at historical cost, in that and subsequent years. The inflation-adjusted historical cost of fixed assets is thus their inflation-adjusted historical cost at the start of 1929 (the first year for which the BEA reports the GDP price index) plus the running total of all inflation-adjusted net investments in fixed assets, valued at historical cost, in 1929 and subsequent years. To obtain an estimate of the fixed assets' inflation-adjusted historical cost at the start of 1929, I divided the unadjusted figure for the net stock of corporations' fixed assets, valued at historical cost, by the GDP price index of 1929. The inflation-adjusted net investment of any year is the net investment of that year divided by the GDP price index of that year. The MELT-adjusted historical costs of fixed assets and net investments were computed in an analogous manner.

The GDP price index is reported in NIPA Table 1.1.4, line 1. The MELT is the amount of new value, in money terms, that is created by an hour of labor. Because capitalism is now a global system, there exists a single MELT throughout the world. But because reliable international data are not available, I used U.S. data to approximate the MELT.

In Marx's theory, the labor that creates new value is, roughly speaking, the labor of workers who are engaged in activities that both (a) produce a good or service that commands a price and (b) do not transfer ownership of, protect, or keep track of value that already exists beforehand. (Sales activities, labor performed in financial, real-estate, and insurance industries, and legal activities transfer ownership of already-existing value; the labor of security personnel and some managerial activity protects already-existing value; and the labor of accountants and bookkeepers and some other managerial labor keeps track of already-existing value.) It would be a formidable task to estimate the amount of such labor that is performed in the U.S. with any degree of precision. I therefore assumed that value-creating labor has been a constant share of the total. (This share need not be estimated, since it appears in both the numerator and the denominator of the MELT-adjusted rates of profit and therefore cancels out.)

To avoid even further complications, I excluded government workers and used BEA figures for "full-time equivalent employees" in private industries, reported in NIPA Table 5.5A–D, line 3, as my estimate of the total amount of labor performed. As a measure of the corresponding amount of new value created, I used figures for the net value added of the business sector, reported in NIPA Table 1.9.5, line 2.

The series I obtained for the MELT is a rough estimate. If value-creating labor has actually fallen as a share of the total, which seems to be a reasonable assumption, then my estimated MELT-adjusted rates of profit *underestimate* the extent to which the actual MELT-adjusted rates have fallen over time. (If value-creating labor is a declining share of the total, then the MELT has actually risen faster than I estimate it has risen, which implies that *current* MELT-adjusted profit is actually smaller, in relationship to *past* MELT-adjusted investment, than my estimates suggest.)

6
The Current-cost "Rate of Profit"

Chapter 5 showed that the rate of profit of U.S. corporations failed to experience a sustained recovery after the slumps of the 1970s and early 1980s, and that the fall in the rate of profit accounts for the fall in the rate of accumulation. Although the evidence is clear, physicalist economists—including radical and Marxist physicalists—reject it. The rates of profit presented above measure profit in relationship to the actual amounts of money advanced as capital in the past (minus depreciation), but physicalists contend that profit must instead be measured in relationship to the amount of money that businesses would now need to spend in order to replace their fixed assets—the assets' current cost (replacement cost).[1] In this chapter, I discuss this and other reasons why they reject the conclusions of chapter 5, and why they are wrong to do so.

Let me make clear at the outset that I have no objection to current-cost accounting as such, or to the valuation of fixed assets in current-cost terms. These procedures are appropriate for some purposes. My point is simply that the current cost of fixed assets is not the same thing as the capital that has been advanced, and profit as a percentage of the current cost of fixed assets is not a rate of profit in any normal sense of the term.

DISMISSAL OF THE LAW OF THE TENDENTIAL FALL IN THE RATE OF PROFIT

Radical physicalist economists have frequently asserted that, prior to the recent financial crisis and Great Recession, the rate of profit in the U.S. recovered—almost completely—from the fall it experienced through 1982. They have therefore argued that Marx's law of the tendential fall in the rate of profit (LTFRP) is of little value, if any, when trying to explain the roots of the latest slump. Instead, they have attributed it to the "financialization" of capitalism and problems stemming from it (and to more immediate financial-sector phenomena), which they portray as largely unrelated to and separable from movements in profitability.

For instance, in the midst of the financial crisis, in July 2008, Fred Moseley (2008) wrote:

> Three decades of stagnant real wages and increasing exploitation have substantially restored the rate of profit [in the U.S.], at the expense of workers. This important fact should be acknowledged ... The main problem in the current crisis is the financial sector ... The best theorist of the capitalist financial system is Hyman Minsky, not Karl Marx. The current crisis is more of a Minsky crisis than a Marx crisis.

In early 2009, despite the fact that the crisis had worsened considerably in the meantime, Moseley (2009) argued that the substantial restoration of the rate of profit verges on "almost complete recovery":

> ... the rate of profit is now approaching the previous peaks achieved in the 1960s ... The last several years especially, since the recession of 2001, ha[ve] seen a very strong recovery of profits ... I conclude that there has been a very substantial and probably almost complete recovery of the rate of profit in the U.S.[2]

Estimates by Gérard Duménil and Dominique Lévy (2005) indicated that the rate of profit of the overall business sector in the U.S. did not recover so substantially. Yet with regard to the corporate sector, their view echoed Moseley's; as of 1997, the rate of profit of the "Corporate sector ... recovered to its level of the late 1950s ... Considering the evolution of the profit rate since World War II, the recovery of the profit rate appears nearly complete within the entire Corporate sector" (Duménil and Lévy 2005: 9, 11, emphases omitted). Duménil therefore argued that "the crisis was of financial origin and that the profit rate had been relatively steady and had little to do with it" (Beggs 2009; cf. Harman 2009: 386 n73).[3]

In their new book, Duménil and Lévy present a markedly revised view of the trajectory of the rate of profit: "a *slight upward trend* of the corporate profit rate *á la Marx* was established within neoliberalism from the low levels of the structural crisis of the 1970s[,] but rates remained inferior to those prevailing during this crisis decade" (2011: 60; emphasis added). (*Á la Marx* means that property income or a close substitute is used to measure profit.) Yet for reasons they do not make clear, they still maintain that the latest crisis "was not the effect of deficient profit rates" (ibid.: 33), and they therefore regard it as a "crisis of neoliberalism" rather than as a crisis of capitalism. In any case, it is important to examine the evidence that supposedly supported their original view that the recovery of the rate of profit "appears nearly complete," since it has served as *the main empirical foundation* of a widespread conclusion that the latest crisis and slump are rooted in neoliberalism and financialization, rather than in capitalist production.

CHERRY PICKING TROUGHS AND PEAKS

One reason why Moseley and Duménil-Lévy claimed that the rate of profit recovered almost completely is that they failed to distinguish between cyclical variations and longer-term (secular) trends in profitability. It is obvious that, in order to ascertain the trend, one needs to set aside or control for cyclical effects. Otherwise, one might take a completely *trendless* data series (such as the sine wave depicted in Figure 6.1) and conclude that it exhibits a rising trend simply by cherry picking a trough point (A) and comparing it to a later peak point (B). Or one might say that the series exhibits a falling trend, simply by cherry picking a peak point (B) and comparing it to a later trough point (C).

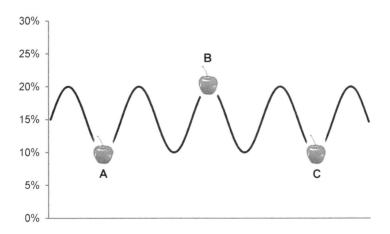

Figure 6.1   Cherry Picking Troughs and Peak

Yet this is exactly what Moseley and Duménil-Lévy did. When he asserted that the rate of profit had almost completely recovered from its prior fall, Moseley compared his rate of profit during *trough* or near-trough years (from the mid-1970s through the early 1980s) with the rate during a *peak* period (2004–07 or 2005–07). He did so even though he knew that a massive and unsustainable asset-price bubble had formed in the housing sector during the latter period (Moseley 2009, esp. section 5). Had he compared the troughs in his data, Moseley would have reported a rise in the rate of profit from 10 percent in 1980 to 14 percent in 2001, rather than the rise of twice that amount (to between 17 percent and 19 percent) that induced him to refer to an "almost complete recovery" of the rate of profit. And he would have reported *no recovery* in trough rates of profit from 1987 through 2001, the most recent trough year prior to the latest crisis.

Similarly, Duménil and Lévy (2005) chose to analyze movements in profitability only through 1997. They made this choice, for reasons they do not explain, even though their paper actually presented data through 2000, and even though a few more years of data, including data for the trough year of 2001, were available when they published the 2005 version of their paper. But 1997 was a peak profit-rate year, and the rate of profit declined markedly over the next four years. Thus, when they stated that the corporate sector's rate of profit fell sharply through 1982 and then experienced a recovery that "appears nearly complete," Duménil and Lévy were comparing a *trough* to a *peak*.[4]

Why did Moseley, and Duménil and Lévy, choose to cherry pick their data in this manner? I do not know. I can only speculate that a preanalytic "vision" (Schumpeter 1954: 41) led them to regard the increases in profitability, but not the subsequent declines, as significant. The vision was that of *Capital Resurgent* (Duménil and Lévy 2004)—a neoliberal counterrevolution that ushered in a new, sustainable boom on the backs of the working class.[5]

LOGICAL AND METHODOLOGICAL BASES OF THE DISMISSAL

Two main reasons why the LTFRP is dismissed as irrelevant to an explanation of the latest economic crisis and downturn are not empirical, but logical and methodological. The logical reason is that physicalist economists have long dismissed the law, and have even regarded reference to it as a sign of dogmatism and obscurantism, on the grounds that it is *logically impossible*. While Marx argued that labor-saving technical change produces a tendency for the rate of profit to fall, Okishio's (1961) theorem supposedly proved that profit-maximizing capitalists would never adopt any labor-saving technical changes that have this effect. The theorem supposedly demonstrated that, if a business adopts a technical change that raises its own rate of profit, given current prices and wages, then the economy-wide rate of profit will also always be higher (or constant) when all is said and done.

Okishio's theorem has since been disproved by proponents of the temporal single-system interpretation (TSSI) of Marx's value theory (see Kliman 2007, esp. Chapter 7). Yet the myth still prevails that Okishio showed that the rate of profit cannot possibly fall for the reasons Marx stated. The myth affects the debate over the causes of the current crisis, by making it less than respectable to even consider Marx's law as a potential determinant of the crisis.

For instance, Robin Hahnel, a radical physicalist economist, recently wrote:

> The idea that capitalism contains *internal contradictions* which act as seeds for its own destruction is simply wrong and needs to be discarded once and for all …

> Marx hypothesized that when individual capitalists substitute machinery for labor to lower production costs they witlessly produce a *long-run tendency for the rate of profit to fall* because in the final analysis capitalist profits derive from exploiting labor … But thanks to work begun by Nobuo Okishio, modern political economists now know better. To make a long story short: labor-saving, capital-using technical change does nothing, in-and-of itself, to depress the rate of profit in capitalism and thereby generate a *crisis of capitalism*. (2010a, emphases in original)

And in a subsequent comment on this article, Hahnel added:

> When nothing useful has come from a literature that is now hundreds of years old, I personally cannot justify "keeping up with it" at the expense of reading and following literatures that bear juicy fruit.

> I cannot tell you that Kilman [*sic*] has not finally figured out a way to save what has literally become a Holy Grail for some Marxists. But I can tell you that I am willing to bet my house that he has not.

BTW 1: The Okishio theorem is a mathematical theorem and does not contain any logical flaws. One can object to its assumptions as being inappropriate or not the same as Marx's assumptions. Or one can object to how someone interprets the theorem. But the theorem is logically sound. My PhD students learned how to prove it every year for 25 years.

BTW 2: I also don't read literature by creationists, so I can't swear they fail to make sound arguments. Nor do I read literature by climate denialists. In this case I do check from time to time to see if the overwhelming concensus [*sic*] of the world scientific community that climate change is real and stems from human economic activiity [*sic*] has weakened. (Hahnel 2010b)

This is an equivocal argument. Now that the disproofs of Okishio's theorem have become more widely known, attempts to defend it in this manner have become common. Yet equivocation—using the same term in different senses within the same argument—is a logical error; it renders the argument invalid.

In the present case, Hahnel appealed to what we may call OT1, a theorem about *real-world capitalism* that supposedly shows that "labor-saving, capital-using technical change does nothing, in-and-of itself, to depress the rate of profit in capitalism." But after this claim was questioned, he appealed to what we may call OT2, a *purely mathematical* theorem. "The Okishio theorem is a mathematical theorem [which] does not contain any logical flaws" and which is therefore a true theorem—even if its assumptions are "inappropriate" (at variance with real-world capitalism) and even if "someone" wrongly interprets this purely mathematical theorem as a demonstration that labor-saving, capital-using technical change does nothing, in-and-of itself, to depress the rate of profit in capitalism.

Once we have distinguished OT1 from OT2, it becomes clear that "the" Okishio theorem can do no damage to the LTFRP or to the idea that capitalism contains internal contradictions. OT1, the theorem about capitalism, does no damage because it is false: Okishio failed to prove that it is impossible for the equilibrium rate of profit to fall under the conditions he assumed, because he failed to prove that the mathematical object that cannot fall, which he called "the rate of profit," is the same thing as the equilibrium rate of profit of real-world capitalism or the LTFRP. (It is not the same thing as either of them.) OT2, the disinterested exercise in applied mathematics, does no damage because its "rate of profit" is only a mathematical object, not the rate of profit of real-world capitalism or Marx's law.

There is also a methodological reason why the LTFRP is dismissed, and the valuation of profitability in historical-cost terms is dismissed along with it. In an effort to be scientific, or at least be good economists, mainstream Marxist, Sraffian, and other radical economists have long embraced equilibrium modeling and the physicalism to which it leads, and physicalism compels one to measure the rate of profit in current-cost terms. So the rate of profit valued at historical cost is dismissed simply because one would violate the methodological norms of equilibrium economics and physicalism if one were to use it to assess movements in profitability.[6] And since the reclamation of the LTFRP against the Okishio theorem requires repudiation of current-cost valuation, the LTFRP must also be dismissed, despite the fact that the theorem has been disproved, in order to protect these methodological norms. Thus, although Duménil and Lévy (2005, 2011) have studied a great variety of measures of the rate of profit, capital investments are valued at their current cost in every single one of these measures.

WHAT IS AT STAKE ETHICALLY?

> I don't know what you mean by "glory," Alice said.
> Humpty Dumpty smiled contemptuously. "Of course you don't—till I tell you. I meant 'there's a nice knock-down argument for you!'"
> "But 'glory' doesn't mean 'a nice knock-down argument,'" Alice objected.
> "When I use a word," Humpty Dumpty said, in rather a scornful tone, "it means just what I choose it to mean—neither more nor less."
> "The question is," said Alice, "whether you *can* make words mean so many different things."
> "The question is," said Humpty Dumpty, "which is to be master—that's all."
>
> —Lewis Carroll, *Through the Looking Glass*

Before turning to the empirical and theoretical aspects of this controversy, I wish to comment on what is at stake ethically. The ethical issue has to do with the responsibility of intellectuals when communicating with the public.

When physicalists use the terms *rate of profit* or *profit rate*, what they mean is profit as a percentage of the amount of money that businesses would currently need in order to replace their capital assets—the assets' current cost (replacement cost). To almost everyone else, however, what these terms mean is profit as a percentage of the book value of the capital assets. The book value is the money actually advanced (invested) in the past in order to purchase the capital assets—their historical cost—minus depreciation and similar charges. For instance, this is how the term is defined in the *MIT Dictionary of Modern Economics* (1992):

> profit rate. PROFIT expressed as a proportion of the book value of capital assets.

This is how it is defined in the *Encyclopedia of Small Business* (www.enotes.com/small-business-encyclopedia/profit-margin):

> the rate of profit (sometimes called the rate of return) ... comprises various measures of the amount of profit earned relative to the total amount of capital invested ... the profit rate measures the amount of profit per unit of capital advanced ... .

And this is how Marx defined it:

> The surplus-value [*s*] or profit ... is consequently an excess over and above the total capital advanced. This excess then stands in a certain ratio to the total capital, as expressed by the fraction *s/C*, where *C* stands for the total capital. We thus obtain the *rate of profit*[,] *s/C* ... .

> Profit ... expresses in fact the increment of value which the total capital receives at the end of the processes of production and circulation, over and above the value it possessed before this process of production, when it entered into it. Marx (1991a: 133, emphasis in original; 1991b: 91)

Because this is what *rate of profit* means to almost everyone, people who read or hear that "the rate of profit" has consistently risen since the early 1980s are seriously misled into thinking that there has been a recovery of what businesses, investors, Marx, and they themselves mean by the rate of profit. Yet as we have seen, no such recovery has taken place.

Physicalist economists therefore have a responsibility, when engaging in public communication, to avoid saying things that will inevitably be understood as statements that there *has* been such a recovery. Ideally, they should avoid trying to make *rate of profit* mean just what they choose it to mean—neither more nor less—and find a different term for what they now insist upon calling "the rate of profit." But if this is somehow too much to ask, they should at the very least let the public know that "what we mean by 'the rate of profit'—which is not what businesses and investors mean, or that Marx meant, but is instead the ratio of profit to the replacement cost of capital—has consistently risen since the 1980s."

Definitions of one's variables that are buried in the middle of technical papers are not adequate substitutes for such clarifications. Most people who hear speeches or read interviews will not read the technical papers. Even those who do read them will frequently not realize that "fixed assets valued at current cost" differs from "the amount of money actually spent to acquire fixed assets, minus depreciation" unless this is pointed out explicitly. But intellectuals—especially radical intellectuals—have a responsibility to promote understanding, not misunderstanding, among the public. If they instead become the masters of words, they likewise become the masters of public discourse rather than its servants.

DIVERGENT TRENDS IN PROFITABILITY

Although the rates of profit we considered above, which employ historical-cost valuation, did not rebound after the early 1980s, current-cost "rates of profit" did recover to some extent. Yet Figure 6.2 shows that one can conclude that the recovery was nearly complete only if one cherry picks troughs and peaks, and that there was very little recovery after 1984 in the property-income "rate of profit."[7] More than 99 percent of the increase in this rate between 1982 and 2007 took place between 1982 and 1984. More than three-fifths of the increase in the before-tax profit rate also took place during these two years. Thus, even these current-cost measures fail to lend much support to the notion that neoliberalism succeeded in restoring the rate of profit through increased exploitation of workers. (Since the property-income rate did not rise after 1984, the rise in the before-tax profit rate after that year is due, not to increased exploitation, but to the fact that two items which are part of property income but not before-tax profit—interest payments and "taxes on production and imports"—declined as a share of corporations' property income.)

Figure 6.2   Current-cost "Rates of Profit," U.S. Corporations
(profits as percentages of current cost of fixed assets)

Nonetheless, current-cost "rates of profit" have diverged significantly during the last three decades from the historical-cost rates we considered in Chapter 5. Figure 6.3 compares the property-income rates. Between 1982 and 1997, the current-cost rate rose by 44 percent but the historical-cost rate of profit (with depreciation valued at historical cost) fell by 3 percent; *it was lower at the height of the dot-com bubble than during the depth of the recession of the early 1980s.* Both rates then fell to a similar degree between 1997 and 2001, but this left the current-cost rate 15 percent higher at the 2001 trough than at the 1982 trough, while the historical-cost rate was 27 percent lower in 2001 than in 1982.

Following a presentation by Gérard Duménil at a recent conference, a colleague noted that the historical-cost rate of profit measures what businesses care about—profit as a percentage of their actual past investment—and she asked why he instead assessed movements in profitability using the current-cost rate. Duménil replied that historical-cost rates of profit value depreciation at

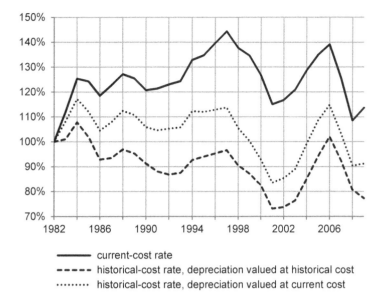

Figure 6.3   Property-Income Rates of Profit
(percentages of 1982 rates, U.S. corporations)

historical cost, which is not meaningful to businesses that must replace depreciated assets at their current cost.[8] This answer does not address the question that was asked, because one can value depreciation at current cost without using the current-cost "rate of profit" to assess movements in profitability. What makes the current-cost rate a bogus rate of profit is not the manner in which it treats depreciation, but the fact that it is not a measure of profit as a percentage of actual past investment. It is not such a measure because it retroactively *revalues* past investments:

> ... for historical-cost estimates ... the change in the net stock [that is, advanced capital] from the end of one year to the next equals investment less depreciation ... [This] relationship does not hold for current-cost estimates because end-of-year price indexes are used to *revalue* constant-dollar estimates of net stocks to the prices of each year ... . (U.S. Department of Commerce, Bureau of Economic Analysis, 2003: M-10, emphasis added)

A third rate of profit shown in Figure 6.3, the dotted curve, helps to clarify this point. It has the same numerator as the current-cost "rate of profit," property income with *depreciation valued at current cost.* Its denominator, advanced capital, is last year's advanced capital, plus this year's (gross) investment less *depreciation valued at current cost.*[9] It is nonetheless a historical-cost rate of profit, because "the change in the net stock from the end of one year to the next equals investment less depreciation." While the current-cost "rate of profit" trended upward between 1982 and 2007, this historical-cost rate trended downward, and between 1986 and 2007, it fell even more sharply than did the other historical-cost rate. In the trough of 2001, it was 16 percent lower than in the trough of 1982. Its movements lend no support to the notion that neoliberalism succeeded in restoring profitability.

Figure 6.4 shows the relationship between the current-cost and the standard historical-cost rates of profit since the end of the Great Depression. When property-income rates of profit are considered, the ratio of the current-cost rate to the historical-cost rate falls by 33 percent from 1941 to 1947, then rises by 43 percent from 1947 to 1965, then falls by 39 percent from 1965 to 1981, and then rises again, by 67 percent from 1981 to 2002. When before-tax profit rates are considered, the relationship is even more volatile; the percentage changes during the same four sub-periods are –35 percent, 47 percent, –47 percent, and 89 percent. The fall in the ratios that took place from the mid-1960s through the early 1980s was the result of the accelerating inflation of that sub-period, and the subsequent rise in the ratio is the result of the deceleration of inflation (disinflation) that took place thereafter. In other words, because replacement-cost measures retroactively revalue capital assets instead of valuing them at the prices at which they were acquired, they inflate the denominator of the rate of profit in periods of rising inflation, artificially lowering the rate of profit, and they deflate the denominator in periods of disinflation, artificially raising the rate of profit.

Because the relationship between current-cost and historical-cost rates of profit has been quite unstable, judgments as to whether profitability has or has not recovered since the early 1980s depend largely upon which of the two rates is discussed. And claims that financial-sector problems and the process of financialization were the only underlying sources of the latest crisis and slump, because profitability rebounded after the early 1980s, can be correct only if the current-cost rate of profit is a valid measure of profitability. *Replacement-cost versus historical-cost measurement is thus a matter of considerable empirical significance.*[10] *A choice must be made.*

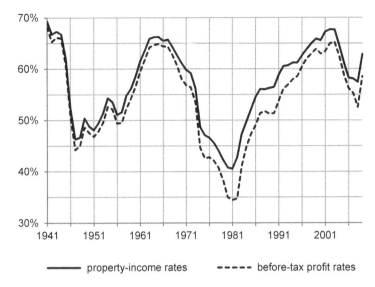

Figure 6.4   Relationship between Current-Cost and Historical-Cost Rates of Profit (current-cost rates as percentages of historical-cost rates)

WHY THE CURRENT-COST "RATE OF PROFIT" ISN'T ONE

It is therefore worth assessing the theoretical case for current-cost valuation of capital investments and profitability. Physicalist economists have now used the current-cost "rate of profit" to assess movements in profitability for at least a half-century, since Okishio (1961). Is it really the case that they have all been guilty of an outright error?

My answer is an unqualified "yes." The current-cost "rate of profit" is simply not a rate of profit in the normal sense of the term.[11]

First of all, the current-cost rate is not what businesses and investors seek to maximize. They base their investment decisions on measures of profitability such as net present value and internal rates of return. Whereas the current-cost "rate of profit" uses *today's* prices to value both current investment expenditures and future receipts, these measures use today's prices to value current investment expenditures but *expected future prices* to compute future receipts. Consequently, the current-cost rate is not an accurate measure of the expected future rate of profit that businesses and investors seek to maximize.

Secondly, the current-cost "rate of profit" fails to accurately measure businesses' and investors' actual rates of return, their profits as a percentage of the original amount invested. The discrepancy can be very large. Imagine, for instance, an investment that would generate a constant revenue stream forever, if the price of the product produced by means of the investment remained constant. If the price instead rises or falls by a constant percentage per period, it is easy to show that the actual rate of return r^A and the current-cost "rate of profit" r^C are related as follows:

$$r^A = (1 + \dot{p})r^C + \dot{p}$$

where $\dot{p}$ is the per-period percentage change in the product's price (in decimal form).[12] Thus if $r^C = 10$ percent (that is, 0.10) but the price of the product falls by 2 percent per period (that is, $\dot{p} = -0.02$), then r^A is 7.8 percent.

Third, contrary to what proponents of simultaneous valuation (for example, Laibman 1999: 223) often claim, the current-cost "rate of profit" fails to accurately measure businesses' and investors' expected future rates of return. Imagine that a firm invests in new equipment that costs $100,000 at today's prices, and that the resulting increase in its output, if valued simultaneously—that is, also on the basis of today's prices—is $10,000 per annum. The current-cost "rate of profit" on this investment is 10 percent. Yet if the price of its product is expected to decline by 2 percent per annum, as in the example above, only the most naïve firm would overlook this information and expect a 10 percent, rather than a 7.8 percent, rate of return on its investment.

Fourth, the relationship between the rate of capital accumulation and the rate of profit is perhaps the main reason why the latter is of economic importance, but the current-cost "rate of profit" bears no clear relationship to the rate of accumulation. Indeed, although U.S. corporations' rate of accumulation has fallen markedly over the last three decades, the current-cost "rate of profit" has risen. Proponents of current-cost valuation of profitability (for example, Duménil and Lévy 2004, Husson 2008, Stockhammer 2009) argue that these two rates have diverged because of a unique neoliberal "regime of accumulation" that encourages financial speculation instead of investment in the "real" economy. As Chapter 5 showed, however, that argument is false, at least in the U.S.'s case, and there has been a remarkably close relationship between U.S. corporations' rate of accumulation and their *actual* rate of profit during the last

40 years. Thus, *the divergence between the rate of accumulation and the current-cost "rate of profit" is actually crucial evidence that the latter is not a rate of profit in any meaningful sense.* As Figure 5.8 made clear, corporations' investment behavior was regulated by movements in the actual (historical-cost) rate of profit, not the current-cost rate.

To see why the current-cost rate and the rate of accumulation can diverge markedly (in the absence of distinctively neoliberal "regime of accumulation"), imagine an economy without fixed capital, in which seed corn and labor are the only inputs, corn is the only output, and workers are paid in corn. At the start of the year, the capitalist farmers obtain one-year loans totaling $40 million from their bankers. Since the price of corn is $5/bushel, they use the $40 million they have borrowed to purchase 8 million bushels of corn, which they then plant as seed and use to hire farmworkers. At year's end, 10 million bushels of corn are harvested.

Now imagine that the price of corn has fallen in the meantime to $4/bushel.[13] Sales revenue is $4 × 10 million = $40 million, and the cost, at the *end* of the year, of the 8 million bushels of corn invested at the *start* of the year is $4 × 8 million = $32 million. Profit computed on the basis of current costs is therefore $40 million – $32 million = $8 million, and so the current-cost "rate of profit" is $8 million/$32 million = 25%. In terms of value (or price) however, there is no profit—even if we ignore the interest that the capitalist farmers must pay the bankers. The $40 million in sales revenue received at year's end is no greater than the $40 million invested at the start. The actual value (or price) rate of profit is therefore 0 percent.

Which of these two rates of profit, 25 percent or 0 percent, more accurately depicts the maximum rate of capital accumulation—that is, the farmers' ability to expand their operations next year? Proponents of current-cost valuation contend that the maximum rate of accumulation is 25 percent. The farmers initially invested 8 million bushels of corn, but end the year with 10 million bushels, which is a 25 percent increase. Hence, they can supposedly expand their operations by up to 25 percent, by investing 10 million bushels of corn at the start of next year instead of the 8 million bushels that they invested at the start of the current year.

The farmers themselves, however, are a wee bit disappointed. Their one-year loans must now be repaid, and they have to use their entire sales revenue of $40 million to repay the $40 million that they borrowed at the start of the year. The farmers' net worth has not increased at all and, after repaying their loans, they have nothing left over with which to expand their operations. They are unable to accumulate, *even in physical terms*. Moreover, they have not yet paid, and cannot pay, the interest they owe the bankers. If the same situation occurs year after year—with corn output exceeding corn input by 25 percent each year, but the price of corn falling by 20 percent—the farmers are soon drowning in debt.[14]

Fifth, current-cost "rates of profit" seem to bear no relationship to equity-market rates of return. Table 6.1 reports results of regressions that measure the ability of different rates of profit to predict the earnings-to-price ratio of Standard and Poor's 500 (S&P 500) corporations during the 1947–2009 period.[15] (The earnings-to-price ratios are lagged by one year, so the rate-of-profit data are for 1946 through 2008.) Using the coefficient of determination, R^2, as the measure of the rate of profit's predictive power, we see that historical-cost rates of profit outperform current-cost rates as predictors of the earnings-to-price ratio to a huge extent. The small t-statistics associated with the current-cost rates' slope coefficients indicate that these rates have no statistically significant influence, at normal levels of testing, on the earnings-to-price ratio. And the slope coefficient associated with the after-tax current-cost rate has the wrong sign. These results are an additional indication that historical-cost rates of profit are more closely related to what it is that actual capitalist firms and investors care about and mean by profitability.

Table 6.1   Rates of Profit and Equity-market Rates of Return

Independent variable (rate of profit)	Constant	Slope	R^2
After-tax, historical-cost rate	−0.022	0.769	0.354
	(−1.340)	(5.780)	
After-tax, current-cost rate	0.087	−0.261	0.017
	(5.588)	(−1.034)	
Before-tax, historical-cost rate	−0.001	0.371	0.354
	(−0.059)	(5.782)	
Before-tax, current-cost rate	0.060	0.113	0.010
	(3.917)	(0.786)	

Note: In all regressions, the dependent variable is the earnings-to-price ratio (the reciprocal of P/E ratio) of the S&P 500. N = 63. Figures in parentheses are *t*-statistics.

MIS-MEASURING INFLATION

My final reason why the current-cost rate is not a rate of profit in the normal sense of the term has to do with inflation. I noted above that Husson and Duménil have recently defended the use of the current-cost rate on the ground that the historical-cost rate of profit is affected by inflation, while the current-cost rate eliminates that effect. Yet the current-cost rate adjusts for inflation in an improper manner. What it adjusts for is actually not inflation—a general, economy-wide increase in the price level—but increases in the prices of each type of capital asset.

It might make sense to adjust for inflation in this manner if there were no changes in the composition of capital assets over time. In that case, changes in the prices of capital assets acquired in the past would accurately reflect the changes in capital-asset costs that businesses currently face. But when, for instance, businesses were in the process of buying computers instead of *replacing* their worn-out typewriters, changes in the *replacement cost* of typewriters became an ever less meaningful measure of the inflation (or deflation) they experienced. The replacement cost of typewriters became ever less meaningful even for businesses that continued to use typewriters, because they did not replace the typewriters when they wore out, but bought computers instead.

But current-cost measures are, precisely, replacement-cost measures. They measure changes in the cost of replacing the entire current stock of capital assets, which contained a relatively large number of typewriters, not changes in the cost of the capital assets that businesses are actually acquiring currently. The latter contained a relatively large number of computers and relatively few typewriters.

Thus, in order to properly adjust rates of profit so as to remove the effects of inflation, one needs to adjust for changes in the *general* price level, not compute the current-cost "rate of profit." This is what I did when I computed the inflation-adjusted rates of profit discussed in Chapter 5. My estimates indicate that movements in the inflation-adjusted rates of profits since the early 1980s did not diverge substantially from movements in the nominal historical-cost rates of profit.

Mis-measurement of inflation is responsible for almost the entire rise in the property-income current-cost "rate of profit" between 1980 and the latest crisis. The reasoning underlying this conclusion is not difficult, but it is somewhat complex, so I will proceed step by step, beginning with why and how the current-cost rate mis-measures inflation-adjusted profit.

The current-cost rate is the ratio of nominal profit to the current cost of fixed assets, and the current cost of fixed assets can be decomposed into an index of the price of fixed assets times an index of the physical quantity of fixed assets:

$$\frac{\text{current-cost}}{\text{"rate of profit"}} = \frac{\text{profit}}{\begin{array}{c}\text{current cost}\\\text{of fixed assets}\end{array}} = \frac{\text{profit}}{\left(\begin{array}{c}\text{price of}\\\text{fixed assets}\end{array}\right) \times \left(\begin{array}{c}\text{physical quantity}\\\text{of fixed assets}\end{array}\right)}$$

If we now divide the numerator and denominator of the expression on the right-hand side by the index of the price of fixed assets, we obtain:

$$\frac{\text{current-cost}}{\text{"rate of profit"}} = \frac{\text{profit} \Big/ \left(\begin{array}{c}\text{price of}\\\text{fixed assets}\end{array}\right)}{\left(\begin{array}{c}\text{physical quantity}\\\text{of fixed assets}\end{array}\right)}$$

The measure of "real" profit in the numerator of the right-hand-side expression is a measure of the quantity of fixed assets that can be bought with the profit. But if we wish to control for inflation, changes in the *general price level*, we need to divide money profit by the GDP price index (or some similar index) rather than by the index of the price of fixed assets. The "real" (physicalist) rate of profit is therefore not the current-cost rate but

$$\frac{\text{"real" rate}}{\text{of profit}} = \frac{\text{profit} \Big/ \left(\begin{array}{c}\text{GDP Price}\\\text{Index}\end{array}\right)}{\left(\begin{array}{c}\text{physical quantity}\\\text{of fixed assets}\end{array}\right)}$$

(I am not *recommending* that this "real" rate be used to measure movements in profitability. It is not a rate of profit in the normal sense of the term any more than the current-cost rate is. My point is rather that the "real" rate properly measures the conception of the rate of profit to which *physicalist economists* themselves subscribe— the physical "quantity" of profit as a percentage of the physical quantity of fixed assets—while the current-cost rate does not.)

The trajectories of these two rates will differ substantially whenever fixed-asset prices rise or fall substantially in relationship to the general price level. As I will show presently, this is indeed what occurred in the 1970s and 1980s. Thus, by focusing on the current-cost "rate of profit" instead of the alternative "real" rate, physicalist economists have misunderstood the last three decades of U.S. capitalism—even in terms of their own perspective. They have greatly overestimated the extent to which the physical rate of profit has recovered. And they have regarded the rise in the current-cost rate as a sign of the success of neoliberalism, although most of this rise was, as we shall see, simply the result of short-term variations in fixed-asset prices in relationship to the general price level.

The "real" rate of profit differs from the current-cost rate in one respect only; it deflates profit by the GDP price index instead of by an index of fixed asset prices. Yet *this one difference is responsible for the majority of the rise in the current-cost "rate of profit" since the early 1980s.* As Figure 6.5 shows, the current-cost and

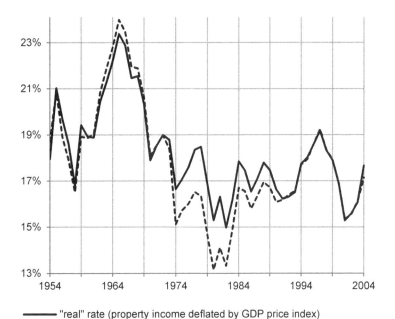

——— "real" rate (property income deflated by GDP price index)

- - - - - current-cost rate (property income deflated by fixed-asset price index)

Figure 6.5 Current-cost and "Real" Rates of Profit, U.S. Corporations (deflated property income as percentage of physical quantity of fixed assets)

alternative "real" rates have hardly differed throughout most of the last half-century.[16] But between 1974 and 1980, fixed-asset prices rose much more sharply than did prices in general. This caused a temporary but sharp fall in the current-cost "rate of profit" in relationship to the alternative "real" rate. During the next decade, on the other hand, the rise in fixed-asset prices was significantly smaller than the rise in the general price level, and so the current-cost rate rose sharply in relationship to the "real" rate.

Consequently, while the current-cost "rate of profit" rose by 16.6 percent between the trough of 1980 and 2001, the latest trough-profit-rate year before the recent crisis, the "real" rate of profit was unchanged. And during the 1980–2006 period as a whole, the current-cost rate was on average 25.9 percent greater than in 1980, while the "real" rate was on average only 12.1 percent greater than in 1980 (see Figure 6.6). Thus, the majority of the rise in the current-cost rate since 1980 was produced by an exceptional decline in the relative price of fixed assets.

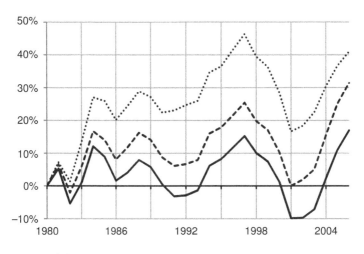

Figure 6.6   Current-cost, "Real," and Inflation-Adjusted Rates of Profit, U.S. Corporations

(cumulative percentage changes since 1980 in property-income rates)

Actually, almost the entire rise in the current-cost rate is due to the exceptional decline in fixed assets' relative prices. The "real" rate of profit eliminates only some of this effect. While it deflates profit—the numerator of the rate of profit—by the general price level, it continues to deflate the sum of net investments—the denominator of the rate of profit—by the prices of fixed assets, just as the current-cost "rate of profit" does. If we deflate the net investments as well as property income by the GDP price index, we obtain the inflation-adjusted rate of profit shown in Figure 6.6. Its average level between 1980 and 2006 was just 3.6 percent greater than its level in 1980.[17] The remainder of the 25.9 percent increase in the current-cost rate is thus attributable to the elimination of the temporary spike in fixed-asset prices relative to the general price level. In other words, *86 percent of the rise in the current-cost "rate of profit" is attributable to mis-measurement of inflation—not to neoliberalism, and not to an increase in the degree of exploitation.*

7
Why the Rate of Profit Fell

This chapter attempts to account for why the rate of profit fell. The first section looks at the distribution of corporate output, or income, between profit and compensation of employees.

The second section decomposes movements in the rate of profit in a manner that will be familiar to readers familiar with Marxist economists' discussions of changes in the rate of profit. However, I find such procedures inadequate and difficult to interpret. They decompose the rate of profit into complexly determined variables instead of simple ones, they are not truly causal analyses, and they focus on nominal and/or physical variables but disregard MELT-adjusted ones. Thus, in the third section, I decompose movements in the rate of profit in a different manner. The key result of my analysis is that Marx's LTFRP fits the facts remarkably well; the relationship on which the law is based—slow growth of employment in relationship to the accumulation of capital—accounts for the lion's share of the fall in the nominal rate of profit since World War II.

The final section of the chapter argues that the revolution in information technology had led to an increase in depreciation due to obsolescence, and it discusses how this increase has affected profits and the rate of profit. I argue that it has led to significant destruction of capital value during the last few decades. Since the destruction of capital value is an indicator of economic weakness that nonetheless boosts profitability, weakness resulting from technical progress has been even more significant than the decline in the measured rate of profit would suggest. My estimates indicate that, once we control for the boost to profitability that results from depreciation due to obsolescence, the fall in the rate of profit during the last few decades becomes substantially greater, and large portions of the increases in the rate of profit during the bubbles of the 1990s and 2000 are eliminated.

Only the property-income rate of profit will be considered in this chapter, because I will be concerned with how the distribution of income between classes—compensation of employees vs. property income—has affected the rate of profit. In this context, it would not be useful to consider the before-tax profit rate, because before-tax profit is only part of property income.

THE PROFIT SHARE OF INCOME

The failure of the rate of profit to recover might seem curious, since so much has been written about the stagnation of real (inflation-adjusted) wages, and about the alleged redistribution of income from wages to profits, that have taken place during the past four decades. Yet the stagnation of wages is a very misleading phenomenon, and the redistribution from wages to profits is not actually a fact. It is true that wages and salaries in the *narrow* sense have not risen markedly. However, as I will discuss in more detail in Chapter 8, other components of employees' compensation—employer-provided health and retirement benefits and employers' Social Security and Medicare tax payments—have increased far more rapidly than have wages and salaries. As a result, *total* compensation has not declined as a share of corporate income, nor has profit increased as a share of corporate income. In other words, income has not been redistributed from wages to profits; it has been redistributed from wages to other forms of employee compensation.

Although total compensation has not stagnated, it has indeed increased more slowly in recent decades than it did in the early post-World War II period. Figure 7.1 presents data on the average annual growth rates of the real output (net value added) produced, and the real employee compensation paid, by U.S. corporations. If we use the GDP price index to adjust for inflation, we find that the annual growth rate of real compensation was 41 percent lower between 1973 and 2007 than between 1947 and 1973. If we use the consumer price index (CPI-U) to adjust for inflation, we find that the average growth rate was 56 percent lower. As the graph makes clear, the fall in compensation growth went along with, and can be attributed almost completely to, a comparable fall in the growth of corporations' net value added.[1]

The slowdown in the growth of employee compensation is consequently not a distributional phenomenon. It stems from the relative stagnation of capitalist production. As Figure 7.2 shows, corporations' profit (property income) has not increased as a percentage of their net value added. On the contrary, this percentage, which I will call the profit share, has declined slightly over time. Between 1947 and 1965, the profit share averaged 32.2 percent,

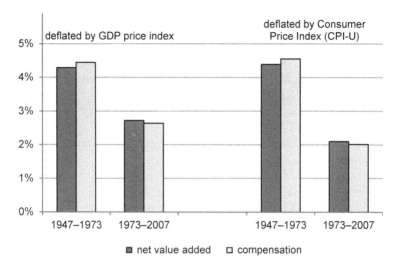

Figure 7.1   Net Value Added and Compensation of Employees, U.S. Corporations (average annual growth rates)

Figure 7.2   Profit Share of U.S. Corporations' Net Value Added
(property income as percentage of net value added)

but it fell significantly during the next five years. Between 1970 and 2007, it averaged 29.0 percent and was completely trendless.

In principle, the finding that compensation has been a constant share of net value during the last four decades might be misleading, since BEA figures include compensation of managers. If managers' compensation had increased especially rapidly, then "regular" workers' compensation would have fallen significantly as a share of net value added, despite the constancy of the overall compensation share. However, the data that are available suggest that managers' compensation has *not* increased especially rapidly. Between December 1985 and December 2007, hourly compensation of all private-industry workers increased by 120 percent in nominal terms, while hourly compensation of private-industry employees in "management, business, and financial operations" occupations increased only slightly more rapidly, by 128 percent.[2]

Since the share of people employed in these occupations is less than 10 percent of the total, the growth rate of other employees' compensation was close to the growth rate for all private-industry workers, 118 percent according to my estimate. If we assume that these growth rates apply to corporations, and that managers received between 12 and 27 percent of total compensation in December 1985, which was almost certainly the case, straightforward computations indicate that the changing composition of compensation between then and the end of 2007 caused nonmanagerial employees' share of net value added to decline only slightly, by between 0.3 and 0.7 percentage points. Because the available data are so limited and fragmentary, more than this cannot be said.[3]

In any case, the slight decline in "regular" workers' share has not resulted in a rising profit share, and it has not lessened the fall in corporations' rate of profit, because *corporations* have not been the beneficiaries of the decline in regular workers' share. *Managerial employees* have been the beneficiaries. Since some portion of top executives' compensation, and perhaps some portion of the compensation received by other managers and professionals, is actually surplus-value rather than labor income, the growth in their share of total compensation is relevant if one is analyzing the distribution of income, the distribution of surplus-value, or the causes and effects of changes in the ratio of surplus-value to advanced capital. But it is not very relevant here, where I am analyzing changes in the *corporations'* rate of profit. Managers' compensation is not corporate profit; it does not belong to corporations. On the contrary, it is a cost that reduces their profits.

Commenting on this issue, Husson (2010) recently wrote:

Kliman makes [wages of managers] a category apart which is neither surplus value, nor variable capital, and stresses that these incomes escape the enterprises. It is a very debatable argument: on this account, the dividends paid to the shareholders would not be surplus value either, since, by definition, these profits are not retained by companies.[4]

But the issue is not whether a certain type of income is "retained by" or "escapes" corporations. The issue is whether that type of income belongs to the corporations in the first place. Dividend payments do, while compensation of managers does not.

The data reviewed above have several important implications. First of all, *while the failure of the rate of profit to recover since the early 1980s seems paradoxical if we imagine that the profit share rose thereafter, the paradox disappears once we know that the profit share was constant.* Secondly, the relative constancy of the profit share implies that the decline in the rate of profit is not mostly a distributional phenomenon. Figure 7.3 helps to clarify this fact. The constant-profit-share rate of profit is what the rate of profit would have been if property income had been a constant percentage of net value added throughout the 1929–2007 period.[5] Movements in the constant-profit-share rate are very similar to those of the actual

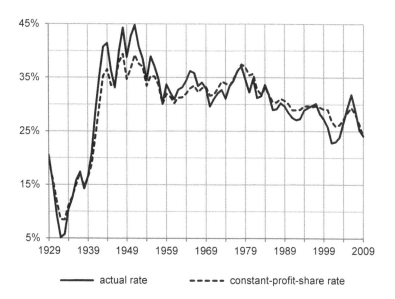

Figure 7.3   Actual and Constant-Profit-Share Rates of Profit (property-income rates)

rate of profit, because the actual profit share has in fact remained relatively constant.

Third, however, the slight fall in the profit share during the post-World War II period helps to account for a *bit* of the fall in the rate of profit.[6] Notice that the actual rate of profit in Figure 7.3 almost always exceeded the constant-profit-share rate between 1940 and 1969, but almost always fell short of it since 1970. This reversal reflects the significant decline in the profit share that occurred in the latter half of the 1960s. Between 1947 and 2007, the property-income rate of profit fell by 27.6 percent while the profit share fell by 2.7 percent. The remainder of the fall in the rate of profit is attributable to the 25.5 percent decline in the constant-profit-share rate or, equivalently, the 25.5 percent decline in the ratio of net value added to advanced capital. (Changes in this ratio are the only sources of changes in the constant-profit-share rate.) About 10 percent of the fall in the rate of profit is thus attributable to the fall in the profit share.

Yet it is misleading to attribute even 10 percent of the fall in the rate of profit to the decline in the profit share. As Figure 7.2 showed, the profit share did not change significantly between 1947 and 1965 or between 1970 and 2007, so almost none of the fall in the rate of profit during these periods can be attributed to a declining profit share.

THE "RATE OF SURPLUS-VALUE" AND THE "ORGANIC COMPOSITION OF CAPITAL"

I am frequently asked how much of the decline in the rate of profit was caused by a fall in the rate of surplus-value and how much was caused by a rise in the organic composition of capital. The simplest answer I can give is this: since the profit share was basically constant, so was the ratio of property income to employee compensation. Consequently, almost the entire fall in the rate of profit was due to an increase in the ratio of advanced capital to employee compensation.

This answer is simple, but it may seem to evade the actual question that was asked because it uses different terminology. The following answer uses the questioner's terminology, but is far more complicated.

Complications arise partly because, as I discussed in the appendix to Chapter 5, I am not interested here in measuring or decomposing "the Marxian" rate of profit, and the variables I employ in this book are based on the BEA's concepts, not Marx's concepts. Moreover, the ratio of constant to variable capital, which Marx called the value composition of capital, differs from what he called the organic composition of capital. (As I shall discuss in greater detail below, changes in the organic composition are basically due to technical change, while the value composition is also affected by other factors.) Complications also arise because BEA data are in nominal terms, not adjusted for changes in the MELT.

That said, and bearing in mind that we are using terms differently from Marx, we can employ the heuristic device of re-describing the variables that enter into the determination of the rate of profit in the following manner:

Variable	Heuristic re-description	Symbol
Property income	Surplus-value	s
Historical cost of fixed assets	Constant capital	c
Compensation of employees	Variable capital	v
Ratio of property income to compensation of employees	Rate of surplus-value	s/v
Ratio of historical cost of fixed assets to compensation of employees	Value composition of capital	c/v

If one wishes, one can think of the variables in the left-hand column as proxies for Marx's variables. If one does not wish to do so, one should not. It would be pointless to argue about whether these are good proxies or not, since "the Marxian" rate of profit, if such a thing exists, is not my concern here. The variables have the same meaning and significance whatever one calls them.

Since compensation of employees does not appear in the denominator of the particular rate of profit under discussion— property income as a percentage of the historical cost of fixed assets—this rate of profit is

$$\frac{s}{c} \equiv \left(\frac{s}{v}\right)\left(\frac{v}{c}\right)$$

where v/c is the reciprocal of the value composition of capital. When the value composition rises (falls), v/c falls (rises). Although the rate of profit could be expressed as the rate of surplus-value divided by the value composition of capital, the above expression allows us to decompose changes in the rate of profit into the sum of two parts, since

$$\text{\% change in } \frac{s}{c} \approx \text{\% change in } \frac{s}{v} + \text{\% change in } \frac{v}{c}$$

Figure 7.4 shows the cumulative percentage changes since 1947 in the rate of profit and its components. On the one hand, we see that short-term movements in the rate of profit were strongly driven by movements in the rate of surplus-value; the former rose and fell along with the latter. Yet since the rate of surplus-value remained roughly constant over the entire period—its value in 2007 was just 3.9 percent less than its value in 1947—its long-term influence on the rate of profit was very minor. In contrast, the reciprocal of the value composition fell by 24.6 percent between 1947 and 2007. The rate of profit fell by only a bit more, 27.6 percent. Almost all the decline in the rate of profit during the 60-year period, 89 percent, can therefore be attributed to the rise in the value composition of capital.

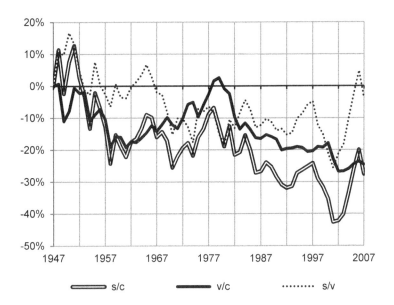

Figure 7.4   Standard Decomposition of the Rate of Profit
(percentage changes since 1947 in property-income rate and components)

Figure 7.4 also indicates that between 1947 and 1968, and again between 1970 and 2003, there was very little change in the rate of surplus-value. This implies that almost all the decline in the rate of profit over the course of these two subperiods is also attributable to the rise in the value composition of capital.

The results of this section are consistent with Marx's LTFRP. The law says that labor-saving technical progress under capitalism causes the technical and organic compositions of capital to increase, that the value composition of capital consequently tends to increase as well, and that the increase in the value composition in turn tends to lower the rate of profit. Periods such as 1965–70, when a sharp fall in the rate of surplus-value led to a sharp fall in the rate of profit, are compatible with the law insofar as they are exceptions rather than the rule.[7]

Although these results are consistent with Marx's law, I would not wish to claim that they confirm the law. A single country, not the world's total social capital, has been analyzed here, and the variables that have been considered are, at best, proxies for Marx's.

One difference between Marx's variables and those considered above is that my measure of variable capital is total compensation of employees rather than compensation of regular workers (proletarians). But since, as I discussed in the last section, regular workers' compensation has increased almost as rapidly as total compensation during the last quarter-century, the use of total compensation figures does not substantially affect my estimates of the growth rates of s/v and v/c.

Another important difference is that my variables are in nominal terms, and are therefore affected by changes in the MELT. In contrast, Marx's discussion of the LTFRP implicitly abstracted from changes in the MELT. Statements such as "the total labour of these 2 million workers always produces the same magnitude of value" (Marx 1991a: 323) would otherwise be ridiculous.

Adjustment for changes in the MELT would not affect the rate of surplus-value, since the same MELT is used to deflate both surplus-value and variable capital. But a rise in the MELT causes variable capital to increase by a greater percentage than constant capital, *ceteris paribus*. This is because all of the variable capital increases as a result of the rise in the MELT, but only a small portion of the constant capital increases—the investment that took place after the rise. Increases in the MELT thus tend to lower the nominal value composition of capital. This is why the reciprocal of the nominal value composition rose substantially between 1961 and 1979 (see Figure 7.4), a period of accelerating inflation. Once changes in the MELT are removed, the reciprocal of the value composition falls by 5 percent during that period.[8]

Thus, while the fall in the nominal value composition of capital may seem at first to contradict a key premise of Marx's law, it does not actually do so.

Figure 7.5 makes clear that movements in the nominal value composition are quite different from those of the MELT-adjusted value composition to which the LTFRP implicitly refers, and from movements in the technical and organic compositions of capital. The technical composition, a measure of technical change, is an index of the quantity of means of production divided by the number of employed workers. By definition, the percentage growth rate of the organic composition is identical to the percentage growth rate in the technical composition, since Marx's definition of the organic composition states that it is "determined by [the] technical composition and mirrors the changes in [it]" (1990a: 762). To obtain an approximation of the growth rates of the technical and organic compositions, I divided an index of the physical quantity of corporations' fixed assets by the number of "full-time equivalent" employees in private industries and computed the percentage changes in the ratio.[9]

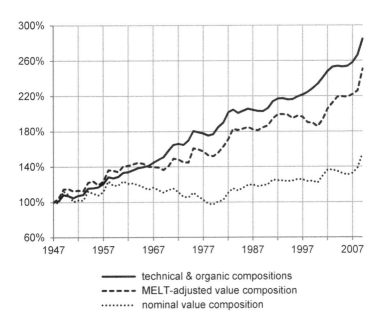

Figure 7.5 Compositions of Capital, U.S. Corporations
(as percentages of 1947 compositions)

The technical and organic compositions of capital have risen almost continually, and rather rapidly, during the last six decades. Their average annual growth rate between 1947 and 2009 was 1.7 percent. On the whole, the MELT-adjusted value composition has tracked the technical and organic compositions closely and it has risen almost as quickly, by 1.5 percent per year on average. In contrast, the nominal value composition of capital has increased much more slowly. Its *total* increase between 1961 and 1999 was less than 0.1 percent.

Changes in the MELT can also produce a discrepancy between movements in the observed nominal rate of profit, which has been analyzed here, and movements in the MELT-adjusted rate of profit to which the LTFRP refers. Consequently, an analysis that deals only with movements in the nominal rate and its components cannot properly test the law. As a test of the law, and as an explanation of the observed movements in the rate of profit in the U.S. corporate sector, the following decomposition analysis is much superior, since it isolates changes in the MELT as a distinct variable, a distinct source of changes in profitability. Thus, to repeat, the results reported above are *consistent* with Marx's law, but I do not claim that they *confirm* it.

ALTERNATIVE DECOMPOSITION OF THE NOMINAL RATE OF PROFIT

One factor that affects the nominal rate of profit is the profit share. As we have seen, the profit share fell only a bit over the last six decades, and it has been constant since 1970, so this factor accounts for very little of the fall in the rate of profit.

Another factor that affects the nominal rate of profit is the MELT. If commodities' prices rise in relationship to their labor-time values, which is almost always the case, the MELT rises. But this does not mean that the nominal rate of profit almost always increases in relationship to the MELT-adjusted rate. *If the MELT rises, but its rate of growth remains constant, the relationship between the nominal and MELT-adjusted rates of profit will remain unchanged* (see Kliman 2007: 129–32). However, if the MELT rises more (less) rapidly, commodities' nominal prices also rise more (less) rapidly in relationship to their labor-time values. As a result, the nominal rate of profit rises (falls) in relationship to the MELT-adjusted rate of profit.

Figure 7.6 shows that this factor has also had little effect on the rate of profit. The gap between the nominal and MELT-adjusted rates of profit has fluctuated within a relatively narrow band. Moreover, the gap has been almost trendless during the last six decades (the dotted line is the trendline).[10] In other words, the nominal and MELT-adjusted rates of profit have fallen by almost the same amount.

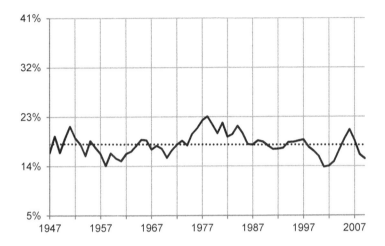

Figure 7.6   Gap Between Nominal and MELT-Adjusted Rates of Profit
(percentage-point difference between property-income rates)

Since changes in the profit share and the MELT had little effect on the rate of profit, almost all of the decline in the nominal rate can be attributed to the decline in the rate of profit we obtain when we hold the profit share constant and we also adjust for changes in the MELT. I will call this latter rate of profit the constant-profit-share MELT-adjusted (CPS-MA) rate. It is what the nominal rate of profit would have been if property income had remained exactly constant as a share of net value added *and* if prices had not risen in relationship to commodities' labor-time values. As Figure 7.7 shows, nominal, MELT-adjusted (MA), and CPS-MA rates of profit all fell by almost the same amounts—13.2, 13.7, and 12.4 percentage points, respectively—between 1947 and 2004. The fall in the CPS-MA rate of profit therefore accounts for 94 percent of the fall in the nominal rate during that period.

But why did the CPS-MA rate of profit decline? What changed during the course of the post-World War II period that caused it to decline? The answer turns out to be that not much changed—but

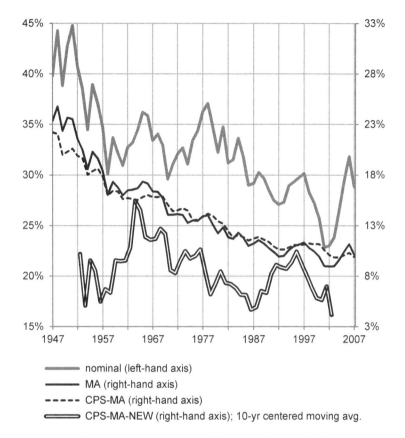

Figure 7.7   Alternative Decomposition of the Nominal Rate of Profit
(property-income rates)

nothing much *needs* to change in order for something to decline. Imagine that a couple of 22-year-olds host a party. The average age of the people at the party is therefore 22 when the party begins. Then the guests start to arrive. All of the guests are 10 years old. As more and more guests arrive, the average age of the people at the party gets closer and closer to 10. So the average age of the people at the party continually declines, even though nothing changes *during* the party. The first guests and the last guests, and all of the guests in between, are 10 years old.

What happened in the case of the rate of profit is similar. At the start of the post-World War II period, the CPS-MA rate of profit was 22 percent. But as Figure 7.7 shows, the CPS-MA rate of profit on *new* investments (CPS-MA-NEW), the *additional* profit as a percentage of the *additional* advance of capital, was much lower.[11] Between 1948 and 2000, it averaged 10 percent. The overall CPS-MA rate of profit therefore fell further and further; between 1991 and 2000, its average value was less than 11 percent.

CPS-MA-NEW trended downward, but its decline through 2000 was modest and not statistically significant at normal levels of testing.[12] Hence, little of the fall in the overall rate of profit is attributable to the *decline* in the rate of profit on new investments. The main reason why the overall nominal rate of profit fell is that CPS-MA-NEW was almost always *lower* than the currently existing CPS-MA rate of profit, that is, the average CPS-MA rate of profit generated by past investments. Putting the same point differently, the nominal rate of profit that existed at the start of the postwar boom fell, and had to fall, because it was unsustainably high. And it was unsustainably high because, throughout the entire six decades that followed, the rate of return on new investments, in CPS-MA terms, was too low to allow it to be sustained.[13]

But why was the rate of return on new investment too low? The answer is that *employment increased less rapidly than advanced capital* throughout the entire period. This is how Marx's LTFRP explains the tendency of the rate of profit to fall, and it is what is implied by the facts, namely the low level of CPS-MA-NEW and the relative constancy of the profit share.

In other words, if CPS-MA-NEW is low and the profit share is relatively constant, this means, almost as a matter of definition, that employment growth is low in relationship to capital accumulation. I say "almost as a matter of definition" because, owing to the lack of data on corporate employment, we must make an assumption in order to estimate its growth. It is very reasonable to assume that net value added per employee has increased at the same rate in the corporate sector and in the private-business sector as a whole. Given this assumption, it then follows—from the definition of CPS-MA-NEW and the relative constancy of the profit share—that the rate of return on new investments in MELT-adjusted terms is approximately equal to the percentage growth rate of corporate employment divided by the additional capital that corporations accumulate (expressed as a share of their profit). Thus, if employment grows slowly in relationship to the accumulation of capital, the MELT-adjusted rate of return on new investments will be low.

This result is derived in an appendix at the end of this chapter. The derivation is somewhat tedious and not very enlightening. Here, it may be helpful to show that Marx's theory implies a very closely related result.

Let s stand for surplus-value and C stand for total advanced capital, both expressed in terms of labor-time. Marx's rate of profit is $\dfrac{s}{C}$; the associated rate of profit on new investments is $\dfrac{\Delta s}{\Delta C}$.

Now,

$$\Delta s \equiv \Delta\left(\left[\frac{s}{E}\right]E\right)$$

where E is the number of workers employed. Let us assume that the intensity of labor is constant; E is then an exact measure of the amount of living labor performed. In Marx's theory, new value added in terms of labor-time is also equal to the living labor performed, since living labor creates all new value. It follows that, if the profit share—here, the ratio of surplus-value to new value added—is constant, then $\dfrac{s}{E}$ is constant. Hence,

$$\Delta s \equiv \Delta\left(\left[\frac{s}{E}\right]E\right) = \left(\frac{s}{E}\right)\Delta E = s\left(\frac{\Delta E}{E}\right) = s(\%\Delta E),$$

where $\%\Delta E$ is the percentage growth rate of employment. The rate of profit on new investments is therefore

$$\frac{\Delta s}{\Delta C} = \frac{s(\%\Delta E)}{\Delta C} = \frac{\%\Delta E}{\left(\dfrac{\Delta C}{s}\right)},$$

the ratio of the growth rate of employment to the additional capital accumulated (expressed as a share of surplus-value). If this ratio is lower than $\dfrac{s}{C}$, then $\dfrac{s}{C}$ must fall.

The results reported in this section therefore indicate that Marx's law of the tendential fall in the rate of profit fits the facts remarkably well. The dominant cause of the fall in the nominal rate of profit was the pronounced tendency for the rate of profit to fall toward a lower rate of profit on new investments. The latter rate is determined by the same relationship that the law singles out—the relationship between the growth rate of employment and the accumulation of capital.

The fact that CPS-MA-NEW was lower than the overall CPS-MA rate of profit throughout the whole post-World War II period is therefore tremendously important. In light of this fact, the fall in the rate of profit is no longer a mystery. It is exactly what we should expect. The rate of profit fell because new investments of capital persistently failed to generate enough additional employment of living labor to sustain the rate of profit at its current level (and because the tendency for the rate of profit to fall that this produced was not offset by a rise in the profit share or a more rapid rate of growth of the MELT).

MORAL DEPRECIATION: ONGOING DESTRUCTION OF CAPITAL VALUE

One reason why means of production depreciate (lose value) is that they become obsolete. Marx called this phenomenon "moral depreciation":

> … in addition to the material wear and tear, a machine also undergoes what we might call a moral depreciation. It loses exchange-value, either because machines of the same sort are being produced more cheaply than it was, or because better machines are entering into competition with it. (Marx 1990a: 528)

In this section, I will show that the revolution in information technology of the last few decades has led to a substantial increase in moral depreciation. Since the BEA and Marx treat moral depreciation differently, its increase has caused profit as measured by the BEA to decline substantially in relationship to surplus-value. However, the effects of moral depreciation on the *rate* of profit are more complex, since depreciation affects advanced capital as well as profit. My estimates indicate that additional moral depreciation reduced advanced capital by more than it reduced profit. The rate of profit based on BEA concepts therefore fell by a good deal less than the ratio of surplus-value to advanced capital. This suggests that the rate-of-profit data discussed above make the performance of U.S. capitalism in recent decades appear better than it actually was.

The destruction of capital value that has been taking place as a result of the revolution in information technology is much like the destruction of capital value that occurs in a crisis, except that it has been taking place in a more gradual and protracted fashion. The technological revolution thus seems to be a significant cause of the relative stagnation of the economy during the last several decades.

DEFINITIONS

BEA profit measures are poor proxies for surplus-value—in other words, profit from production—largely because of the manner in which the BEA treats moral depreciation. Such depreciation does not affect the amount of surplus-value that is created, but it does lower profit as measured by the BEA.

The BEA defines depreciation as "the decline in value due to wear and tear, obsolescence, accidental damage, and aging" (Katz and Herman 1997: 70). Since it does not distinguish between obsolescence and other sources of depreciation, it regards them all as factors that reduce profit and the net stock of advanced capital. However, Marx treated the decline in fixed assets' values caused by obsolescence differently from the decline in their values caused by wear and tear.[14]

The difference is a consequence of his theory that the value of any commodity is the monetary expression of the average amount of labor (living and past) currently needed to *reproduce* commodities of the same kind. If a fixed asset undergoes moral depreciation, some of the labor expended in its production is no longer needed to reproduce new fixed assets of the same kind, and this reduces the values of the commodities produced by means of it. Thus, some of the money that was spent to acquire the fixed asset will not be recovered if (as is true in the aggregate, according to Marx's theory) these commodities are sold at their values. In contrast, if the depreciation resulted from material wear and tear of the fixed asset, all of the labor used to produce it is still needed in order to produce fixed assets of the same kind. Hence, the money that was spent to acquire it will be recovered in full, if the commodities produced by means of it sell at their values.

For instance, consider a machine purchased for $10,000. If the only depreciation it undergoes is depreciation due to wear and tear, the whole $10,000 will be recovered, *ceteris paribus*. In Marx's terminology, the using-up of this machine "transfers" a value of $10,000 to the products produced by means of it. If, on the other hand, the price of such machines falls to $7,000 because of a technological improvement, even before this particular machine can be used in production, 30 percent of the labor that was expended to produce it is no longer needed to produce machines of this kind, and so 30 percent of its original cost, $3,000, will not be recovered if the products produced by means of it are sold at their value. The using-up of this machine therefore "transfers" a value of only $7,000 rather than $10,000 to the products: "If, as a result of a new invention, machinery of a particular kind can be produced with a lessened expenditure of labour, the old machinery undergoes a certain amount of depreciation, and therefore transfers proportionately less value to the product" (Marx 1990a: 319).

In short, when a fixed asset undergoes moral depreciation, its owners realize a loss. Thus Marx speaks of "the danger of moral depreciation," and he argues that because capitalists try to avoid this danger by using up their machines quickly, before they become obsolete, "It is … in the early days of a machine's life that this special incentive to the prolongation of the working day makes itself felt most acutely" (ibid.: 528).

In Marx's theory, workers' surplus labor is the exclusive source of surplus-value (profits generated in production). Since moral depreciation does not alter either of the two factors that determine the amount of surplus labor, workers' wages and the amount of labor they perform, it does not alter surplus-value. But the BEA treats moral depreciation just like material wear and tear, and therefore deducts it from profit. Consequently, its profit figures are not measures of surplus-value, but measures of surplus-value *minus* losses due to moral depreciation.

Because the BEA does not estimate how much depreciation is due to obsolescence, and no independent estimates seem to be available, it is not possible to directly gauge the magnitude of the difference between surplus-value and realized profit. This might not be a significant problem if moral depreciation were roughly constant as a percentage of advanced capital. In that case, although moral depreciation would alter the level of the rate of profit, it would not greatly affect the trend.

INCREASE IN MORAL DEPRECIATION

However, there are good reasons to suspect that moral depreciation has increased markedly as a percentage of advanced capital. First of all, the rate of depreciation, depreciation as a percentage of advanced capital, has risen substantially during the last half-century. Secondly, this rise is due entirely to increased employment of software, computers, and other information-processing equipment, which depreciate particularly rapidly. Finally, almost all of the depreciation they undergo seems to be moral depreciation. Taken together, these three points imply that moral depreciation has greatly increased as a percentage of advanced capital.

Here are the most salient facts. As Figure 7.8 shows, the average rate of depreciation, which had been constant in the 1950s, rose rapidly between 1960 and 2000, from about 7 percent to about 11 percent.[15] During the same period, of course, businesses' use of information-processing equipment and software (IPE&S) increased phenomenally, rising from less than 5 percent of their fixed assets to more than 18 percent.[16] Since most IPE&S depreciates far more rapidly than do other fixed assets, this caused the average rate of depreciation to rise.

Figure 7.8   Rate of Depreciation, U.S. Corporations
(historical-cost depreciation as percentage of historical cost of fixed assets)

For instance, estimates published in "BEA Depreciation Estimates" (U.S. Department of Commerce, 2008) indicate that prepackaged software has the shortest "service life" of the 107 different kinds of equipment and software listed in the report, while custom-made and "own-account" software have shorter lives than any of the other kinds of equipment on the list except for nuclear fuel (see Table 7.1).[17] The estimated service life of "office, computing, and accounting machines" is also well below average and has fallen since 1978. Table 7.1 also provides data, taken from another BEA publication (U.S. Department of Commerce, Bureau of Economic Analysis 2003, M–30, Table B), on the resale value of 5-year-old used cars and computer equipment. Not surprisingly, whereas 5-year-old used cars were worth almost one-third of what new cars were worth, 5-year-old used personal computers and printers were worth less than 14 percent of new ones.

Table 7.1   Rapid Depreciation of Computer Equipment

	Service life
Prepackaged software	3 yrs
Custom software	5 yrs
Own-account software	5 yrs
Nuclear fuel	4 yrs
Office, computing, and accounting machines	
before 1978	8 yrs
since 1978	7 yrs

	Service lives of private non-residential equipment					
Number of years	3–5	6–10	11–15	16–20	21–25	> 25
Percentage of all 107 equipment categories	3.7%	14.0%	38.3%	25.2%	12.1%	6.5%

	Value of 5-year-old asset, as percentage of the price of a new asset
Automobiles	32.6%
Computers and peripheral equipment	
Personal computers	10.6%
Printers	13.4%
Computer storage devices	17.7%
Terminals and displays	22.2%
Tape drivers	29.2%

Note: All data in this table come from U.S. Department of Commerce, Bureau of Economic Analysis (2003) and U.S. Department of Commerce (2008).

In a 2003 paper, Tevlin and Whelan pointed out that increased use of computers is the source of most of the rise in the rate of depreciation of fixed assets during the 1990s: "once computers are excluded, the estimated depreciation rate shows only a slow and modest upcreep over time" (2003: 7). It is important to note that they excluded only "computers and peripheral equipment," which account for only a small percentage of the total depreciation of businesses' IPE&S assets. In 2009, 49 percent of total IPE&S depreciation was depreciation of software, while depreciation of computers and peripheral equipment constituted only 17 percent of the total.

If we exclude *all* IPE&S fixed assets, it turns out that the entire rise in the rate of depreciation during the post-World War II period disappears. As Figure 7.9 shows, *the average rate of depreciation of all other fixed assets of U.S. businesses has been trendless and quite stable throughout the whole period. The entire rise in the rate of depreciation is therefore attributable to businesses' increased employment of rapidly depreciating IPE&S.*

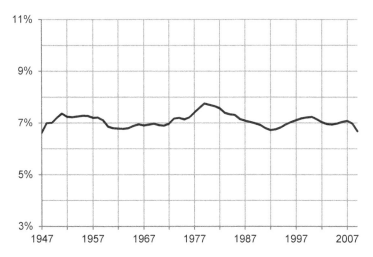

Figure 7.9   Rate of Non-IPE&S Depreciation, U.S. Business Sector
(IPE&S = information-processing equipment & software)

Now, almost all of the depreciation of computer and computer-related equipment seems to be moral depreciation. Software undergoes no physical wear and tear. As for computer hardware, in a paper that examined depreciation of Compaq and Gateway computers produced between 1984 and 2001, Geske, Ramey, and Shapiro (2004, Table 9) estimated that, on average, only one-eighth of their total depreciation was due to wear and tear ("age-related"). The rest was moral depreciation; half was due to "obsolescence" in the strict sense, while three-eighths of total depreciation was the depreciation of "age-zero" computers, which occurs when they are taken out of the box.

Since increased employment of IPE&S assets is responsible for all of the increase in the rate of depreciation, and almost all depreciation of computers and software is moral depreciation, it is reasonable to assume that the entire increase in the rate of depreciation is the result of additional moral depreciation. Simulation results suggest that this assumption is quite realistic: the portion of the increase in the rate of depreciation caused by additional moral depreciation is unlikely to have differed greatly from 100 percent.[18]

LOSSES DUE TO INCREASED MORAL DEPRECIATION

On the basis of this assumption, I have computed losses, reductions in profit, resulting from increased moral depreciation. The estimated increase in moral depreciation—the loss—is the difference between the depreciation figure reported by the BEA and my estimate of what the depreciation figure would have been if total depreciation had increased at the same rate as did the depreciation of corporations' non-IPE&S fixed assets.[19]

Losses due to increased moral depreciation, as a percentage of adjusted profit (profit as reported by the BEA plus the estimated increase in moral depreciation), are shown in Figure 7.10. During the early to mid-1980s, such losses increased rapidly, reaching surprisingly high levels. The losses have subsequently remained quite high in percentage terms (except during the middle of the last decade, when profits temporarily skyrocketed). Between 1990 and

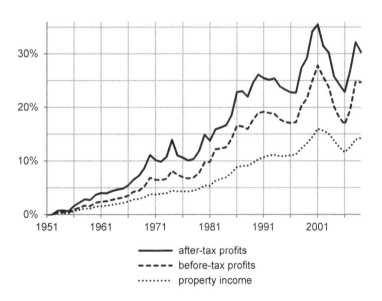

Figure 7.10 Losses Due to Additional Moral Depreciation, U.S. Corporations (percentages of adjusted profits)

2009, they were on average equal to 27 percent of after-tax profits, 21 percent of before-tax profits, and 13 percent of property income.

This means that a large share of surplus-value has not been realized as profit, because of losses stemming from moral depreciation. There is no way to know exactly how large that share is, because we do not know the extent of total moral depreciation; I have estimated only the increase. If we assume, unrealistically, that there was no moral depreciation prior to the increase produced by the revolution in information technology, then the percentages reported in the preceding paragraph are the percentages of surplus-value that was not realized as profit during the 1990–2009 period. But they are *minimum* percentages. Every additional dollar of moral depreciation would raise both losses and adjusted profits by a dollar, and this would boost losses as a percentage of adjusted profit (since the numerator, being smaller than the denominator, would experience a greater relative increase).

We will see below how the increased moral depreciation affected estimates of the rate of profit. Before doing so, however, we need to note that it affected the denominator of the rate of profit, the advanced capital, as well as the numerator. This is because my advanced capital data refer to the "net stock" of capital. The addition to the net stock of capital, net investment, is gross investment *minus* depreciation. Moral depreciation therefore reduces both profit *and* advanced capital as measured by the BEA. In principle, the effect of moral depreciation on the rate of profit is indeterminate. Over time, however, the advanced capital tends to be reduced by a relatively larger amount than profit, because reductions in the net stock of capital, unlike reductions in profit, are cumulative and permanent. For instance, if a machine undergoes $3,000 worth of moral depreciation, the net stock of capital is reduced by $3,000 forever after.

The numerator of the BEA-based rate of profit is therefore realized profit (surplus-value minus losses due to moral depreciation), while the denominator is advanced capital *minus* losses due to moral depreciation. But what was the ratio of surplus-value to advanced capital? Again, we do not know, because we do not know how much of the depreciation reported by the BEA is moral depreciation. It is nonetheless possible to estimate the effect of *increased* moral depreciation on the rate of profit.

My estimate of the increase in moral depreciation was explained above. To compute the effect of this increase on the property-income rate of profit, I obtained adjusted profit estimates by adding the estimated additional depreciation of each year to the BEA-based estimate of the year's property income. Estimates of advanced capital were obtained by adding the estimated additional depreciation of each year to net investment (in terms of historical cost). Whereas the BEA figure for advanced capital at the start of a year is the advanced capital at the start of the prior year plus the net investment of the prior year, my adjusted figure for advanced capital also includes the estimated additional depreciation of the prior year.

Figure 7.11 shows how the adjustments affect the two variables. The adjusted measure of advanced capital increases by a greater percentage than the adjusted measure of property income because, as noted above, additional depreciation lowers the advanced capital, but not profit, permanently and in a cumulative manner.

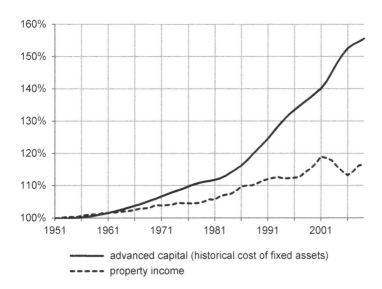

Figure 7.11   Variables Adjusted for Excess Depreciation
(as percentages of unadjusted variables)

Figure 7.12 shows how the adjustments affected the property-income rate of profit. Between the trough of 1982 and the trough of 2001, the BEA-based ratio of property income to the historical cost of the net stock of fixed assets fell by 26.9 percent (from 31.2 percent to 22.8 percent). When the estimated excess depreciation is added back into the numerator and denominator, the rate of profit falls by 34.7 percent (from 29.7 percent to 19.4 percent). The percentage decline in the ratio of surplus-value to advanced capital was therefore 29 percent greater than the percentage decline in the BEA-based rate of profit. It is also noteworthy that the adjustment eliminates most of the rise in the rate of profit during the 1990s, and almost half of the rise that took place between 2001 and 2006, which suggests that these increases in the BEA-based rate were largely due to the fact that the BEA does not distinguish moral depreciation from wear and tear.

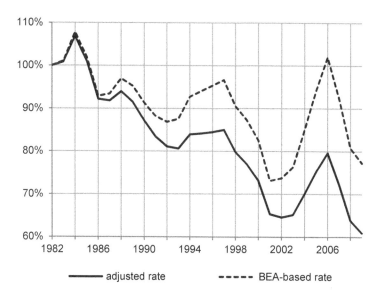

Figure 7.12   Adjusted and BEA-Based Rates of Profit

(as percentages of 1982 rates; property-income rates)

The above analysis suggests that the measured rate of profit tends to rise in relationship to the ratio of surplus-value to advanced capital when moral depreciation is not distinguished from depreciation due to wear and tear. It therefore suggests that careful attention to moral depreciation is needed when assessing the impact of technological progress on profitability or testing Marx's law of the tendential fall in the rate of profit. Finally, it suggests that the fall in the BEA-based rate of profit significantly understates the fall in the ratio of surplus-value to advanced capital that has occurred since the early 1980s. We thus have one more result that calls into question the vitality of capitalist production under neoliberalism.

Technological progress results in moral depreciation, and moral depreciation tends to prop up the measured rate of profit. This does not imply that technological progress tends to raise the rate of profit. On the contrary, it means that one way in which technological progress lowers profitability is *by way of* moral depreciation, since it causes realized profit to fall short of the surplus-value generated in production. Just as other sorts of destruction of capital value first lead to losses that lower profitability, and then raise profitability after the losses are written down and the value of advanced capital is reduced accordingly, so too in the case of moral depreciation. Moral depreciation ultimately boosts the measured rate of profit because it *first* causes the rate of profit to fall. In other words, the subsequent rise in the rate of profit is not due to technological progress itself, but to the writing-down of losses.

MATHEMATICAL APPENDIX

Theorem

If the profit share of net value added is relatively constant, and net value added per employee grows at the same rate in the corporate and total private-business sectors, then the rate of return on new investments in MELT-adjusted terms is approximately equal to the percentage growth rate of corporate employment divided by the additional capital that corporations accumulate (expressed as a share of their profit).

Definitions

A	average profit share
ΔC_{MA}	additional capital accumulated, in MELT-adjusted terms
E_c	corporate employment
E_p	private business-sector employment
M	monetary expression of labor-time (MELT)
N_c	net value added of corporations
N_p	net value added of private business sector
π_c	corporations' nominal profit
π_{cMA}	corporations' MELT-adjusted profit

Proof

The numerator of the CPS-MA rate of profit is $\dfrac{A \cdot N_c}{M}$. The numerator of CPS-MA-NEW is the change in this expression. Since A is a constant, the numerator of CPS-MA-NEW is

$$A\Delta\left(\frac{N_c}{M}\right) = A\left(\frac{N_c}{M}\right)\left(\frac{\Delta[N_c/M]}{N_c/M}\right). \tag{1}$$

Since the profit share is relatively constant, A is approximately equal to the actual profit share, $\frac{\pi_c}{N_c}$, and so

$$A\left(\frac{N_c}{M}\right) \approx \left(\frac{\pi_c}{N_c}\right)\left(\frac{N_c}{M}\right) = \frac{\pi_c}{M} = \pi_{cMA}. \tag{2}$$

Substituting (2) into (1), we obtain

$$\pi_{cMA}\left(\frac{\Delta[N_c/M]}{N_c/M}\right) \tag{3}$$

as the approximate value of the numerator of CPS-MA-NEW. And since my proxy for M is, $\frac{N_p}{E_p}$, (3) can instead be expressed as

$$\pi_{cMA}\left(\frac{\Delta[N_c/N_p]E_p}{[N_c/N_p]E_p}\right) \tag{3'}$$

Now, if net value added per employee grows at the same rate in the corporate and total private-business sectors,

$$\frac{N_c}{E_c} = \alpha\left(\frac{N_p}{E_p}\right)$$

where α is a constant, which implies that

$$\frac{N_c}{N_p} = \alpha\left(\frac{E_c}{E_p}\right)$$

so that

$$\left(\frac{N_c}{N_p}\right)E_p = \alpha\left(\frac{E_c}{E_p}\right)E_p = \alpha E_c \tag{4}$$

Substituting (4) into (3''), we find that the numerator of CPS-MA-NEW is approximately equal to

$$\pi_{cMA}\left(\frac{\Delta[\alpha E_c]}{\alpha E_c}\right), \tag{3''}$$

and since α is constant, (3'') can be rewritten as

$$\pi_{cMA}\left(\frac{\alpha \Delta E_c}{\alpha E_c}\right) = \pi_{cMA}\left(\frac{\Delta E_c}{E_c}\right) = \left(\pi_{cMA}\right)(\%\Delta E_c) \tag{3'''}$$

where $\%\Delta E_c$ is the percentage growth rate of corporate employment.

Dividing (3''') by the denominator of CPS-MA-NEW, ΔC_{MA}, we obtain

$$\frac{\left(\pi_{cMA}\right)(\%\Delta E_c)}{\Delta C_{MA}} = \frac{\%\Delta E_c}{\Delta C_{MA}/\pi_{cMA}}$$

the percentage growth rate of corporate employment divided by the additional capital that corporations accumulate (expressed as a share of their profit), as the approximate value of CPS-MA-NEW. ∎

8
The Underconsumptionist Alternative

This chapter critically examines the underconsumptionist account of the Great Recession's underlying causes as well as the theoretical foundations of underconsumptionism. In the next chapter, I will discuss the political implications of the theory, about which I am quite worried at this historical moment. I believe that it induces false hope that capitalism can be made more equitable and relatively crisis-free, and that failure of attempts to achieve this aim may well lead to disillusionment and a turn to the right. Some readers may wish to read that discussion first, but I have deferred it until later in order to avoid giving the impression that I am dismissing underconsumptionism for political reasons, rather than criticizing it on empirical and logical grounds.

I have argued in this book that the roots of the Great Recession lie in a massive build-up of debt during the last several decades, that the debt build-up is traceable to a persistent fall in profitability, and that the fall in profitability was caused by insufficient growth of employment in relationship to the rate at which capital was accumulated. Underconsumptionist authors, among others, agree that the debt build-up played a key role. They contend, however, that it was rooted in falling pay for workers and/or a fall in their share of income, which led to a lack of consumption spending—or what would have been a lack, if consumption had not been propped up by debt. I will argue, to the contrary, that the latest crisis cannot be traced back to a decline in the compensation that U.S. workers received, or a decline in their share of income—because *neither of these things declined*.

Yet even if underconsumptionist writers were right about the facts, I will then argue, we would still have to reject their account of the crisis, because the underconsumptionist theory of crisis upon which it rests is unsound. I will critique the intuition that lies behind the theory, and I will argue that the defense of the theory contained in a key underconsumptionist text, Paul A. Baran and Paul M. Sweezy's *Monopoly Capital*, rests on a logical error and is seriously flawed on empirical grounds.

LIES, DAMNED LIES, AND UNDERCONSUMPTIONIST STATISTICS

> There are three kinds of lies: lies, damned lies, and statistics.
> — Adage popularized by Mark Twain; origin unknown

The evidence that follows shows that the underconsumptionist account of the underlying causes of the Great Recession is incorrect. Contrary to what underconsumptionist writers argue, the share of national income received by the U.S. working class has not fallen; it has remained about the same for 40 years, and it is a good deal higher than in 1960. Moreover, during the last three decades (the period for which reliable data exist), compensation of U.S. workers has *risen*—by as much as 37 percent, according to one measure—even after we adjust for inflation.

Workers' Share of National Income

Elsewhere in this book, I have discussed the claim that the latest economic crisis is an irreducibly financial crisis, a crisis of a particular form of capitalism dominated by finance, instead of a crisis of capitalist production. John Bellamy Foster and Fred Magdoff (2008), two writers for *Monthly Review*, a publication that has long been sympathetic to underconsumptionism and the so-called "left-Keynesian" tradition, have recently fused the financial-crisis notion with underconsumptionism:[1]

> It was the reality of economic stagnation beginning in the 1970s … that led to the emergence of "the new financialized capitalist regime," … whereby demand in the economy was stimulated primarily "thanks to asset-bubbles." … But such a financialized growth pattern was unable to produce rapid economic advance for any length of time, and was unsustainable … .
>
> A key element in explaining this whole dynamic is to be found in the falling ratio of wages and salaries as a percentage of national income in the United States. Stagnation in the 1970s led capital to launch an accelerated class war against workers to raise profits by pushing labor costs down … Chart 3 shows a sharp decline in the share of wages and salaries in GDP between the late 1960s and the present.

Foster and Magdoff's Chart 3 uses official U.S. government data to show that wages and salaries fell from 52 percent of GDP in

1960 and 53 percent in 1970 to about 46 percent in 2007. It looks convincing—unless you also look at the government's categories and realize that the chart leaves out big and growing chunks of working people's incomes. Data for these other components of workers' incomes are readily available; they are reported in the same table that Foster and Magdoff used to get their wage and salary figures.

Essentially the same chart appears without comment in Harvey (2010: 13), and Rick Wolff (2008a) reproduced it and employed it as a basis for his own analysis in a piece published in *Monthly Review's MRZine*. More recently, Wolff and Stephen Resnick published an interpretation of the economic crisis which highlighted the fact that "real wages paid workers in manufacturing remained more or less constant and even fell a bit from [the late 1970s] to today" (Resnick and Wolff 2010: 176), but disregarded the other components of manufacturing workers' incomes.

Several months before Foster and Magdoff published Chart 3, Martin Feldstein, then president of the National Bureau of Economic Research, wrote that it is a "measurement mistake" to "focus on wages rather than total compensation," and that it "leads to a mistaken view of how the shares of national income have evolved. *A very misleading number—the ratio of wages and salaries to GDP—fell from 53 percent in 1970 to 46 percent in 2006*" (2008: 2, 4; emphasis added). He also noted that this mistake has "led some analysts to conclude that the rise in labor income has not kept up with the growth in productivity" (ibid.: 2).

What is left out when one restricts one's attention to wages and salaries? First, workers' total compensation also includes the health and retirement benefits that many employers pay, and the portion of Social Security and Medicare taxes that employers pay on their workers' behalf. Since the U.S. population is getting older and living longer after retirement, and health-care costs are rising especially quickly, these nonwage components of compensation have increased twice as fast as wage and salary income since 1970. In effect, workers are drawing less of their compensation now, and saving more of it for when they're older.[2]

Secondly, the government pays people, especially the working class, a lot of "social benefits": Social Security and Medicare benefits, veterans' benefits, and other items such as welfare assistance and unemployment insurance benefits. As the population has gotten older and more people have come under the Social Security and Medicare systems, these social benefits have also increased as a share of national income. Of course, working people are also putting more money into the Social Security and Medicare funds than before. So we need to subtract what they contribute through their taxes; we should add to total compensation only the *difference* between the social benefits provided by government and the tax contributions that partly pay for them. I'll call this difference "net government social benefits." Since 1970, net benefits have increased almost four times as fast as wage and salary income.

Although Foster and Magdoff's Chart 3 expressed workers' incomes as a share of GDP, this is another measurement error (see Feldstein 2008: 4). About one-eighth of U.S. GDP consists of the "consumption" (loss of value) of existing fixed assets, which is not part of anyone's income, and which the BEA and other national accounting agencies subtract when computing national income. Analyses of the distribution of income should therefore consider shares of national income, not shares of GDP.

Figure 8.1 compares Foster and Magdoff's results with those we obtain when we add in nonwage compensation and net government social benefits, and when we measure workers' income as a share of national income rather than as a share of GDP. Between 1960 and 2007, the wage-and-salary shares of GDP and national income fell by 6.2 and 5.8 percentage points. But the total compensation share

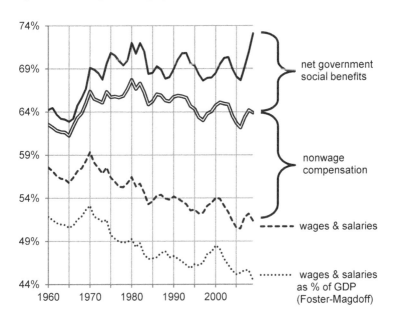

Figure 8.1   Workers' Share of U.S. National Income, 1960–2009

of national income *rose* by 0.8 points, and when net government social benefits are also included, workers' share of national income *rose* by 5.0 points. Between 1970 and 2007, the wage-and-salary shares of GDP and national income fell by 7.5 and 7.6 percentage points. But the total compensation share of national income fell by only 3.0 points, and when net government social benefits are also included, workers' share of national income *rose* by 0.1 percentage point.[3]

I do not mean to imply that working people are living well. That isn't the case. They were not well-off in the mid-1970s, and their incomes have grown only slowly since then. But the reason they aren't living well has nothing to do with a *decline* in their share of national income, because no such decline occurred. And as I discussed in Chapter 7, the slowdown in the growth of corporate employees' compensation is likewise not a distributional phenomenon, but a consequence of the slowdown in the growth of total corporate income (net value added). Since corporate income has not been growing quickly and working people have been getting a close-to-constant share of it, their compensation has increased only slowly.

Real Compensation

Foster and Magdoff then write that the fall in the wage-and-salary share of GDP

> … reflected the fact that real [inflation-adjusted] wages of private nonagricultural workers in the United States (in 1982 dollars) peaked in 1972 at $8.99 per hour, and by 2006 had fallen to $8.24 (equivalent to the real hourly wage rate in 1967), despite the enormous growth in productivity and profits over the past few decades.

One problem with this statement is that it, too, considers only wages and salaries, not the total compensation of a working population that is receiving an increasing portion of its compensation after retirement. Another problem is that there are different ways of adjusting for inflation. The method they chose makes the growth in real pay seem smaller. To remove the effect of inflation, they used the Consumer Price Index for urban wage earners (CPI-W). A readily available and widely used alternative is the PCE price index. Because the CPI-W (like other versions of the CPI) is not a consistent series— for years prior to 1985, its estimates of homeowners' housing costs are based on the values of the homes, but for subsequent years, they are based on rental costs of similar homes (see Bosworth and Perry 1994: 320–21)—its usefulness in analyses that span these two periods is limited. In any case, Foster and Magdoff should have informed readers of the different methods of inflation adjustment and the different results to which they lead.

A third problem is that they use pay data for "production and nonsupervisory workers." Several years ago, the BLS announced that it would discontinue publication of this series; it later decided to keep the series but also publish an alternative measure that takes all private-sector workers into account. One reason for the planned discontinuation was that the production and nonsupervisory worker category did not make much sense to the people who answered the government's survey questions. As the U.S. Department of Labor (2005) noted:

> … the production and non-supervisory worker hours and payroll data have become increasingly difficult to collect, because these categorizations are not meaningful to survey respondents. Many survey respondents report that it is not possible to tabulate their payroll records based on the production/non-supervisory definitions.

For this reason, Figures 8.2 and 8.3 also consider data for all U.S. workers in the private sector. Data on their wages and salaries are available only since 1976; data on their hourly total compensation are available only since 1980. Hourly total compensation data for production and nonsupervisory workers are available only for the June 1981–December 2005 period. The other total compensation figures for these workers are my estimates.[4]

Figure 8.2 makes clear that real hourly total compensation has *risen significantly*, not fallen, and that the rise in production and nonsupervisory workers' real compensation has been above average. When we use the PCE price index to adjust for inflation, we find that their compensation rose by 37 percent between 1980 and 2009, while compensation of all workers rose by 35 percent. When we use the CPI-W to adjust for inflation, we find that production and nonsupervisory workers' compensation rose by 27 percent, while compensation of all workers rose by 25 percent.

If we use the PCE price index to adjust for inflation, we find that real wages and salaries have also *risen*, not fallen, as Figure 8.3 shows. Between 1972 and 2009, wages and salaries of production

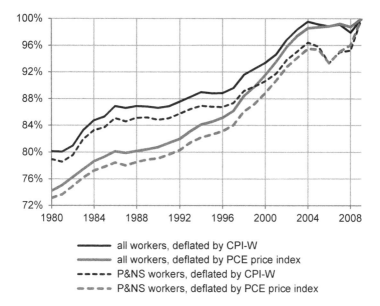

Figure 8.2   Real Hourly Compensation, Private-Industry Workers in U.S. (as percentage of 2009 level)

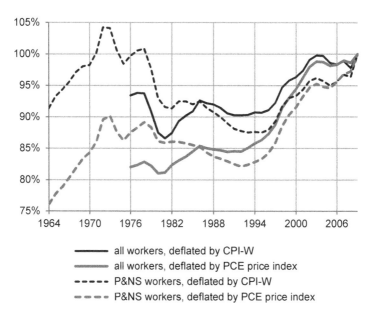

Figure 8.3   Real Hourly Wages and Salaries, Private-Industry Workers in U.S. (as percentage of 2009 level)

and nonsupervisory workers rose by 12 percent. Between 1976 and 2009, their wages and salaries rose by 14 percent, while those of all private-industry workers rose by 22 percent. Even when we use the CPI-W to adjust for inflation, we find that wages and salaries of all private-industry workers rose by 7 percent. The only series that declines is the one that Foster and Magdoff presented—wages and salaries of production and non-supervisory workers deflated by the CPI-W—which has fallen by 4 percent since 1972.

The upshot of the above analysis is that one must do *all* of the following in order to conclude that workers' real pay has declined:

(1) look only at wages and salaries, and ignore the more meaningful total compensation figures;
(2) use only the CPI-W to adjust for inflation, ignoring the PCE price index, and
(3) look only at the production and nonsupervisory workers series, ignoring the figures for all workers.

But even when one does all this, one still finds that the pay of U.S. workers has risen in real terms under neoliberalism. When the CPI-W is used as the inflation measure, real wages and salaries of nonproduction and supervisory workers have risen by 9 percent since 1981, the year in which Ronald Reagan took office.

According to widely publicized studies by Thomas Piketty and Emmanuel Saez (for example, Piketty and Saez 2003), dramatic increases in income inequality and wage inequality have taken place in the U.S. in recent decades. This might seem to suggest that managers and professionals have received whopping increases in pay, while "regular" workers' pay has stagnated or fallen. However, as I discussed in the last chapter, nonmanagerial employees' share of U.S. corporations' net value added did not decline substantially between 1985 and 2007, and Figure 8.3 offers independent support for this conclusion. Although data for production and nonsupervisory workers are problematic, as I noted above, they are the best available source of information on regular workers' real wages and salaries, since they exclude owners of companies, employees who are "primarily employed to direct, supervise, or plan the work of others," and "employees [in service-providing industries who are] not directly involved in production."[5] As Figure 8.3 shows, *real wages and salaries of production and nonsupervisory workers increased at the same rate between 1986 and 2009 as did the real wages and salaries of private-industry workers as a whole.*

In marked contrast, Piketty and Saez's data lead to the conclusion that the average real wage of the bottom 90 percent of the population rose by 17.9 percent between 1986 and 2008, while the average real salary of the top 10 percent rose almost three times as rapidly, by 48.2 percent.[6] It is not immediately apparent why Piketty and Saez's data yield results that differ so drastically from those reported by the BLS, but it is clear that their dataset is highly atypical. It is based on the wage and salary income that people report on their income tax returns, the limitations of which are obvious. The BLS wage and salary data are based on a survey of business establishments.

Moreover, while the BLS data pertain to *individuals*, Piketty and Saez's wage and salary data pertain to *tax units*. If the number of wage earners per tax unit declines faster at the bottom of the wage distribution than at the top, the measured increase in inequality will be misleadingly large. Results of a recent study suggest that this may well have occurred. In the U.S., a tax unit is either an unmarried person or a married couple who file a joint tax return (and, in both cases, any dependent children), so a decline in the marriage rate tends to lower the number of wage earners per tax unit. The study found that the marriage rate has declined much more sharply among less educated people. For instance, between 1970 and 2007, the percentage of native-born 30-to-44 year old males who were married fell by 39 points among those without a high-school diploma, but by only 19 points among college graduates (Fry and Cohn 2010: 19). Since less educated people generally receive lower wages, this suggests that the fall in the number of wage earners per tax unit may well have been disproportionately large at the bottom of the wage distribution, causing Piketty and Saez's data to exaggerate the increase in inequality.

A new study by Burkhauser, Larrimore, and Simon (2011) suggests that Piketty and Saez's findings are also very misleading with respect to income inequality, because they define income in a quite unusual way. Table 8.1 shows the total percentage changes in real income for quintiles (groups of 20 percent) of the U.S. population between 1979 and 2007. In the first row, income is defined as Piketty and Saez define it; in the second row, it is defined in the manner "most often used in the United States poverty, income, and income inequality literatures" (Burkhauser 2011: 8).[7] All three definitions of income lead to the conclusion that income inequality increased, but the extent of the increase is far greater when Piketty and Saez's definition is employed, and their definition is the only one which leads to the conclusion that the real incomes of low- and middle-income Americans fell or stagnated.

Table 8.1   Real Income Growth, U.S., 1979–2007

	Quintile				
Definition of income	*bottom*	*2nd*	*middle*	*4th*	*top*
Before-tax income of tax units; transfer payments excluded (Piketty-Saez definition)	–33.0%	–5.5%	2.2%	12.3%	32.7%
Before-tax income of households, adjusted for size; transfer payments included (most common definition)	9.9%	8.6%	22.8%	29.2%	42.0%
After-tax income of households, adjusted for size; transfer payments and health benefits included	26.4%	25.0%	36.9%	40.4%	52.6%

THE UNDERCONSUMPTIONIST INTUITION

I argued above that phenomena which underconsumptionist writers present as crucial underlying causes of the latest economic crisis and slump turn out, on closer examination, to be nonexistent phenomena. If this were all that was wrong, we could conclude that underconsumption should be rejected as an explanatory factor in the present case, but not necessarily everywhere and always. However, as I will now argue, it should indeed be rejected everywhere and always, because underconsumptionist *theory* rests on an elemental (and elementary) logical error that makes it untenable. Before discussing that error, it will be helpful to examine the underlying intuition that gives rise to it.[8]

Underconsumptionist theory holds that economic crises and recessions are caused by a lack of spending that supposedly results when workers are paid too little.[9] This implies, conversely, that if workers do better, then the economy will also do better. Since we are dealing here with a *capitalist* economy, this notion seems rather strange. When workers' pay is reduced, their loss is a gain for the companies that employ them, extra profit, and profit is the fuel that powers the capitalist system. What creates problems for the system is not a rise in the rate of profit, but a fall.

However, the underconsumptionist camp points to the fact that workers, being less well off than managers, owners, and so on, spend a bigger fraction of their incomes on consumer goods and services. So, if workers' pay and/or share of income fall, personal consumption demand will tend to fall. This would indeed reduce profits, and it could set the stage for an economic crisis or recession, *unless the decline in personal consumption demand is offset by a rise in another component of demand.*

Let us consider businesses' *productive* consumption demand—in other words, their investment demand. It consists of spending by businesses to build structures (factories, malls, offices, and so on), as well as purchases of machinery, other equipment, and software. If investment demand rises, and the rise is large enough to offset the fall in personal consumption demand, a decline in wages or workers' share of income does not lead to a decline in *total* demand. It therefore does not lead to an economic crisis or recession.

Underconsumptionists claim, however, that investment demand *cannot* grow faster than personal consumption demand in the long run. Why not? Well, they say, if businesses invest in new factories and machines and so on, and use them to produce more stuff, they then have to sell the stuff. This is obviously correct. But then comes the underconsumptionist intuition: the businesses ultimately have to sell the stuff to *people.*

Underconsumptionists do recognize that investment goods are produced, and that some investment goods are used to produce more investment goods. But their intuition tells them that the process *ultimately* results in more shoes and iPods, and only as many additional investment goods as are needed to produce more shoes and iPods. In the long run, there cannot be more investment goods that do not result in additional shoes and iPods.

Why not? Why can't businesses ultimately sell to each other, instead of to people? For instance, why can't there be a process in which mining companies sell iron to companies that use the iron to make steel; and the steel producers sell the steel to companies that use the steel to make mining equipment; and the mining-equipment producers sell the mining equipment, not to the iPod and shoe producers, but to the mining companies that then use the equipment to mine more iron, … and so on and so forth? (Of course, I am not referring to a system without *any* production of consumer goods, just one in which production of consumer goods and the demand for them rise less rapidly than production of and the demand for investment goods.)

The underconsumptionist answer is that "the process of production is and must remain, regardless of its historical form, a process of producing goods for human consumption" (Sweezy 1970: 172). *However, neither Sweezy nor any other underconsumptionist author has ever provided any evidence or argument to support this claim.* It is merely the underconsumptionist intuition presented in a dogmatic fashion, as if it were an established fact.

In the next section, I will examine a seemingly more robust argument for underconsumptionist theory that Sweezy and Baran later provided. For now, let me just say that although their argument is clearly inspired by the above intuition, it is rather different from it. The intuition has to do with the purpose of production—producing goods *for* human consumption—while Baran and Sweezy's argument does not. And while the intuition is that production of investment goods to produce more investment goods is ultimately impossible, Baran and Sweezy sought to show only that such a process is unlikely.

In any case, the underconsumptionist intuition leads to a theory of economic downturns in the following way. The demand for consumer goods sets an ultimately rigid limit to investment demand, and total demand is therefore held down by the restricted growth of consumption demand. But technological progress leads to a quicker growth of *potential* output. It follows from this contradiction that a chronic, structural tendency exists for aggregate supply to exceed aggregate demand. This situation is of course unsustainable in the long run. When the growth of output does temporarily exceed the limit set by consumption demand, "overproduction crises" must be the result. Either production and employment must decline, or prices must fall, or some combination of the two.

Some other theories simply assume that demand does not keep pace with production. That underconsumptionists have tried to explain why it does not keep pace is a considerable merit. Yet the crucial claim that the expansion of capitalist production *must* eventually be held back by limited consumption demand happens to be false, as was first demonstrated by Marx's schemes of reproduction in *Capital*, Volume 2.[10] He did not dispute the tendency toward underconsumption, but showed that this tendency constitutes no insurmountable obstacle to the expansion of production (Dunayevskaya 2000: 126).

One part of total output consists of consumption goods, and another of investment goods (means of production) that will be used, directly or indirectly, to produce consumption goods in the future. Consumption demand *does* set a limit to the expansion of these parts of output. Yet the reproduction schemes demonstrated, first, that there exists a final part of output, means of production that will be used to produce additional means of production, which themselves then produce even more means of production, and so on—as in the iron → steel → mining equipment → iron ... example. Nowhere down the line is it the case that *all* iron, steel, and mining equipment enters into the production of consumer goods. *The growth of this final part of output is not constrained by "human consumption," since its demanders are not humans, but capitalist companies.*

The reproduction schemes also demonstrated that an increase in the rate of economic growth under capitalism generally requires an expansion of this final part of output in relation to the total, as Table 8.2 illustrates. Machines are used to produce machines and to produce food. Assume that each machine lasts only one year. In both Year 1 and Year 2, the economy's total output is $100, and, in each department, the value of used-up machines and the new value added in production are each equal to half of the value of output. But the value of the boldfaced final part of output—the machines that Department I uses to produce new machines—is only $25 in Year 1 but $30 in Year 2. This creates additional employment opportunities for workers in Department I and, since Department I now has more machines and workers, the value of output in Department I is greater. (The increase in the number of machines and workers employed in Department I is initially made possible by a downsizing of Department II.)

Table 8.2   The Final Part of Output and Economic Growth

	Department	Value of used-up means of production	Value added	Value of output
Year 1	I	$25	$25	$50 worth of machines
	II	$25	$25	$50 worth of food
	Total	$50	$50	$100
Year 2	I	$30	$30	$60 worth of machines
	II	$20	$20	$40 worth of food
	Total	$50	$50	$100

Now in Year 1, the economy cannot grow. The $50 worth of machines produced at the end of the year is just enough to replace the $50 worth of machines used up during the year in the two departments; and without additional machines, growth is not possible. But in Year 2, $60 worth of machines is produced at the end of the year, which is 20 percent more than is needed to replace the $50 worth of machines that were used up during the year. So if there is *investment demand* for the additional machines (and if 20 percent more workers are hired), the value of output in the total economy will increase by 20 percent next year. In other words, the economy's growth rate will increase from 0 percent to 20 percent. The increase in the growth rate is made possible by the increase in the number of machines that produce machines, and the resulting relative increase in the production of machines at the expense of food production.

In principle, the rate of growth would also increase if fewer machines were needed to produce the same number of new machines or the same amount of food, but the capitalistic tendency to replace workers with machines makes that less likely to happen. Thus, rather than being a system that produces for consumption's sake, capitalism increasingly becomes a system of production for production's sake, the production of machines in order to produce more machines.

Underconsumptionists have not attempted to disprove what the reproduction schemes show to be possible: growth can occur indefinitely, despite a relative decline in consumption demand, by means of an increase in the demand for machines to produce new machines and a relative expansion of machine production. They simply dismiss the reproduction schemes in favor of what they believe to be reality, namely the dogma that all production, even under capitalism, is production for the sake of consumption.[11] The problem with this appeal to reality is that the schemes are not models of real-world capitalism that can properly be rejected on the grounds that they supposedly fail to model the actual growth paths of Departments I and II. The schemes are explanatory devices that reveal, among other things, that it is *logically possible* that production can take place for the sake of production, indefinitely and to an increasing degree. Any attempt to get away from this fundamental fact by appealing to reality represents a flight from logic.

Because the demand for machines to produce additional machines is not ultimately constrained by the limited demand for food, it can be an increasing share of total demand. So total demand can grow faster than demand for food, and this allows total production to grow faster than food production, even in the long run.

This implies that underconsumptionism cannot account for downturns in the economy. Imagine that the value of the economy's total output is $100 but consumption demand is only $80. If investment demand is sufficiently strong, at least $20, no downturn will occur, despite the limited consumption demand. If, on the other hand, investment demand is too weak, say $15, a downturn will occur. *But it doesn't occur because of limited consumption demand.* Consumption demand is only $80 if there is a downturn, but consumption demand is also only $80 if there is not. (In the 65 years from 1943 to 2007, real personal consumption spending in the U.S. declined only twice, in 1974 and 1980, while there were 23 years in which real gross private domestic investment spending declined. Moreover, the percentage decline in consumption spending in 1974 and 1980 was on average just 7 percent of the percentage decline in investment spending.) So the causes of the downturn are the phenomena that have resulted in investment demand of $15 rather than $20. And since the lack of investment demand is not caused by underconsumption, neither is the downturn.

It is widely recognized that what actually drives productive investment spending is profitability—past profits to fund investment spending and expectations of future profitability to provide the incentive to do so. Behind sluggish investment spending, therefore, is the tendency of the rate of profit to fall, as Chapter 5 showed.

In general, underconsumptionists agree. They contend, however, that the lack of demand in the market is what depresses the rate of profit, and that this in turn leads to an insufficient volume of investment. Yet, as has just been shown, the insufficiency of investment spending is what *causes* the lack of demand—if investment spending had been sufficiently strong, there would have been no lack of demand. And profitability problems are what cause the insufficiency of investment spending. Once all this is recognized, it is clear that underconsumptionism mistakes the effect, lack of demand, for the cause, and the cause, insufficient past profitability and expected future profitability, for the effect. As Dunayevskaya argued:

> The crisis ... is not caused by a shortage of "effective demand." On the contrary, it is the crisis that causes a shortage of "effective demand." The ... "inability to sell" manifests itself as such *because of the fundamental antecedent decline in the rate of profit, which has nothing whatever to do with the inability to sell.* (1991: 43, emphasis in original)[12]

Although underconsumptionists dismiss the implications of Marx's reproduction schemes, many of them nonetheless argue that their theory is rooted in his work. They (for example, Sweezy 1970: 177;

Desai 2010: 115) are particularly fond of taking out of context a sentence in which Marx writes, "The ultimate reason for all real crises always remains the poverty and restricted consumption of the masses" (1991a: 615). Let us put this sentence back in the context of the paragraph in which it appears.

Marx notes that if "the whole society [were] composed simply of industrial capitalists and wage-labourers," total income (= net output) would be divided between the profits of the former and the wages of the latter. If we assume that workers spend their whole income on consumption goods and services, then a lack of demand, and hence "a crisis[,] would be explicable only in terms of" two things. First, all income might be spent on goods and services, but there could be a lack of demand in some branches of production (and too much demand in others)—"a disproportion in production between different branches." Secondly, industrial capitalists' demand might be less than their accumulated profit; in this case, there would be "a disproportion between the consumption of the capitalists themselves and their accumulation."[13] "But as things actually are, [demand] depends to a large extent on the consumption capacity of non-productive classes; while the consumption capacity of the workers is restricted" (Marx 1991a: 614–15). In other words, workers receive only part of the income that isn't profit, while third parties, who are neither capitalists nor workers but instead belong to "non-productive classes," receive the rest, and there would be a crisis if the consumption demand of the latter were significantly less than their income.

Thus, "The ultimate reason for all real crises"—*besides the two reasons that Marx referred to in the same paragraph, only two sentences earlier*—"always remains the poverty and restricted consumption of the masses" in the sense that this creates the *possibility* that third parties, who receive income that the workers would otherwise receive, *might* not spend it all on goods and services. Or, if we set aside, as something other than "real crises," those caused by the first kind of disproportionality, then the workers' restricted consumption is the ultimate reason in the sense that this creates the *possibility* that industrial capitalists and third parties receive some income that they *might* not spend on goods and services. And these possibilities in turn "imply the possibility of crises, *though no more than the possibility*. For the development of this possibility into a reality a whole series of conditions is required" (Marx 1990a: 209, emphasis added).

Nothing in these passages even hints at the idea that crises are caused by chronic structural problems in capitalism that result from persistently inadequate personal consumption demand. And nothing in them even hints at a denial that investment demand can grow more quickly than consumption demand, even in the long run. Marx is certainly *not* "frontally challenging any idea that the 'fundamental' cause of capitalist crises lay in some separate sphere of production" (Desai 2010: 115), since the passages only discuss factors that make crises *possible*; they do not discuss the fundamental conditions that turn "this possibility into a reality."

The leading underconsumptionist of the twentieth century noted that the "ultimate reason" sentence—a single out-of-context sentence in a somewhat opaque paragraph of a manuscript that Marx did not prepare for publication!—"appears to be Marx's most clear-cut statement in favor of an underconsumption theory of crises" (Sweezy 1970: 177). If that is the best evidence that Marx was an underconsumptionist—and it is—I would hate to see the other evidence.

BARAN AND SWEEZY'S LOGICAL ERROR

Baran and Sweezy's celebrated *Monopoly Capital* may seem at first reading to be mostly a description of post-World War II capitalism in the U.S. But the point of the description is to answer the book's central theoretical question: how can monopoly capitalism avoid stagnation or another Great Depression, since this requires that "the surplus" be "absorbed," but the continual growth of the surplus makes its absorption increasingly difficult? This question does not arise out of the facts. It arises out of their underconsumptionist theory. It makes sense only in light of that theory, and if that theory is irredeemably flawed, the many phenomena they describe—the growth of military spending, "wasteful" business expenditures, and so on—do not have the same functions or significance that Baran and Sweezy attribute to them.

Thus, although their defense of the underconsumptionist theory of economic crises and slumps is little more than one page long, it is the lynchpin of the entire book. Almost everything else stands or falls together with it. Since *Monopoly Capital* continues to be a great influence in parts of the academic and political left, and since its brief defense of underconsumptionist theory plays such a central role, I will discuss and critique it in its entirety.

After reiterating their claims that the surplus has a tendency to rise in relationship to total income, but that capitalists' personal consumption demand absorbs an ever-smaller share of the surplus, Baran and Sweezy ask whether investment demand can "absorb a rising share of a rising surplus." They answer the question as follows:

> The logic of the situation is as follows: if total income grows at an accelerating rate, then a larger and larger share has to be devoted to investment; and, conversely, if a larger and larger share is devoted to investment, total income must grow at an accelerating rate. What this implies, however, is nonsensical from an economic standpoint. It means that a larger and larger volume of producer goods would have to be turned out for the sole purpose of producing a still larger and larger volume of producer goods in the future. Consumption would be a diminishing proportion of output, and the growth of the capital stock would have no relation to the actual or potential expansion of consumption. (Baran and Sweezy 1966: 81)

The second sentence is false, as we shall see. Everything else in this paragraph is correct, if the ratio of potential output to the capital stock remains constant. That is the assumption that Evsey Domar's (1957) growth model makes, and Baran and Sweezy cite Domar in a footnote to the paragraph, so presumably they are also assuming that the potential-output/capital ratio remains constant. I will therefore assume this as well. It follows from this assumption that the capital stock and potential output grow at the same percentage rate; if they grew at different rates, their ratio would change over time.

Explosive Growth?

Baran and Sweezy's next sentence begins as follows: "Quite apart from the fact that such an explosive growth process would sooner or later exceed the physical potentialities of any conceivable economy … ."

Thus, one reason why this growth process supposedly has "nonsensical" implications—an increasing share of production that is not production for human consumption—is that the process is supposedly explosive. "Explosive" is a technical term in growth theory; here it means that the percentage growth rate of output and the capital stock increases in an *unbounded* manner; in other words, there is no limit to the increase in their growth rate. This is why the growth process would eventually outstrip the physical potentialities of any economy. But Baran and Sweezy have done nothing to demonstrate that the growth process under discussion must be explosive. In fact, it does not have to be explosive, as the following example shows.

Assume that (a) The potential-output/capital ratio remains constant; (b) actual output is initially equal to potential (maximum) output; (c) workers' consumption is initially equal to 75 percent of income; (d) the remainder is "the surplus," initially 25 percent of income; (e) capitalists' consumption is initially equal to 20 percent of income; (f) the final 5 percent of income is invested, used to purchase additional capital stock, and so the entire surplus is "absorbed"; and (g) the potential-output/capital ratio is 0.15. (See Table 8.3.)

Table 8.3   Initial Situation

	Percentages of income				
(1)	*(2)*	*(3)*	*(4)*	*(5)*	*(6)*
		Capitalists'	*Needed*	*Output-*	*Growth rate of*
Workers'	*Surplus =*	*personal*	*investment*	*capital*	*capital and*
consumption	*100% – (1)*	*consumption*	*= (2) – (3)*	*ratio*	*output*
					= (4) × (5)
75%	25%	20%	5%	0.15	0.75%

Assumptions (f) and (g) have several implications. First, since investment is initially equal to 5 percent of potential output and the potential-output/capital ratio is 0.15, investment is initially equal to $5\% \times 0.15 = 0.75\%$ of the capital stock. Secondly, this implies that the capital stock is initially growing at 0.75 percent per year, since the ratio of investment to the capital stock is the percentage growth rate of the latter (the increase in the capital stock as a percentage of the total capital stock). Finally, since potential output grows at the same percentage rate as the capital stock, it is also initially growing at 0.75 percent per year.

What happens next? Baran and Sweezy argue that workers' consumption falls over time as a share of income, so that the surplus rises, but the portion of the surplus that is absorbed by capitalists' personal consumption also falls over time. So let us imagine that the share of income consumed by workers falls from 75 percent to 74 percent to 73.1 percent to 72.29 percent, and so on; each year it declines by 9/10ths as much as it declined the year before. The end result is that the workers' share will fall *forever*, but not in an *unbounded* manner. It will move closer and closer to 65 percent of total income, without ever going below or even reaching that lower limit (see Figure 8.4). (In the same way, if you save $400 this week, $200 next week, $100 the following week, and so on, your total savings will increase forever, but not unboundedly. Your total savings will always be less than $800.) Imagine that capitalists' personal consumption gradually falls in the same way, from 20 percent of income to 19.5 percent to 19.05 percent, and so on. It will approach a lower limit of 15 percent. Thus, in keeping with Baran and Sweezy's prior argument, the surplus rises, from 25 percent of income toward an upper limit of 100% − 65% = 35%,[14] and the share of the surplus that is absorbed by capitalists' personal consumption falls over time, from 20%/25% = 80% toward a lower limit of 15%/35% = 42.9%.

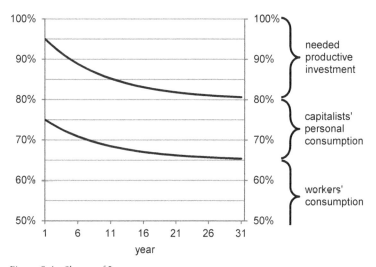

Figure 8.4   Shares of Income

Because workers' and capitalists' personal consumption demand is declining as a share of income, actual output will drop below potential output unless investment spending gradually rises from 5 per cent of total income toward an upper limit of 100% − 65% − 15% = 20% of total income. Let us assume that it does rise in this manner. Since we are assuming that the potential-output/capital ratio remains constant at 0.15, the income that is invested gradually approaches an upper limit of 20% × 0.15% = 3% of the capital stock. Given our other assumptions, this implies that the economy's growth rate gradually rises and approaches an upper limit of 3 percent.

But this means that the growth rate *never exceeds* 3 percent. In other words, there is no explosive growth here. A growth rate of 3 percent is not particularly rapid. It is a bit less than the average growth rate of real GDP in the U.S. since 1929. Our example therefore demonstrates that, contrary to what Baran and Sweezy assert, (1) the surplus can rise *forever* as a share of income, and (2) the share of output that is consumed by people and the share of the surplus that is absorbed by capitalists' personal consumption can fall *forever*, but that (3) all of the surplus can nonetheless be absorbed, *forever*, if (4) an ever-increasing share of income is devoted to investment, and that (5) *this process does not ever have to lead to explosive growth that eventually outstrips the physical potentialities of the economy.*

As we will now see, the above demonstration also demolishes *Monopoly Capital's* main argument on behalf of the underconsumptionist theory of economic crisis. The argument reads as follows:

> If accelerating growth [that is, an increasing rate of growth] is ruled out as totally unrealistic, one is left with the inescapable conclusion that the actual investment of an amount of surplus which rises relatively to income must mean that the economy's capacity to produce grows more rapidly than its output. Such an investment pattern is certainly not impossible; indeed, it has frequently been observed in the history of capitalism. But what is impossible is that it should persist indefinitely. Sooner or later, excess capacity grows so large that it discourages further investment. When investment declines, so do income and employment and hence also the surplus itself. In other words, this investment pattern is self-limiting and ends in an economic down-turn—the beginning of a recession or depression. (Baran and Sweezy 1966: 81)

Everything in this chain of reasoning hinges on the claim that an increasing rate of growth can be "ruled out as totally unrealistic." As the above example has shown, this claim is unsubstantiated and unwarranted. So we are not left with the inescapable conclusion that the capital stock (the "capacity to produce") and potential output must continually grow more rapidly than actual output if there is a continual rise in investment as a share of income. In our example, there is never a gap between potential and actual output, much less a growing one. To assure readers that there is no sleight-of-hand here, Table 8.4 presents the first ten periods of the economy's

Table 8.4 First Ten Periods

| Year | C_W | C_C | I | Y | Percentages of Y | | | $K = last\ year's\ K + I$ | Q_{MAX} | $\frac{Q_{MAX}}{K}$ | Growth rate (of Y, Q_{MAX}, and K) |
					C_W	C_C	I				
1	450	120	30	600	75.0	20.0	5.0	4000	600	0.15	
2	447	118	39	605	74.0	19.5	6.5	4030	605	0.15	0.75%
3	446	116	48	610	73.1	19.1	7.8	4069	610	0.15	0.97%
4	446	115	56	618	72.3	18.6	9.1	4117	618	0.15	1.18%
5	448	114	64	626	71.6	18.3	10.2	4173	626	0.15	1.36%
6	451	114	71	636	70.9	18.0	11.1	4237	636	0.15	1.52%
7	454	114	78	646	70.3	17.7	12.0	4308	646	0.15	1.67%
8	459	114	84	658	69.8	17.4	12.8	4385	658	0.15	1.80%
9	465	115	91	670	69.3	17.2	13.5	4470	670	0.15	1.92%
10	471	116	97	684	68.9	16.9	14.2	4560	684	0.15	2.03%

C_W = workers' consumption; C_C = capitalists' personal consumption; I = net productive investment; Y = actual output = income = total consumption & investment spending; K = capital stock; Q_{MAX} = potential output. Most figures are rounded to the nearest whole number.

evolution. Readers can verify that all of the numbers conform to our assumptions, and that they do not violate any of Baran and Sweezy's assumptions concerning changes in shares of income and a rising growth rate. *Yet actual and potential output are always equal* (in the example).[15]

And thus we are not left with the inescapable conclusion that excess capacity increases. Consequently, despite what Baran and Sweezy assert, a rise in the investment share of income need not lead to an eventual decline in investment, income, employment, and the surplus. In other words, the argument has done *nothing* to show that "this investment pattern is self-limiting and ends in an economic down-turn."

The Real World

Let us return to Baran and Sweezy's assertion that "if a larger and larger share [of income] is devoted to investment, total income must grow at an accelerating rate. What this implies, however, is nonsensical from an economic standpoint." One justification of this assertion is the explosive-growth argument. Their only other justification is that

> Quite apart from the fact that such an explosive growth process would sooner or later exceed the physical potentialities of any conceivable economy, there is simply no reason to assume that anything like this has ever occurred or is likely to occur in the real world. Manufacturers of producer goods do not provide each other with an infinitely expanding market for each others' output and they know it. In particular, it is sheer fantasy to imagine the cautious, calculating giant corporations of monopoly capitalism planning and carrying out the kind of snowballing expansion programs which this case presupposes.

The final two sentences, which refer to an "infinitely expanding market" and "snowballing expansion," clearly presuppose that the growth process in question must be explosive, which has already been shown to be false. As for the first sentence, there is *very* good reason to "assume" that accelerating growth has occurred. Table 8.5 presents estimates of the worldwide growth rate of real GDP since 1600, based on data published by the late Angus Maddison and the World Bank.[16] The table provides extremely strong evidence that acceleration of real GDP growth was the norm in the world as a whole for almost four centuries. Through 1973, the average growth rate continually rose, except between 1913 and 1950, a period during which the Great Depression and two world wars took place.

Table 8.5 Worldwide Growth of Real GDP since 1600

Years	*Average annual percentage growth rate (exponential)*								
	1600–1700	1700–1820	1820–1870	1870–1900	1900–1913	1913–1950	1950–1960	1960–1973	1973–2008
Maddison (international $)	0.11	0.52	0.94	1.92	2.51	1.81	4.58	4.93	3.31
World Bank (U.S. $)								5.21	2.95

In the case of the U.S., there is also *very* good evidence that the share of income devoted to investment rose, and the share devoted to consumption fell, during the three-quarters of a century following 1933, the trough of the Great Depression. Owing to the accounting identity between expenditures on output and the production of output, the real GDP, private fixed nonresidential investment, and

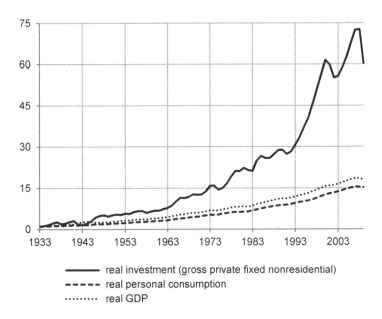

Figure 8.5 Growth of Investment, Consumption, and GDP in U.S., 1933–2009 (multiples of 1933 values)

personal consumption figures plotted in Figure 8.5 are demand data as well as actual-output data.[17] Everything fell in 2009 because of the recession, but in 2008, investment demand was 72.7 times as large as in 1933, while GDP was only 18.5 times as large and personal consumption demand was only 15.4 times as large. So private investment demand grew almost *four* times as rapidly as GDP and almost *five* times as rapidly as personal consumption demand. Putting the same point differently, the investment share of income almost quadrupled while the consumption share fell by 16 percent.

According to *Monopoly Capital* and underconsumptionist theory in general, "there is simply no reason to assume that anything like this has ever occurred or is likely to occur in the real world." But it *did* occur, for at least 75 years in the U.S. And it almost certainly occurred on a world scale throughout the last four centuries. How else could one account for almost four centuries of accelerating growth? If actual and potential output are equal and the potential-output/capital ratio is constant, an x percent rise in the investment share of income results in an x percent rise in the rate of growth of output.[18] Under these conditions, a rise in the investment share of income would fully account for the rise in the rate of economic growth. Of course, actual and potential output are not always close to being equal, the potential-output/capital ratio is not exactly constant, and lots of other things matter. Nonetheless, as a study that reviewed the literature on the determinants of economic growth concluded:

> ... investment may not be the sole engine of growth[, but this] does not alter the fact that capital accumulation remains a *centerpiece* of that engine. In general, it is hard to find countries that have been able to grow at high and sustained rates for long time periods without an important effort of capital formation—a fact noted long ago by economic historians such as Rostow [1960] or Gerschenkron (1962). (Schmidt-Hebbel et al. 1994: 20, emphasis in original)

Table 8.6, which is based on data reported in the same study, illustrates this fact. Differences in the investment share of GDP accounted for 91 percent of the differences in the GDP growth rate between 1965 and 1992.

Table 8.6 Investment and growth, 1965–92 averages

	East-Asian Tigers	OECD countries	Other LDCs	Latin America & Caribbean	Africa
Gross domestic investment (% of GDP)	28.8	23.8	21.3	20.8	19.2
GDP growth rate (%)	4.8	2.8	2.7	1.5	0.6

Note: The East-Asian Tigers are Hong Kong, Singapore, South Korea, and Taiwan. The OECD is the Organization for Economic Cooperation and Development; at the time, almost all of its members were advanced industrialized countries. LDCs are less-developed countries.

Measurement Issues

I showed above that private fixed nonresidential investment demand in the U.S. grew almost four times as fast as GDP and almost five times as fast as personal consumption demand between 1933 and 2008. This finding is quite important, since it flatly refutes the underconsumptionist claim that "there is no reason to assume that anything like [a long-term rise in the investment share of income] has ever occurred or is likely to occur in the real world." Careful discussion of measurement issues related to this finding is therefore in order.

The BEA does not publish inflation-adjusted measures of total investment demand and total consumption demand that can validly be compared with one another. This is the main reason why the investment data in Figure 8.5 exclude some components of real investment and consumption demand—spending to construct homes, government spending, and spending on imports and exports. Also, it is impossible to draw any conclusion about the exports and imports, because the BEA's data for them begin only with 1967 and because the statistical tables fail to break down spending on some imports and exports, like food and beverages, and cars and trucks, into investment spending and consumption spending.

Because there are no inflation-adjusted data for the total economy, we have to examine the home construction and government spending components separately. Real spending on the construction of homes (NIPA Table 1.1.3, line 12) was 26.7 times as great in 2008 as in 1933. It is difficult to assess the significance of this figure, because the status of spending on home construction is ambiguous. On the one hand, the BEA classifies it as investment spending. On the other hand, people purchase homes in order to consume the "housing services" they provide; such purchases are really consumption spending. On the third hand, as the old joke about economists' answers goes, demand for new homes is often, in part or whole, demand for an asset, an alternative to putting money in the bank or buying securities, and thus neither (productive) investment spending nor consumption spending.

To help resolve this problem, we can use personal consumption spending on housing services and utilities (NIPA Table 1.5.3, line 16) as a proxy for the personal-consumption component of home construction spending. In real terms, it was 17.4 times as great in 2008 as in 1933, which is very similar to the growth factor of total personal consumption spending, that is, 15.4. It is therefore safe to say that home construction spending has not had a sizable impact on the relative growth of productive investment and personal consumption.

Real gross government investment spending (NIPA Table 3.9.3, line 3) was 21.5 times as great in 2008 as in 1933, while real government consumption spending (NIPA Table 3.9.3, line 2) was only 14.4 times as great. The latter figure is very similar to the growth factor of private consumption spending. Using the relative sizes of private nonresidential investment spending (NIPA Table 1.5.5, line 28) and government investment spending (NIPA Table 1.5.5, line 53 plus line 56) to weight their growth factors, we can get a rough estimate of the total growth of real investment. I estimate that it grew somewhat more than 60-fold between 1933 and 2008, about four times as fast as total consumption spending. And since we have to exclude imports and exports because of a lack of data, and we can exclude home construction because of its lack of impact, I also estimate that total investment spending in the U.S. grew about four times as fast as total consumption spending.

To measure investment, I used figures for gross investment rather than net (post-depreciation) investment. Gross investment spending is the appropriate measure here, since it is the same thing as the total production of investment goods. (This follows from the fact that everything that is produced is either an investment good or a consumption good or service, and the fact that consumption spending is in effect the same thing as the production of consumption goods and services.) In other words, gross investment would be the same thing as the Department I of Marx's reproduction schemes in Volume 2 of *Capital* if we were to add in production of raw materials, while consumption spending is Department II.

In any case, real net private nonresidential investment (NIPA Table 5.2.3, line 12) was negative in 1933, so it is impossible to estimate its growth rate since that year. It was also negative throughout the whole 1931–44 period, except in 1937, 1940, and 1941. Between 1945 and 2008, real net private nonresidential investment grew 7.0 times as fast as real personal consumption spending, and 9.9 times as fast as real GDP. But because net investment is extremely volatile, the amount by which it increased between a certain year and 2008 is greatly affected by the choice of the starting year. If I had chosen 1930, 1937, 1940, or 1941 as the starting year, the results would have been quite different. Real net investment would have grown between 4.3 and 93.4 times as fast as real personal consumption spending and between 4.5 and 89.5 times as fast as real GDP.

In nominal terms—that is, when no adjustment is made for inflation—gross private nonresidential investment (NIPA Table 1.1.5, line 9) grew 3.0 times as fast as personal consumption spending (ibid., line 2), and 2.6 times as fast as GDP (ibid., line 1), between 1933 and 2008. Net private nonresidential investment grew 2.4 times as fast as personal consumption spending, and 3.1 times as fast as GDP, between 1945 and 2008.

In sum, we have extremely robust evidence that nonresidential investment spending grew significantly faster than consumption spending and GDP during the past three-quarters of a century. All of the various measures of their relative growth that we have considered confirm that this has been the case.

Yet why did I begin my analysis with 1933, or as close to it as possible? In that year, the trough of the Great Depression, investment spending was exceedingly low. Did I not cherry pick the data and thereby exaggerate the increase in investment demand? No. This starting point is the right one to select in order to test what under-consumptionists claim. They regard the Depression as a return to equilibrium, the point at which growth of means of production, which had temporarily outstripped growth of personal consumption, was forcibly brought back in line. As Baran and Sweezy put it, in a passage quoted above, "investment of an amount of surplus which rises relatively to income … is self-limiting and ends in an economic down-turn—the beginning of a recession or depression." Elsewhere in *Monopoly Capital*, they made the point even more clearly: "the Great Depression [… was] the *normal outcome* of the workings of the American economic system[,] … *the realization in practice of the theoretical norm toward which the system is always tending*" (Baran and Sweezy 1966: 235, emphases added).

Because they consider 1933 or thereabouts as an equilibrium, underconsumptionists would predict that the relationship between investment and consumption spending that existed in or around 1933 is the relationship that is sustainable in the long run. In other words, they would predict that any subsequent increases in investment relative to personal consumption would be only temporary and self-negating. In fact, underconsumptionists such as Alvin Hansen *did* predict a return to Depression conditions after World War II, and Baran and Sweezy argued more than two decades later that "monopoly capitalism without external stimuli is powerless to pull itself out of a state of stagnation" (ibid.: 239).

WHITHER UNDERCONSUMPTIONISM?

Of course, underconsumptionists may well invoke "external stimuli" in an effort to explain away the evidence that investment spending in the U.S. grew significantly faster than consumption spending for at least 75 years. In her underconsumptionist writings of a century ago, Luxemburg (e.g. Luxemburg 1964) invoked an external stimulus, imperialism, in order to explain how capitalist economies are able to grow at all, and the *Monthly Review* school has long pointed to external stimuli—innovation, consumerism, and U.S. hegemony, as well as military spending, finance, marketing, and other forms of "waste"—in order to explain away the fact that U.S. capitalism did not reach a point of absolute stagnation long ago. Various religious cults have been similarly adept at finding ad hoc rationalizations to explain away the failures of their prophecies of doom or salvation.

Supporters of *Monopoly Capital* may point to the fact that it held that investment spending cannot rise in relationship to consumption spending *indefinitely*. But 75 years is a long time. Moreover, even after the very severe recent slump, we are still very far away from the "equilibrium" between real gross private domestic nonresidential investment and personal consumption spending that existed in 1933. Re-establishment of that "equilibrium" would require that investment spending fall by 79 percent from its 2008 peak, even without any fall in consumption spending.[19] The massive decline in investment that occurred in 2009 only reduced it by 17 percent. How much longer must we wait before it is agreed that the evidence has shown underconsumptionist theory to be false? *Indefinitely*?

Yet even if the theory put forward in *Monopoly Capital* did not require ad hoc rationalizations and indefinitely long waiting times in order to fit the facts, it would remain fatally flawed for another, more fundamental reason. That reason is the one stressed above: the conclusion that an ever-rising investment share of income and an ever-rising growth rate are "totally unrealistic" is rooted in an elementary logical error: the incorrect inference that if something increases forever, it must also increase boundlessly. In principle, the economy's growth rate and the investment share of income could rise forever but remain within realistic bounds.

9
What is to be Undone?

A NEW MANIFESTATION OF STATE-CAPITALISM

In March 2008, the U.S. government "bailed out" Bear Stearns, Wall Street's fifth largest investment firm. In July of that year, it "bailed out" Fannie Mae and Freddie Mac, huge mortgage lenders and backers of mortgage loans, and officially nationalized them two months later. Once panic struck in mid-September, other nationalizations followed. The government effectively nationalized AIG, a giant insurance company, by purchasing the vast majority of its stock. More than 700 banks, as well as General Motors and Chrysler, also became partly government-owned shortly thereafter, as the government used TARP funds to supply them with capital.

Throughout the political spectrum, some commentators regarded these moves as efforts to make the rich richer, while some on the left regarded them as progressive in some sense, since they marked an ideological shift away from the free market and neoliberalism. I think both notions are seriously mistaken.

These interventions—and the government's aggressive fiscal and monetary policies generally—were a new manifestation of state-capitalism. It is not the state-capitalism of the former U.S.S.R., characterized by central "planning" and the dominance of state property. It is state-capitalism in the sense in which Dunayevskaya (2000: 258ff) used the term to refer to a new global stage of capitalism, characterized by permanent state intervention, that arose in the 1930s with the New Deal and similar policy regimes. The purpose of the New Deal, just like the purpose of the latest government interventions, was to save the capitalist system from itself.

Because many liberal and leftist commentators chose to discuss the interventions in distributional terms—who is the government rescuing, rich investors and lenders, or laid-off workers and average homeowners facing foreclosure?—let me stress that I mean "save the capitalist system" in the literal sense. The purpose of these interventions was not to make the rich richer, or even to protect their wealth, but to save the system *as such*.

Government officials have not hidden the fact that this has been their aim. In testimony before the Financial Crisis Inquiry Commission, Federal Reserve Chairman Ben Bernanke (2010) stated:

> Governments provide support to too-big-to-fail firms in a crisis not out of favoritism or particular concern for the management, owners, or creditors of the firm, but because they recognize that the consequences for the broader economy of allowing a disorderly failure greatly outweigh the costs of avoiding the failure in some way.

Consider the "bailout" of Bear Stearns. The Fed attempted to sell it off to JP Morgan Chase for the fire-sale price of $2 per share, a tiny fraction of what its assets were worth on the open market and one-fifth of the ultimate sale price. Bear was in serious trouble, but there were other ways of dealing with its troubles. Had it been able to borrow at the Fed's "discount window," Bear might have been able to weather the immediate crisis it faced, which was due to a lack of cash, and limp along until TARP came to the rescue six month later. But the Fed waited until *the day after* Bear was sold to JP Morgan Chase to announce that it would now open the discount window to Wall Street firms. Alternatively, if Bear had been allowed to file for bankruptcy, it could have continued to operate, and its owners' shares of stock would not have been acquired at a fraction of their market value. Instead, the Fed forced it to be sold off.

It is thus quite misleading to refer to the takeover of Bear Stearns as a "bailout." The Fed was definitely not trying to bail out the company's owners. Nor was the Fed out to enrich the owners of JP Morgan Chase; Chase was selected as the new owner of Bear's assets because it was the only financial firm big enough to buy them. The Fed acted in the manner it did in order to send a clear signal to the financial world that the U.S. government would do whatever it could to prevent the failure of any institution that is "too big to fail," because such a failure could set off a domino effect, triggering a panicky withdrawal of funds large enough to bring the financial system crashing down.

And consider the government's "bailout" of Fannie Mae and Freddie Mac. This came about because of a sharp decline in their stock prices. But the government didn't rescue them in order to prop up the price of their stock. Their stock prices continued to decline after the rescue plan was announced, precisely because the government's motivation was *not* to bail out the firms' shareholders.

Indeed, the shareholders did not receive any money from the government. Only the institutions and investors that lent to them were bailed out, and the government had seriously considered not bailing out the holders of risky subordinated debt. Just like in the Bear Stearns case, the point of the intervention was to restore confidence in the financial system by assuring lenders that, if all else fails, the U.S. government will be there to pay back the moneys that are owed to them.

The new manifestation of state-capitalism is essentially non-ideological in character. Henry Paulson, Treasury Secretary under George W. Bush, was certainly no champion of government regulation or nationalization. But once panic followed the collapse of Lehman Brothers, he rushed to the rescue with TARP. At a moment when "this sucker could go down" (George W. Bush, quoted in Herszenhorn, Hulse, and Stolberg 2008), ideological scruples simply had to be set aside. So did concerns that governmental rescues of too-big-to-fail firms lead to moral hazard and excessive risk-taking. The be-all and end-all priority is to serve the interests of capitalism—capitalism itself, as distinct from capitalists. As Marx noted, "The capitalist functions only as *personified capital* ... the rule of the capitalist over the worker is [actually] the rule of things [capital] over man ... of the product [capital] over the producer" (1990b: 989–90). The goal is the continued self-expansion of capital, of value that begets value to beget value, the accumulation of value for the sake of the accumulation of value—not for the sake of the consumption of the rich.

The movement away from free-market, neoliberal capitalism, and back to more government control and even ownership, is a pragmatic matter rather than an ideological one. There is nothing inherently progressive about it. Indeed, greater government intervention has recently been accompanied by—or, more precisely, has increasingly taken the form of—austerity measures. In the U.S.'s case, the government has simply been doing what it must, whatever it must, to prevent a collapse of the capitalist system. When it needed to borrow massively in order to calm the panic in the financial markets and prevent the recession from turning into a depression, it borrowed massively. But the resulting explosion of Treasury debt—an increase of more than 50 percent in the three years since Lehman Brothers collapsed—has itself become a potential threat to the stability of the system, so discussion of economic policy now focuses on austerity measures to bring deficit spending under control.

The U.S. government operated for many decades under the doctrine that the big commercial banks are so crucial to the system that they are too big to fail. During the latest crisis, this doctrine was extended for the first time to institutions other than commercial banks, such as Bear Stearns and AIG. The extension of the too-big-to-fail doctrine reflects the fact that the recent crisis posed a threat to the financial system in its entirety, and the fact that investment banks, brokerages, and insurance firms have increasingly become "systemically important."[1] Lehman Brothers was allowed to collapse, but that proved to be a mistake, one that the government certainly will not repeat. As James Bullard (2010), president of the Federal Reserve Bank of St. Louis, put it, "the financial crisis revealed that large financial institutions worldwide are indeed 'too big to fail.' ... We can let large financial firms fail suddenly, but then global panic ensues."

Thus, the latest crisis and policymakers' response to it have significantly exacerbated the too-big-to-fail problem. Prior to the crisis, it was not completely clear that, in "unusual or exigent circumstances," the government would use taxpayer money to prop up any and all systemically important financial institutions. Now, however, this *is* completely clear. As a result, moral hazard has increased significantly. Those who lend funds to such institutions, and perhaps their shareholders as well, now have an even greater incentive to engage in risky behavior, secure in the knowledge that taxpayers will be the ones to suffer the consequences of their excessive risk-taking.

It is extremely doubtful that anything can be done within capitalism to stop financial institutions from becoming too big to fail or to permanently downsize those that are already too big. Because capitalism is a value-producing system, cutting costs is of the utmost importance, and this leads inexorably to what Marx called the "centralization of capitals" (1990a: 777). Big firms, which can produce at much lower cost than little ones, beat out the latter, drive them out of business, or take them over. This dynamic is especially pronounced in the financial industry, since a bank needs nowhere near 100 times as much labor or 100 times as many computers in order to lend out $100 million instead of $1 million. In the U.S., the bigness and/or number of too-big-to-fail firms is likely to increase considerably, since its banking industry is not yet nearly as centralized as that of Europe.[2]

Moral hazard, excessive risk-taking, and government bailouts are thus likely to increase considerably as well. The centralization of capitals has thus made capitalism less, not more, stable. This is the very opposite of what orthodox Marxists of a century ago expected.[3]

The recent state-capitalist interventions are perhaps best described as the latest phase of what Marx called "the abolition of the capitalist mode of production within the capitalist mode of production itself" (1991a: 569). There is nothing private about the system anymore except the titles to property. The extension of the too-big-to-fail doctrine to any and all systemically important institutions makes this strikingly clear. And, as I have stressed here, the government has not even been intervening on behalf of private interests. It has been intervening on behalf of the system itself. Such total alienation of an economic system from human interests of any sort is a clear sign that it needs to perish and make way for a higher social order.

IS THE SOLUTION EVEN MORE STATISM?

For decades, and until very recently, we heard a lot about how free-market capitalism is supposedly more successful than forms of capitalism in which state ownership, control, intervention, and/ or regulation play a major role. Now we are hearing a lot about various forms of statist capitalism as the new solution. The key to this dynamic is that those who have not broken completely with capitalist ideology must always try "to pin the blame on something other than capitalism as such" (Harman 2009: 292). They have only two alternatives to choose from—the free market, or state intervention—and they veer from one to the other. The Great Depression appeared to be a crisis of the free market, so they embraced various forms of statism. The global crisis of the 1970s appeared to be a crisis of the interventionist state, so they veered back to the free market. They then veered further when the collapse of the U.S.S.R. and its satellites appeared to be the collapse of capitalism's "other," rather than of capitalism in one of its forms. And now they're veering back to various forms of statism.

SINO-EUPHORIA

We have recently been treated to a lot of euphoric talk about China's miraculous growth—and about how we might avoid a repeat of the recent economic crisis by learning the lessons that China's "state-managed capitalist economy" (Weeks 2011: 150) can teach us. It is worth recalling that we were also treated to a lot of euphoric talk about the causes of Japan's miraculous growth—its work ethic,

Japanese management practices, just-in-time production, and so forth—in the years preceding the bursting of the bubbles in its real-estate and stock markets and the onset of its "lost decade." This was then replaced by a lot of euphoric talk about the miraculous growth of the Asian Tiger countries (Hong Kong, South Korea, Singapore, and Taiwan) and the lessons we could learn from them in the years preceding the Asian currency crisis.

Robert Fogel, the Nobel prize-winning economic historian, has recently predicted that China will become "superrich" during the next three decades (2007: 7; 2010). He forecasts that its economy will continue to grow so rapidly that, by 2040, it will produce two-fifths of the world's GDP—almost triple the U.S.'s share. Inflation-adjusted per capita income in China will be two-and-a-half times as great as U.S. per capita income was in 2000, and "the average Chinese megacity dweller will be living twice as well as the average Frenchman" (Fogel 2010). To justify these astonishing predictions, Fogel points to the following factors: (1) "the enormous investment China is making in education"; (2) his prediction that labor productivity in agriculture will continue to grow quickly; (3) his claim that "Chinese statisticians may well be *underestimating* economic progress"; (4) a political system characterized by "more criticism and debate in upper echelons of policymaking than many realize"; and (5) "China's long-repressed consumerist tendencies" (ibid., emphasis added).

Yet neither of his articles explains how Fogel arrived at his actual numerical growth forecast. His numbers seem to be based largely on the fact that "China has … been able to grow at over 8 percent per capita for more than a quarter of a century" (Fogel 2007: 9), together with an assumption that, owing to the factors he cites, this rate of growth will persist for at least three more decades. Fogel forecasts that China's GDP per capita will grow by 8.0 percent per year between 2000 and 2040 (ibid.: 6).

However, Fogel nowhere mentions the well-known fact that China's recent growth is based largely on *low wages* and repressive labor practices that keep them low, which have enabled it to succeed as an exporter. As Table 9.1 indicates, the average compensation received by Chinese manufacturing workers in 2008 was $1.36 per hour, which is only 4.2 percent of what their U.S. counterparts received.[4] This enormous disparity in pay more than makes up for the disadvantages that China faces due to its lower productivity, distance from some markets to which it sells, and history of political instability.[5] It gives China a decisive competitive advantage in the world market as a low-cost producer. And because of this competitive advantage, China has attracted a great deal of foreign investment and has grown extremely rapidly.

Table 9.1   Pay, Exports, and Economic Growth in the U.S. and China

	Year(s)	U.S.	China
Average hourly compensation costs, all manufacturing employees (in U.S. dollars)	2008	32.26	1.36
Exports of goods and services (% of GDP)	2007	12	38
Annual growth rate of GDP per capita (%)	1990–2007	2.0	8.9

Fogel's omission of these facts is quite significant, since it is hardly credible that a growth rate that has been achieved on the backs of a low-wage workforce will persist in a country in which the "average … megacity dweller will be living twice as well as the average Frenchman." As Gordon G. Chang points out in his critique of Fogel, "he neglects to note that wage rates will increase as China becomes more prosperous. *Already, industry is moving to other countries, such as neighboring Vietnam, to take advantage of even cheaper labor*" (2010, emphasis added).

Then there is John Weeks, a Marxist economist who would have us emulate China's "state-managed capitalist economy" in order to prevent another economic crisis:

Perhaps the strongest evidence of the effectiveness of state interventions and controls in stabilizing and maintaining accumulation was the minor impact that the international financial crisis had on China. In 2007 the average growth rate across the six largest developed capitalist countries was 2.4 percent, which fell to less than 1 percent in 2008 and a negative 4.4 percent in 2009. Over the same three years China's state-managed capitalist economy grew at more than 8 percent annually. Many specific aspects of government economic policy in China explain its apparent immunity to the crisis, and they all have one thing in common: they restrict competition. (Weeks 2011: 150)

Weeks' statistical comparison leaves a lot to be desired. Pre-crisis growth rates are not relevant here, where the issue is the *impact of the crisis* on the growth rates. And while Weeks cites figures for the *change* in the growth rate of "the six largest developed capitalist countries," he tells us only about the *level* of China's growth rate, not how it changed between 2007 and 2009. So the figures he cites do not support his conclusion that the crisis had only a minor impact on China.

In fact, as Figure 9.1 shows, the impact of the crisis on China was not minor. Between 2007 and 2009, the growth rate of its real GDP declined by 5.1 percentage points. Although this decline was somewhat smaller than the decline that occurred in Japan, Germany, and the United Kingdom, it was a bit larger than the decline that occurred in the U.S. and France.[6] Of course, China's growth rate prior to the crisis was much greater than the growth rate of the other six largest countries, so the decline in growth that took place in 2008 and 2009 caused their growth rates to turn negative while its rate remained in positive territory. But, to repeat, pre-crisis growth rates are not relevant here; the evidence indicates that *the impact of the crisis* on China's economy was at least as great as its impact on the economies of the United States and France.[7]

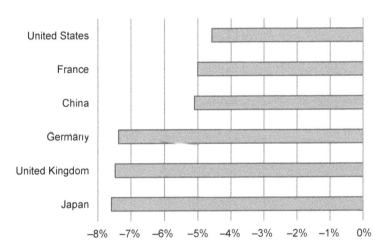

Figure 9.1   Fall in Six Largest Economies' Real GDP Growth, 2007–2009 (percentage-point changes in growth rates)

However, there is an even more basic problem with Weeks' argument. He attributes China's high rate of growth to *restrictions* on competition, but it has actually grown rapidly *because of* competition. Its low wages and repressive labor practices—factors that Weeks, like Fogel, ignores—have enabled it to compete effectively on the world market, and the phenomenal expansion of its export sector has led to rapid growth of GDP.

Weeks goes on to propose a number of reforms, and he assures us that they could bring about "capitalism without severe crises" (2011: 151). The reforms are supposedly based upon the lessons we can learn from China. But because he is evidently unable to recognize that China's growth rests on low-wage, export-led, and market-driven foundations, many of Weeks' proposals either have little to do with recent Chinese experience or run directly counter to it. For instance, one of the restrictions on international competition he proposes is a fixed exchange rate, in order to "reduce currency speculation to [a] marginal role" (ibid.: 151). China does manage its exchange rate, but for a different reason: it keeps the value of the renminbi low in order to enhance its competitiveness in the world market. And while Weeks proposes controls over international capital flows, China's government has done all it can to encourage the massive inflow of capital that has helped fuel its growth.

Another of Weeks' proposals that runs counter to the Chinese experience is his call for a universal guaranteed minimum income program in order to prevent the "use [of] unemployment as a disciplining tool of labor" (ibid.: 151). Unemployment is rampant in China, and it is among the factors that keep wages down. The most recent official unemployment rate, for 2008, was 4.2 percent, but the official statistics exclude both rural workers and migrant workers in urban areas. A mid-2008 survey conducted by the Chinese Academy of Social Sciences found that 9.4 percent of the urban workforce was unemployed, and "Zeng Xiangquan, president of the School of Labor and Personnel at Renmin University in Beijing, reportedly said … that the [National Bureau of Statistics'] initial attempts at using surveys to estimate unemployment have over the past three years come back with a rate of over 20%" (Ye and Batson 2009).

Note that the figures above fail to capture the effect on China of the global economic slump. A January 2009 article (Kolo 2009) stated that Zeng had come out with a new study in which he estimated that China's unemployment rate was 24 percent; and according to an article published in November of that year, he put the rate at 27 percent (Lockrow 2009). In February 2009, a senior Chinese official said that about 20 million migrant workers had returned to the countryside after having failed to obtain jobs (Branigan 2009). Shortly thereafter, a survey conducted by China's National Bureau of Statistics indicated that about 35 percent of the 70 million migrant workers who returned home for the Chinese New Year holiday were without work (*ABC News* 2009). This is not what takes place in an economy that is immune to crisis.

Finally, Weeks proposes "the protection of the right of workers to organize" (2011: 151). Yet China prohibits the formation of independent unions, and the officially recognized unions often fail to defend workers' interests and even oppose them. According to a recent report in *China Labour Bulletin* (2010):

> In May and early June 2010, a two-week-long strike involving more than a thousand workers at the Honda transmission plant in Foshan triggered a wave of strikes across China.
>
> ... Not only did the factory union and the local union federations in Foshan fail to represent workers' interests, or even talk to the workers during the initial stages of the strike, the local township federation actually gathered a mob of so-called union officials to force the strikers back to work, injuring two of the workers in the process.

While these strikes were occurring, we learned about conditions at Foxconn's industrial complex in southern China, at which nearly a half-million workers are employed. (Foxconn is the world's largest producer of electronics components, including the iPod and iPhone.) In the first five months of 2010, at least ten of its workers committed suicide, and the company installed nets outside their dormitories in order to prevent further suicides. Workers are forbidden from talking to one another while on the job, the noise in the factory is evidently loud enough to damage one's hearing even if one wears earplugs, and eight to ten workers live in each dorm room. "Life is meaningless," one Foxconn worker told reporters for Bloomberg News. "Everyday, I repeat the same thing I did yesterday. We get yelled at all the time." Another worker, who said that he had considered killing himself, said "I do the same thing every day; I feel empty inside ... I have no future."

Yet as bad as conditions are at the Foxconn complex, they are apparently not the exception to the rule. According to a Taiwanese professor of business administration cited in the same story, Foxconn's working conditions are among the *best* in China.[8]

In sum, what has enabled China to grow rapidly is that it is so unlike the capitalism of Weeks' dreams. Alienated labor, sweatshop conditions, mass unemployment, repression, and poverty-level wages are key pillars of its success. In contrast, although Weeks tells us that the kinder and gentler capitalism he proposes "was to a great extent achieved in the post-[World War II] period" (2011:

150), such achievements could not and did not persist once the postwar boom petered out. When all is said and done, accumulation and economic growth under capitalism depend upon the extraction of ever-greater amounts of unpaid labor, not reforms that limit that extraction.

REGULATION

What about stricter regulation of the financial industry? Can it prevent the next crisis? To help answer this question, it will be helpful to take a look back at the U.S. savings and loan (S&L) crisis of the 1980s, which took place even through the S&Ls were heavily regulated. Indeed, *the S&L crisis was caused by regulation*.

A federal law imposed a ceiling on the interest rates that S&Ls could pay depositors. About two-thirds of the states also had usury laws that limited the interest they could charge on the mortgage loans they made (home mortgage lending was their main business). The S&Ls were known as a "3-6-3 industry": bring in funds by paying 3 percent on deposits, lend them out at 6 percent, and be on the golf course by 3 o'clock in the afternoon. It was a very boring business, but supposedly one that was very safe and stable.

Yet about half of all S&Ls in existence in 1986 either failed or were taken over by other institutions between that year and 1995 (Curry and Shibut 2000: 26). Depositors of failed S&Ls, whose deposits were insured by the federal government, had to be bailed out, and the bailout cost to taxpayers during the 1986–95 period was $153 billion—not including interest on the bonds that the government issued to pay for the bailout (Curry and Shibut 2000: 31, 33). In contrast, the U.S. Treasury Department recently estimated that the TARP bailout will cost taxpayers less than one-third of that amount (Office of Financial Stability 2010: 1), or about one-fifth, once inflation is taken into account.[9]

Although regulations could control the interest rates that S&Ls paid and charged, they could not control the spiraling inflation that took place in the second half of the 1970s and early 1980s, after the Bretton Woods system collapsed and OPEC raised oil prices. The rate of inflation (as measured by the Consumer Price Index (CPI-U)) averaged 8.0 percent between 1974 and 1978, and 11.7 percent between 1979 and 1981.

When inflation took off, the interest that S&Ls received from their mortgage loans was generally less than the rate of inflation, so in "real" (inflation-adjusted) terms, they were losing money. Moreover, the meager rate of interest that the federal government allowed them to offer depositors was even further below the rate of inflation. Depositors were losing money hand over fist by parking it in S&Ls. This situation stimulated the rapid growth of an unregulated alternative, money-market mutual funds, which were paying interest rates that more than made up for inflation. Depositors were very happy to have this alternative. They fled the regulated S&Ls and put their money in the money-market mutual funds. Thus, regulation and inflation created a situation in which not enough money was coming in and too much money was going out.

In an attempt to keep the S&Ls from collapsing, Congress passed a law in 1980 that nullified the state usury laws. This allowed the S&Ls to charge interest on *new* loans that exceeded the rate of inflation, but it did not solve the fundamental problem: almost all of their income came from interest on *already existing* loans—30-year mortgage loans they had extended in the 1950s, 1960s, and 1970s at low interest rates. The interest on these loans continued to be negative in real terms. The 1980 law also allowed the S&Ls to lend more by holding less capital, and to engage in some speculative real-estate and business lending. Such lending was potentially more lucrative than home-mortgage lending, but also much riskier.

As the crisis continued to worsen, Congress took additional measures to keep the S&Ls from collapsing. In 1982, it passed a law that lifted the ceiling on the rates that the S&Ls could offer depositors. The new law also allowed them to engage in even more speculative lending and further loosened capital requirements. But this was too little, too late. And the provisions in the 1980 and 1982 laws that allowed the S&Ls to try to recoup their losses by making high-risk real-estate and business loans only made matters worse, since a lot of these loans never paid off. The end result was the largest bailout in U.S. history.

Although deregulation of the S&L industry dealt the final blow, it was a failed effort to fix an already critical problem. The original causes of the problem were regulated interest rates and spiraling inflation that Keynesian policies could not prevent. And the reason why the bailout cost taxpayers so much money is that the government guaranteed depositors' funds.

Of course, one could argue that regulation is still effective, since the S&L crisis was limited to one industry in one country, while the latest financial crisis was a general and worldwide one. But the reason why the S&L crisis had such a limited impact is that the scope of regulation was limited. Imagine that all interest rates in the U.S. had been regulated. When inflation accelerated, money would not just have fled from the S&Ls, it would have fled from the U.S. as a whole. There would have been a massive nationwide financial crisis, and a massive crisis in the U.S. might well have triggered crises elsewhere.

There are also a couple of other key problems with the notion that regulations can prevent financial crises. One is that new regulations are always "fighting the last war." As Michael Niemira, a vice-president of and chief economist for the International Council of Shopping Centers said when the U.S. Senate passed the Dodd-Frank financial reform bill, "It is unlikely that the source of the next financial crisis will be identical to the last—it rarely is" (Izzo 2010).

The other key problem was neatly summarized by a cartoon that appeared in *The New Yorker* (Vey 2009), of two accountants in an office. One turns to the other and says, "These new regulations will fundamentally change the way we get around them."

This pessimistic view of regulation is not exceptional. The Dodd-Frank law requires banks to hold more capital, and its provisions will tend to raise their costs and lower their profits. Yet when the Senate and House of Representatives hammered out the final version of the law, banks' stock prices jumped by 2.7 percent. The *New York Times*' Gretchen Morgenson (2010b) commented that this reaction was either "a bit of a mystery" or that "maybe investors are already counting on the banks doing what they do best: figuring out ways around the new rules and restrictions."

Even the staunchest proponents of the view that regulations are a solution, such as Joseph Stiglitz, acknowledge that financial institutions always do find ways to get around them. During the Panic of 2008, he published an article in which he proposed a set of six reforms that were later incorporated into the recommendations of the United Nations' commission on monetary and financial reform that he went on to lead (popularly known as the Stiglitz Commission). Although the article was entitled "How to Prevent the Next Wall Street Crisis," its final paragraph conceded that "These reforms will not guarantee that we will not have another crisis. The ingenuity of those in the financial markets is impressive. Eventually, they will figure out how to circumvent whatever regulations are imposed" (Stiglitz 2008).

So why propose such regulations in the first place? Stiglitz assured us that "these reforms *will* make another crisis of this kind less likely, and, should it occur, make it less severe than it otherwise would be" (ibid., emphasis in original). Yet if, as he said, the financial markets "will figure out how to circumvent whatever regulations are imposed," the regulations will no longer constrain them once they have figured this out, and at that point the next financial crisis becomes just as likely as it would have been otherwise. The best that can be said for new regulations is that they can *delay* the next crisis, while the markets are still finding ways to circumvent them. But a delay of the next crisis means more artificial and unsustainable expansion of the economy through excessive borrowing in the meantime, so that the contraction will be more, not less, severe when the debt bubble does finally burst.[10]

The Dodd-Frank law contains many provisions relating to too-big-to-fail institutions, but it does not break them up nor prohibit government "bailouts" of such institutions, and many analysts contend that it has done little if anything to make major "bailouts" less likely in the future (see, for example, Morgenson 2010b, Ramirez 2010, and Wallinson 2010). Indeed, as Morgenson (2010a) points out, Dodd-Frank has actually created a new too-big-to-fail institution that can be propped up with taxpayers' money "in unusual or exigent circumstances": clearinghouses for derivatives transactions. She quotes Craig Pirrong, a University of Houston finance professor, who said, "Clearinghouses are intimately connected with the financial system and overall banking system ... They are big, interconnected and they can fail when we have big market shocks."

STATE CONTROL AND NATIONALIZATION

Some leftist economists have recently called for state control or nationalization, rather than just regulation, of the financial system. Richard Wolff favors state control. He suggests that there should be "state agencies [to] coordinate[ ] enterprises' interdependent production decisions" and that the U.S. government should require financial institutions "to change into enterprises where employers and employees [are] the same people" (Wolff 2008b). He contends that "workers who also served on their own boards of directors would make different decisions ... than traditional boards elected by shareholders" and that "[w]orkers' broadly defined well-being (an inclusive standard) would displace individual enterprise profits (a narrowly exclusive standard) as the prevailing objective of enterprise decisions" (Wolff 2010).

Fred Moseley (2009) and John Weeks (2011: 150–51) favor nationalization. Noting that policymakers must now either bail out too-big-to-fail firms or allow crises to worsen, Moseley argues that "the only way to avoid this cruel dilemma … is for the government itself to become the main provider of credit in the economy … finance should be nationalized and operated by the government." Like Wolff, he contends that once different people are in charge of financial institutions, the objectives they pursue will, or at least can, be different as well:

> [T]he quasi-nationalization of Fannie Mae and Freddie Mac that has already occurred should be made permanent, and these government mortgage agencies should be used to achieve the public policy goal of decent affordable housing for all, rather than profit maximization. Secondly, major banks … should be nationalized and operated in order to achieve similar public policy objectives. …

> The nationalization of banks is not socialism, but it could be an important step on the road to socialism. The use of government banks to pursue important public policy objectives, rather than profit maximization, would be a model for the rest of the economy.

But there cannot be socialism in one country. What results when you try to have socialism in one country is state-capitalism, a state-run system that is still embedded in the global capitalist economy, and which is still locked into a competitive battle with capitals elsewhere in the world. A state-run bank is still a bank. It still has to obtain funds before it can lend them out, and to do so, it must provide a decent return to those who supply it with funds. (This is true of a worker-run bank as well.) But this means that its investment decisions *cannot* be based on what would enhance workers' well-being or on public policy objectives. If enhancement of workers' well-being or fulfillment of public policy objectives would significantly reduce its profitability in relationship to the profitability of banks with which it competes—and it is hard to imagine circumstances in which this would not be the case—a bank that would dare to pursue these goals would find that lenders and investors would not supply it with the funds it needs in order to compete successfully, or even to remain solvent. In order to survive, a state-run (or worker-run) bank must pursue the goal of profit maximization, just like every other bank.

Moreover, as Egoavil (2009) has emphasized, finance is speculative by its very nature. Lenders essentially place a bet that the future flow of value will be sufficient to allow them to get back more than they lent. This implies that debt bubbles and the bursting of these bubbles are inherent in and inextricable from finance—and that this is just as true when the process of finance is under state-control and/ or ownership as when it is in private hands. Egoavil also suggests that the history of the Crédit Mobiliér, and the recent history of Freddie Mae and Fannie Mae, show that "There is nothing about a government-backed bank which makes it less inclined toward speculative pursuits than private enterprises."

So the notion of state-controlled capital is an oxymoron, like jumbo shrimp. As long as there is capital, what are actually in control are the economic laws of capitalism. Individual capitalists, including individual state capitals and worker-run enterprises, must submit to these laws. As Marx put it in the *Grundrisse*: "Competition executes the inner laws of capital; makes them compulsory laws toward the individual capital" (1973: 752). This is why, although he hailed workers' cooperatives as harbingers of the new society, Marx also cautioned that, as long as they exist within capitalism, "they naturally reproduce in all cases … all the defects of the existing system, and must reproduce them … the opposition between capital and labour is abolished here … only in the form that the workers in association become their own capitalist" (Marx 1991a: 571). In other words, the workers end up exploiting themselves.

In short, "The capitalist functions only as *personified capital*" (Marx 1990b: 989), and whoever or whatever functions in this capacity is a capitalist. Putting different people in "control" does not undo the inner laws of capital; but the inner laws of capital are what must be undone.

"WE SHOULD NOT IMAGINE … THAT IT IS POSSIBLE TO PREVENT ALL CRISES"

In the concluding section of his testimony before the Financial Crisis Inquiry Commission testimony, Bernanke (2010) said, "We should not imagine, though, that it is possible to prevent all crises." On the one hand, this statement was part of a campaign to give the Federal Reserve greater power to function as the safety net of last resort. On the other hand, Bernanke let the cat out of the bag.

Yet Bernanke's explanation of *why* it is impossible to prevent all crises is rather muddled. He makes it seem that financial crises are an inevitable byproduct of any "growing, dynamic economy" whatsoever: "A growing, dynamic economy requires a financial system that makes effective use of available saving[s] in allocating credit to households and businesses. The provision of credit inevitably involves risk-taking." The valid part of this statement is that any growing, dynamic economy requires that additional resources ("savings") be put to effective use, not consumed or hoarded. But a growing, dynamic, *socialist* economy would not require a financial system at all.[11]

In the first place, a tremendous amount of financial-market activity—for instance, currency speculation, derivatives trading, and exchanges involving already-issued bonds, other credit instruments, and shares of stock—is simply gambling. Another large component— for instance, initial offerings of shares of stock—consists of sales and purchases of property rights. None of these activities allocates credit to households or businesses.

Secondly, when Bernanke says that the provision of "credit" inevitably involves risk-taking, he means that lenders temporarily provide funds that they risk not getting back on time from borrowers, along with the agreed-upon interest. This is not a necessary feature of a growing, dynamic economy. *Such risk exists only because lenders and borrowers are separate and opposed entities; it would not exist in a communal society.* Indeed, the very notion of credit would be meaningless in such a society. Just as an individual or household cannot obtain credit from itself, repay itself, or default on its obligation to repay itself—it simply decides whether to use its resources or hold on to them—neither could a communal society. Once all this is understood, the great merit of Bernanke's statement that not all crises can be prevented is that it tacitly concedes that crises are endemic to capitalism and unavoidable under it, because it is a society in which individuals' interests are opposed to one another.

"TRICKLE-UP" ECONOMICS AND ITS POLITICAL IMPLICATIONS

The version of underconsumptionist theory that I discussed in Chapter 8 holds that the ultimate reason for capitalist crises and slumps is that working people are paid too little. This implies, conversely, that crises and slumps can in principle be averted by giving them a bigger slice of the pie. Of course, if they get a bigger slice, the wealthy will get a smaller slice. But working people spend almost all, or more than all, of their income on goods and services, while wealthy people use a lot of their income to buy securities and real estate. So total spending on consumption goods and services will increase if working people get a bigger slice of the pie, and underconsumptionist theory implies that such redistribution can in principle allow the economy to emerge from its latest slump and avoid subsequent ones.

Thus, underconsumptionist economics is "trickle-up" economics. It suggests that what's good for the working class is good for capitalist America. Almost all revolutionary socialists maintain, to the contrary, that the interests of working people and the interests of the system are, in the end, fundamentally opposed, particularly when the going gets tough, as in times of economic crisis.[12] And this is the primary reason why they maintain that revolutionary transformation of society is *needed*.

But if capitalism is capable of doing right by working people, and especially if its interests and their interests go hand-in-hand, as underconsumptionism implies, then socialism would not be something we need, at least not for economic reasons. It might be something you want, but you can't always get what you want. The task of social transformation is so arduous and its realization is so much in doubt that it would be better to forget about what you want, and focus on the here-and-now. One should help make the present system work better, by advocating and fighting for trickle-up policies—especially in the aftermath of a severe slump, when the suffering is so enormous.

I am not suggesting that it is impossible to be a revolutionary socialist as well as an underconsumptionist. Luxemburg, for one, was both. And it is possible to be both without succumbing to outright self-contradiction. Yet there can be a mismatch between theory and political positions besides self-contradiction, for instance what Dunayevskaya called an "abysmal gap." In her critique of Luxemburg's underconsumptionist theory of capitalist accumulation, Dunayevskaya wrote:

> Luxemburg, the revolutionist, feels the abysmal gap between her theory and her revolutionary activity, and comes to the rescue of Luxemburg, the theorist. "Long before" capitalism would collapse through exhaustion of the non-capitalist world, writes Luxemburg, the contradictions of capitalism, *both* internal and external, would reach such a point that the proletariat would overthrow it.

But it is not a question of "long before." No revolutionist doubts that the *only final* solution ... will come in the actual class struggle ... The question *theoretically* is: does the solution come organically from your theory, or is it brought there merely by "revolutionary will." (1991: 45, emphases in original)

Indeed. A proponent of underconsumptionist theory may happen to have a revolutionary perspective, but not because it comes organically from his/her theory.

Some underconsumptionists have disagreed. For instance, the twentieth century's leading underconsumptionist theorist, Paul Sweezy, argued in his 1942 *Theory of Capitalist Development* that the underconsumptionist theory of economic crisis has inherently revolutionary implications:

If the development of capitalism is inseparable from ... consumption demand which tends to lag ever further behind the requirements of production ... then the ills of the system can be expected to grow with age ... [and] the crises which periodically interrupt the economic life of society [must] be regarded as a *memento mori* [reminder of mortality] of the existing social order. But ... if crises are really caused by nothing more intractable than disproportionalities in the productive process, then the existing order seems to be secure enough ... If the first of these alternative views is accepted, socialists must be prepared for stormy weather ahead; they must even be ready, if need be, to force through a revolutionary solution of the contradictions of the existing order. But if the second alternative is accepted, socialists can look forward to an indefinite period of quiet agitational work which, they can at least hope, will eventually be crowned with success in the peaceable adoption, by common consent, of the co-operative commonwealth. (Sweezy 1970: 160–61)

However, it is difficult to know the degree to which Sweezy actually believed, back in 1942, that underconsumptionism necessarily points in a revolutionary direction. After Stalinist Russia disappointed him, and then China deviated from the Maoist road he later championed, and then Stalinist Russia collapsed, he put forward the diametrically opposite argument in *Monthly Review*, the journal he co-edited for a half-century:

If my analysis of the performance of the U.S. economy during the last sixty years is accepted, to what policy conclusions does it point? … public ownership of the means of production and planning to meet the needs of all the people [won't be] a serious option … any time soon. The question should therefore be reformulated: what could be done within the framework of the private-enterprise system to make it work better? …

The second indispensable change needed to make the private-enterprise economy work better is a redistribution of wealth and income toward greater equality. We live in a period in which an unprecedented and growing share of the society's income accrues to corporations and wealthy rentiers, while the share of the underlying population stagnates or declines. This implies a permanent imbalance between society's potential for adding to its stock of capital and its flagging consuming power … Would the capitalist class as a whole, in extremis, be willing to give up half of what it has to save the other half? I have a feeling that the fate of the private-enterprise system may depend on the answer to this question. (Sweezy 1995: 9–11)

Sweezy's 1995 understanding of the political implications of under-consumptionism is identical in substance to what I wrote about it above. And, next to his advocacy of income redistribution in order "to make the private-enterprise economy work better," people who engage in what Sweezy had earlier called "quiet agitational work" on behalf of "the co-operative commonwealth" seem like veritable class warriors.

I am very worried about the political implications of under-consumptionist theory at this juncture in history because, as Sweezy suggests, underconsumptionism implies that a more equitable distribution of income will make capitalism work better. Let me make clear that I am *not* suggesting that working people should refrain from fighting for a bigger slice of the pie or other reforms. The question here is not "reform or revolution?" The question is rather, "is what's good for the working class good for capitalist America?" In light of Chapter 8's critique of underconsumptionism's theoretical and empirical flaws, I must answer in the negative.

Especially during the current slump and its aftermath, working people certainly need to make demands on employers and the governments of their countries and see to it that these demands are met. The fightback that has begun in Greece, France, Spain,

Portugal, the United Kingdom, the United States, and elsewhere is definitely a sign that there is hope for the future. By getting their demands met, working people help themselves in the short run. They are getting concessions from the system. However—and this is the point—they are not putting capitalism on a new path forward, and not solving the economic crisis. The concessions they win are just that, concessions, not a new set of progressive policies that will lead to a prosperous and stable economy.

It is true that a gigantic mobilization of working people during the Great Depression forced the U.S. government to make big and important concessions—the right to bargain collectively, regulation of working hours and minimum wages, the Social Security system, and so on—in order to save the capitalist system in the face of this mobilization. And it is true that such measures, along with a slew of regulations and activist fiscal and monetary policies ("Keynesianism") *seemed* for a time to have permanently done away with major economic downturns and to have re-established capitalism on a sounder and more progressive basis. But it all came tumbling down in the mid-1970s when a severe global economic crisis broke out. Keynesian policymakers and their supporters on the left thought that they could alter the operation of the system by passing laws, but the crisis of the 1970s showed that their policies were no match for the economic laws that actually govern capitalism (see Clarke 1988, Chapters 11 and 12).

To save the system, the gains of the 1930s had to be rolled back. They were rolled back. Of course, Keynesians and their supporters never fail to place the blame for this on Reagan, Thatcher, and neoliberalism, *but they themselves bear most of the responsibility*. The policies they advocated and implemented failed in the end and, because they failed, new people and new ideas naturally came along to replace them and fix the mess. Moreover, the Keynesianism that dominated the left helped to demobilize working people— by encouraging them to trust Keynesian politicians, policies, and doctrines as well the leaders of their unions, instead of trusting their own ability to run their lives themselves and re-establish society on new, human foundations. As a result, the new people and ideas that came along were reactionary ones.

This bit of historical analysis should help make clear that, when push comes to shove, working people's gains are not compatible with the continued functioning of the capitalist system. The reason why they are not compatible is that capitalism is a profit-driven system. So what is good for *capitalism*—good for the *system*, as distinct from what is good for the *majority of people* living under it—is high profits, not low profits. Higher pay for workers cuts into profits, as do increases in corporate income taxes to fund social programs, a shorter work week, health and safety regulations in the work place, and so on. There is no solution to this dilemma within the confines of the capitalist system.

All this would be too obvious to point out were it not for the fact that underconsumptionist theory says the opposite. It says that, by leading to an increase in consumption demand, redistribution of income toward the bottom allows more goods and services to be sold, and this *boosts* profitability.

In Chapter 8, I argued that this notion is incorrect. If my argument is sound, what are the consequences? Well, under capitalism, a new economic boom requires the restoration of profitability, but downward redistribution of income will reduce profitability. It will therefore tend to destabilize capitalism even further. It might trigger renewed panic in the world's financial markets, and who knows what will happen then? In this way, or by causing investment spending to fall, downward redistribution could lead to a deep recession, even a depression. And because progressive policies will have failed, again, to make capitalism work better—for itself—the stage will have been set for other people and other ideas to come along and fix the mess. Even fascism might become a serious option, as it was in Europe during the Great Depression. Working people need to be prepared to confront the fact that their struggles to protect themselves in the face of the economic slump are not in the system's interests, and that successful struggle might well set off a virulent reaction. And they need to be prepared to confront the reaction. But they will not be prepared if they have been led to believe the trickle-up notion that what's good for the working class is good for capitalist America.

FOR A DIFFERENT FUTURE

The latest economic slump and its persistent effects have brought misery to tens of millions of working people. But they are also bringing us a new opportunity to get rid of a system that is continually rocked by such crises. The fundamental instability of capitalism is being acknowledged, not just in the tacit manner in which Bernanke acknowledged it, but explicitly, in leading newspapers and magazines. For instance, Robert Shiller (2008) referred to "the fundamental instability of our system" in a *New*

York Times essay. And in a recent interview with *Harper's Magazine*, Richard Posner, a principal founder of the market-oriented field of law and economics, declared that "Because of the centrality of credit in a capitalist economy, a capitalist economy is inherently unstable" (Silverstein 2010).

An April 2009 Rasmussen poll of 1,000 people throughout the U.S. found that support for capitalism was only marginally greater than support for socialism among low-income people and young adults—and Scott Rasmussen is a Republican pollster. Only 37 percent of respondents under 30 favored capitalism, while almost as many, 33 percent, favored socialism. Respondents whose income was less than $20,000 favored capitalism by only a 35 percent to 27 percent margin (Rasmussen Reports 2009). The poll didn't define "capitalism" or "socialism," so we do not know what the people who expressed a preference for "socialism" meant. But one thing is clear: Margaret Thatcher's TINA doctrine—"there is no alternative" to capitalism—is no longer all-dominating.

Yet we cannot sit back and let the flow of events do our work for us. It is one thing to recognize the instability of capitalism, but another to show that an alternative to it is possible. As Michael Skapinker (2008) argued in the *Financial Times*, the recent crisis and government interventions have put an end to the Reagan-Thatcher era, but "leftwing and far-left websites … clearly have not got a clue" about what might replace it. Encountering answers such as a "world … in which the needs of the many come before the greed of the few," he responded: "Like what, exactly?"

So platitudes do no good, nor does "denounc[ing] with merciless contempt those theorists who demand in advance guaranteed and insured perspectives [… about] the socialist society" (James and Lee, 2006: 103). Such responses are readily recognized as evasive, and they do more harm than good, because they show that one has "not got a clue" about the supposed alternative one is espousing. It is time to recognize that "Like what, exactly?" is an honest and profound question that demands straight and worked-out answers. And it is time to start working out those answers.

I am not advocating abstract revolutionism here. It would be disastrous merely to call for socialism while ignoring the problems of mass unemployment and foreclosed homes that may well persist for many years to come. Merely thinking about alternatives to capitalism while ignoring these problems is no solution either. Working people will have to fight tooth-and-nail just to prevent their living and working conditions from deteriorating further, in the face of efforts to restore profitability and economic growth through austerity measures.

Yet it is wrong to counterpose thought and activity in this manner. They are not opposites, but go hand-in-hand. In the absence of credible answers to the "Like what, exactly?" question, practical struggles of the last couple of decades have quite reasonably been self-limiting. They have not even attempted to remake society totally. When questions about the future are bound up so intimately with day-to-day struggles, a new human society surely cannot emerge through spontaneous action alone. To transcend this impasse, people need to know not just what to be against, but what to be for, not just "what is to be done," but what is to be *undone*—what is it exactly that must be changed in order to have a viable and emancipatory socialism?

Unfortunately, this issue received almost no attention throughout most of the last century. Until the collapse of so-called "communism" and living proof that social democracy is a futile dream, almost everyone on the left simply assumed that socialism was possible, because it actually existed. Some were willing to critique Russia, China, and other state-capitalist countries to varying degrees, but they too tended to think that the *economies* of these countries were socialist or on the road to socialism, so that what was needed was not a different mode of production from theirs but *political* change—"socialism *and* democracy" instead of socialism without democracy, or "socialism from *below*," instead of socialism from above. And other people were confident that effective political action would enable the achievements of social democracy to be sustained and gradually extended to encompass more and more aspects of social and economic existence.

So it is only in recent years that any significant attention has been paid to whether another world is possible. But now, when the future of capitalism is a live issue, it seems to me that this issue needs to be understood as the central problem of revolutionary thought today.

The notion that socialism will come about by means of a party that captures state power and nationalizes the means of production is fundamentally misguided. John Holloway's (2002) book, *Change the World without Taking Power*, had some important things to say about this. (But one has to read it carefully; he wasn't saying that socialism can emerge *without* a challenge to the capitalist state.) I do think that the power of the existing state needs to be broken and that the means of production need to be socialized. But the problem with the above notion is its political determinism; it implies that political and legal changes, not changes in the actual relations of production, are the key determinants of social change. That is a 180-degree inversion of Marx. The horrors of the state-capitalism that called itself "communism," which had everything to do with the notion of "politics in command," as Mao put it, should help make us aware that it is also a 180-degree inversion of the real relationship between these factors.

This simply was not understood by Marxists of the Second International, including Lenin. In *The State and Revolution,* he made a great stride forward by reclaiming Marx's view that the bureaucratic-military machine, through which state power is exercised, cannot be taken over; it has to be broken. Yet in the same work, Lenin wrote that the postal service was a "splendidly-equipped mechanism" that simply needed to be taken over; the immediate aim was to "organise the *whole* economy on the lines of the postal service" (Lenin 1971: 299, emphasis in original).

There is no evidence in this work that Lenin understood that something was wrong with workplace relations under capitalism. (Technological progress had not yet given us the "going postal" phenomenon.) And there is no evidence that he understood that an economic system, unlike a single enterprise such as the postal service, isn't something that one *manages* by issuing directives. It is a network of relationships. These relationships will remain governed by the laws of capitalist production unless and until those laws are broken, and that will require a thorough transformation of the relations of production. Directives will not break the laws of capitalist production. The most important law is the determination of value by labor-time. It compels an enterprise, whoever owns or "controls" it, to minimize costs in order to remain competitive, and therefore to lay off inefficient or unnecessary workers, speed up production, have unsafe working conditions, produce for profit instead of producing for need, and so on. If you are in a capitalist system, you cannot just issue a directive to produce for need, or a directive to refrain from laying off workers. Cutting costs is the key to survival.

This brings me to the notion of developing socialism within capitalism, enlarging the space of the commons or whatever. Unfortunately, it cannot be done. It has been tried (for instance, in the Israeli kibbutzim) and it does not succeed. The economic laws of the larger system will not allow it. If you buy from the capitalist world "outside," you also have to sell to it in order to get the money you need to buy from it, and you will not sell anything if your prices are high because your costs of production are high. And if you have debts, you have to repay them.[13]

I think two main things are needed to move beyond this situation. First, we have to recognize that the emancipation of working people must be their own act. As Eugene V. Debs said, "Too long have the workers of the world waited for some Moses to lead them out of bondage ... if you could be led out, you could be led back again." So the core issue is not one of "taking power," but of what happens *after*, as Dunayevskaya (1978) stressed. There needs to be a new relation of theory to practice, so that regular people are not just the muscle that brings down the old power, but become fully equipped, theoretically and intellectually, to govern society themselves. Nothing short of this can prevent power from being handed over to an elite. It seems very utopian, but there is really no alternative.

Secondly, we have to work out how we can have a modern society that operates without the laws of capitalist production being in control. Very few people on the left have even understood that this is a real problem. Yet no commissar can dictate that the means of production belong to the whole society, or that we will produce for need instead of for profit, and no workers' council can vote these things into being. There must *first* be new relations of production; only then will these things be possible. This too seems utopian, but again, there is really no alternative.

I am painfully aware that these reflections are not yet an answer to the "Like what, exactly?" question. Before events of the last couple of years compelled me to turn my attention to an analysis of the economic crisis, I had been exploring that question. Having completed this book, I can now return to it. Since significant attention was not paid to the question until recently, the lack of an answer at this juncture does not seem to me to be cause for despair or evidence that there is no answer. I suspect that we do not yet have credible answers largely because people have looked for answers in the wrong places. I do think that the above reflections help us to look for answers in the right places.

Unless and until a credible answer is worked out, it seems to me that the most likely alternatives we face are either full-scale destruction of capital value, or persistent economic sluggishness, mounting debt burdens, and recurrent financial crises and downturns. Full-scale destruction of capital value might lead to the restoration of profitability and a new boom, but in the 1930s, capitalism's self-correcting mechanisms proved too weak to bring that about automatically. Recovery also required massive state intervention and the destructiveness of world war. This time around, it is not inconceivable that we would descend into chaos, fascism, or warlordism before that point is reached.

There is also no guarantee that we will avoid such scenarios by accepting a future of relative stagnation, rising debt, and recurrent crises. The U.S. government kept the latest crisis from getting out of hand by restoring investors' "confidence," but the U.S. government can restore confidence only insofar as there is confidence in the U.S. government—that is, in its ability to paper over bad debt with more debt. As the volume of outstanding government debt mounts, confidence in its ability to guarantee debt and repay its own debt—with real money, not printing-press money and a depreciated currency—will move in the opposite direction.

The stakes are high. The time has come to face the future with sober senses.

Notes

1 INTRODUCTION

1. See, for example, "The Economic Crisis: Greed is the Cause" (*Socialist Voice* 2008) and "Greed's the Sole Cause of Every Financial Crisis" (Nakajima 2010).
2. I am indebted to the late Chris Harman for having emphasized that this is an implication of the conventional account. See Harman (2009: 299).
3. See Freeman (2009) for a full-length temporalist critique of Brenner's analysis.

2 PROFITABILITY, THE CREDIT SYSTEM, AND THE "DESTRUCTION OF CAPITAL"

1. I take as read throughout that the falling rate of profit was a cause of the severe slumps of the mid-1970s and early 1980s. This idea is not controversial, although there is a lot of disagreement about why the rate of profit fell.
2. In the same footnote, Brenner also appealed to Okishio's (1961) theorem, which supposedly disproved the LTFRP. However, numerous works by proponents of the TSSI have demonstrated that Okishio's theorem is false. (For one such demonstration, and references to prior ones, see Kliman 2007, Chapter 7.) In order to rescue the theorem, its supporters have taken to defending it on the grounds that it was never intended to be a theorem on Marx's LTFRP (which is not correct; see ibid.: 135–6). In other words, they have implicitly conceded that Okishio failed to show that it is impossible for labor-saving technical change to cause *Marx's* rate of profit to fall. The controversy over Okishio's theorem will be discussed in greater detail in Chapter 6.
3. What "tend" means here is that prices rise by a smaller amount than they would have risen (or fall by a larger amount than they would have fallen) if the increase in productivity had not occurred. The LTFRP does not require that labor-saving technical change lead to deflation, a fall in prices. It requires that such technical change lead to disinflation, a slowdown in the rate of increase in prices. See Kliman (2007: 129–32).
4. This explanation of why prices tend to fall has nothing to do with the irredeemably flawed notion that technical progress causes "overproduction"— the production of too much output in relationship to demand—which in turn forces companies to slash their prices. Companies' decisions about how much output to produce are based on projections of demand for the output. Since technical progress does not affect demand—buyers care about the character-istics of products, not the processes used to produce them—it will not cause companies to increase their levels of output, all else being equal.
5. The rate of profit can be expressed as $\dfrac{a(pY)}{\hat{p}K} = a\left(\dfrac{Y}{K}\right)\left(\dfrac{p}{\hat{p}}\right)$, where a is the ratio of profit to net value added, pY is net value added, p is an index of the *current* price of net physical output, Y is an index of net physical output, $\hat{p}$ is a weighted

average index of the *past* prices at which additions to physical capital have been acquired, and K is an index of physical capital. If the rate of exploitation is constant, then a is constant as well, and if physical output and physical capital grow at the same rate, then $\frac{Y}{K}$ is constant. Under these conditions, the rate of profit will tend to fall as a result of technical progress if, and only if, the increases in productivity that result from technical innovation tend to reduce $\frac{p}{\hat{p}}$. This conclusion helps to clarify why the LTFRP does not require that prices actually decline (see note 3, above): what matters is not whether p is less than $\hat{p}$, but whether $\frac{p}{\hat{p}}$ falls.

6. In principle, a fall in the rate of profit could also induce businesses to redirect investment from productive uses into asset markets (see Potts 2009). However, as I will show in Chapter 5, this did not occur in the U.S. corporate sector in the decades preceding the latest crisis.

7. In testimony before the Financial Crisis Inquiry Commission, Ben Bernanke (2010), the chairman of the Fed's board of governors, stated that the "too-big-to-fail doctrine generates a severe moral hazard ... too-big-to-fail firms will tend to take more risk than desirable, in the expectation that they will receive assistance if their bets go bad ... The buildup of risk in too-big-to-fail firms increases the possibility of a financial crisis and worsens the crisis when it occurs. There is little doubt that excessive risk-taking by too-big-to-fail firms significantly contributed to the crisis, with Fannie Mae and Freddie Mac being prominent examples."

8. Marx regarded "the formation of new independent capitals" as a main form in which capital accumulation appears. For instance, he noted that devaluation of the existing capital "accelerat[es] the accumulation of capital value by the formation of new capital" (Marx 1991a: 358).

9. The term translated here as "swindling"—*Schwindel*—means something like "finagling" or "deceptive business practices," not necessarily fraudulent and illegal ones. German speakers call a person like Bernie Madoff a *Betrüger*; use of the term *Schwindler* would downplay the severity of his actions. (I thank Michael Schmid for clarifying this point.)

10. A bill of exchange is a loan agreement in which the borrower agrees to repay a fixed sum by a given date.

11. It seems that the rise in asset prices led to the temporary rise in the rate of profit largely because consumers regarded the increases in the values of their homes and stock shares as extra income, which they tended to spend and borrow against.

12. Marx's understanding of the dual role played by the destruction of capital came in part from his reading of John Fullarton: "But apart from theory there is also the practice, the crises from superabundance of capital or, what comes to the same, the mad adventures capital enters upon in consequence of the lowering of [the] rate of profit. Hence crises—see Fullarton—acknowledged as a necessary violent means for the cure of the plethora of capital, and the restoration of a sound rate of profit" (Marx 1991b: 105). In the passage to which Marx refers, Fullarton (1845: 171–2, emphasis in original) wrote: "[A] panic ensues, and the bubble bursts, with a destruction of capital which relieves the money market for a season of the load which had oppressed it, abates competition, and restores

the market rate of interest to the level from which it had declined ... [The] periodical destruction of capital ... [enables our social system] to relieve itself from time to time of an ever-recurring *plethora* which menaces its existence, and to regain a sound and wholesome state."

13. Because the new investments that follow the destruction of capital value and the restoration of profitability tend to "embody" new inventions, the concept of "creative destruction" that Schumpeter (1976: 83) popularized—"the ... process of industrial mutation ... incessantly revolutionizes the economic structure from within, incessantly destroying the old one, incessantly creating a new one"—is bound up with the concept of destruction of capital.

14. Much of the problem here stems from the fact that Eduard Bernstein caricatured Marx's view as a theory of collapse in the course of opposing his revolutionary perspective, and from the unfortunate fact that those who then defended this perspective frequently took Bernstein's terminology on board. They argued that capitalism will collapse *by means of* social revolution. Since this is simply a misuse of the word "collapse," much confusion has resulted.

15. For a discussion of the operation of value relations within the U.S.S.R., see Dunayevskaya (2000, Chapter 13).

16. Governmental provision of, and people's entitlement to, some goods and services is now frequently called "decommodification," but it is actually nothing of the sort. Before the government can provide these things, it must either buy them or produce them. If it buys these things, they obviously remain commodities. They continue to be produced in order to expand value. This means that they continue to be produced in a way that minimizes cost and maximizes production, and the consequences of this—exploitation, poor working conditions, unemployment, and falling tendencies of prices and the rate of profit—continue to exist as well. And Marx (1989c: 546) argued that "Where the state itself is a capitalist producer, as in the exploitation of mines, forests, etc., its product is a 'commodity' and hence possesses the specific character of every other commodity." This is so not because he defined it to be so, but because a government that acts as a capitalist producer minimizes costs, maximizes production, and in general behaves just like a private capitalist Nothing is different in this case except that the moneys that purchase the "de-commodified" commodities that the government produces are called tax contributions rather than sales revenues.

3   DOUBLE, DOUBLE, TOIL AND TROUBLE: DOT-COM BOOM AND HOME-PRICE BUBBLE

1. Subprime mortgage loans were those made to less creditworthy borrowers, who did not qualify for traditional (prime) mortgage loans.

2. Bubbles form in the following manner. The demand for an asset such as homes or stock shares increases, which causes the price of the asset to rise in relationship to its underlying value. The wealth of people and businesses therefore increases—on paper. This gives them the means to borrow more, which leads to further increases in demand, in the asset's price, and in paper wealth, partly because the asset's owners become overly confident about the future trajectory of its price as the process unfolds.

3. Japan's malaise has persisted, so journalists have begun to refer to "its two lost decades" (Fackler and Lohr 2010). The Fed's fear that the U.S. is once again

in danger of descending into a Japanese-style lost decade appears to be a main reason why it began a new round of quantitative easing ("printing money") in late 2010.

4. My data on mortgage borrowing come from the annual, seasonally adjusted version of Table D.2 of the *Flow of Funds Accounts of the United States*, which can be downloaded at tinyurl.com/6ko8ka6. My home-price data come from the "nominal home price index" time series constructed by Robert Shiller and others (available at www.econ.yale.edu/~shiller/data.htm); I averaged the quarterly figures reported for 2007 to obtain an annual index number for that year. "After-tax income" refers to the Bureau of Economic Analysis' (BEA) disposable personal income series, reported in National Income and Product Accounts (NIPA) Table 2.1, line 26. "PCE price index" refers to the price index for personal consumption expenditures, reported in NIPA Table 1.14, line 2. "CPI-U" refers to the consumer price index for all urban consumers, available from the Bureau of Labor Statistics (BLS) at www.bls.gov/cpi/.

5. The data in Figure 3.2 come from the BEA's "Comparison of Personal Saving in the NIPAs with Personal Saving in the FFAs" table (available at bea.gov/national/index.htm#gdp). To compute asset acquisition, I added the figures in lines 6 and 7 (net acquisition of financial assets and net investment in tangible assets) and subtracted those in line 12 (net investment in consumer durable goods). I obtained figures for net increases in liabilities from line 8 of this table. The net lending/borrowing figures in Figure 3.3 come from NIPA Table 5.1, line 39, and are for households and nonprofit institutions; data for households alone are not available. The GDP is reported in NIPA Table 1.1.5, line 1.

6. System-wide problems typically have uneven effects. During a recession, for instance, businesses do not all suffer to an equal degree. Only the most vulnerable go bankrupt, and some are hardly affected, but this does not alter the fact that the recession is a systemic problem.

7. These estimates are based on data for prime, alt-A, and subprime mortgages contained in spreadsheet tables available at the "U.S. Credit Conditions" web page of the Federal Reserve Bank of New York, data.newyorkfed.org/credit-conditionsmap/. The foreclosure rates reported in the alt-A and subprime tables are for owner-occupied homes only. To obtain my estimates, I assumed that other homes in these categories were foreclosed upon at the same rates.

8. Your return is the profit minus the interest you owe, $0.04 \times \$97 = \$3.88$, and your rate of return is the difference divided by the $3 of your own money that you invested.

9. However, when Charles Prince, then chief executive officer of Citigroup, told the *Financial Times*, "As long as the music is playing, you've got to get up and dance," he was referring to leveraged buyouts, not mortgage-related securities. See *New York Times* (2007).

10. This widely quoted statistic seems not to be strictly true. According to Shiller's time series (see note 4, above), nominal home prices fell by 2.8 percent in 1991, and did not return to their prior peak level until 1994. They also fell by 8.4 percent in 1941 and by modest amounts in 1959 and 1964.

11. There was a do-over several days later, and this time Congress approved TARP.

12. Paul Krugman (2008) has argued that "Greenspan … dealt with the dot-com bust. He dealt with the '87 stock market crash. He dealt with the Asian financial crisis … In retrospect, his history is one of replacing each bubble with another bubble. And eventually we ran out of bubbles."

13. The S&P 500 index is available at finance.yahoo.com/q/hp?s=^GSPC. Figure 3.5 shows the daily closing values.
14. See the appendix to Chapter 5 for sources of data on, and the methods I used to compute, the after-tax rate of profit.
15. Nonfarm payroll employment data, reported in Table B-1 of the BLS's "Employment Situation" release (available at tinyurl.com/28b7z7q).
16. Target federal funds data are available at www.federalreserve.gov/monetarypolicy/openmarket.htm. To estimate the real federal funds rate, I deflated the nominal rate by the BEA's monthly PCE price index, which is available at research.stlouisfed.org/fred2/series/PCEPI.
17. See note 4, above, for the source of my data on mortgage borrowing. "After-tax income" refers to the BEA's disposable personal income series, reported in NIPA Table 2.1, line 26.
18. My data come from the IMF's *World Economic Outlook* Database, tinyurl.com/2ana4ds. "Excess Savings" refers to the difference between gross national savings and investment. The database expresses these variables as percentages of GDP. To obtain figures for the rest of the world, I multiplied the percentages by the database's figures for current-dollar GDP and then subtracted the U.S. figures from the world figures.
19. It is also not obvious how much of the recent economic malaise has been due specifically to the bursting of the home-price bubble and how much is the combined effect of falling prices in all three markets. The causes of the financial crisis and the causes of the Great Recession are not identical.

4   THE 1970s—NOT THE 1980s—AS TURNING POINT

1. The relationship between Keynesian theory and activist policies—popularly called "Keynesian" policies—that are intended to stimulate the economy is not a simple one. In order to avoid burdening the discussion with repeated qualifications, I will allow readers to infer from the context whether the term "Keynesian" refers to the theory, these policies, or both. Nixon's statement has been widely quoted, for instance in Francis (2007).
2. See Jaclard's (2010) insightful critique of what I am calling "political determinism" and Harman's (2007) discussion of the relationship between this ideology and the use of the term "neoliberalism" to characterize a period of economic development. Chapters 11 and 12 of Clarke (1988) discuss the failures of Keynesian policy and social democracy.
3. My sources are the World Bank, "World Development Indicators & Global Development Finance" databank, databank.worldbank.org/ddp/home.do, and Angus Maddison, "Statistics on World Population, GDP and Per Capita GDP, 1-2008" (available at www.ggdc.net/maddison/). I divided the GDP figures by the population figures reported in each database and then computed exponential annual growth rates.
4. "Potential" does not mean "maximum" here. Potential GDP is what the GDP would be if the entire potential labor force were employed; the potential labor force is the number of people who would be in the labor force if the unemployment rate were equal to (the CBO's estimate of) the minimum unemployment rate that can be attained without causing an increase in the rate of inflation (see Congressional Budget Office 2001: 1, 11ff). Thus, potential GDP is the maximum GDP that can be attained *without causing an increase*

in the rate of inflation. The minimum unemployment rate that can be attained without causing an increase in the rate of inflation is sometimes called the "natural rate of unemployment," a term which suggests that the existence of some unemployment is natural and that there is no real unemployment problem if the actual unemployment rate is at or below the "natural" rate. These notions are certainly dubious and ideology-laden, but I do not think there is anything wrong with measuring the strength or weakness of production and the labor market by comparing actual GDP and the actual labor force to the maximum levels that could be attained without causing an increase in the rate of inflation.

5. I am using the term "cycle" here to mean the period between successive troughs in the percentage gap between actual and potential GDP; this is different from what "business cycle" means. My data for potential real GDP come from the "Quarterly Data" workbook of the CBO's "Key Assumptions in CBO's Projection of Potential Output" spreadsheet (available at tinyurl.com/yfqnp34). My data for actual real GDP come from the BEA's NIPA Table 1.1.6, line 1. To measure the percentage gaps between actual and potential GDP, I de-annualized the annualized quarterly figures by dividing them by four, subtracted potential GDP from actual GDP to obtain the gap, and divided the sum of the gaps during a cycle by the sum of the quarterly potential GDP figures during that cycle. To obtain weighted percentage gaps, I expressed the cycles' lengths as a percentage of the mean length of the cycles and multiplied these by the unweighted percentage gaps. This procedure redistributes the total percentage gap among cycles but leaves the total unchanged.

6. The indexes of industrial production and capacity utilization are available from the Federal Reserve at tinyurl.com/aatcqr. To obtain my measure of industrial capacity, I divided the industrial production index number by the capacity utilization rate.

7. My figures for the Treasury's debt come from the "Gross Federal" debt column of Table B-8 of the 2010 *Economic Report of the President* (available at tinyurl.com/mfvtnf). The gross debt includes the Treasury's debt to the Social Security Administration and other debt not held by the public. My figures for the total domestic nonfinancial debt are the sum of the Treasury debt, the debt of households and nonprofit organizations, the debt of nonfinancial businesses, and the debt of state and local governments. The latter three series come from the annual, seasonally adjusted version of Table D.3 of the *Flow of Funds Accounts of the United States*, which can be downloaded at tinyurl.com/6ko8ka6. Nominal GDP figures are reported in NIPA Table 1.1.5, line 1.

8. Real GDP figures are reported in NIPA Table 1.1.3, line 1. See note 7 for other sources.

9. To obtain the hypothetical nominal GDP that would have existed if real GDP growth had not declined, I computed the hypothetical real GDP figure for 2007 and multiplied it by the GDP price index number. The latter series is reported in NIPA Table 1.1.4, line 1; I rescaled it in order to make the nominal GDP of 1947 equal to the product of that year's price index and real GDP.

10. The household debt figures include the debt of nonprofit organizations. See note 7 for sources. The only other major borrowers are businesses. Borrowing by financial businesses has risen as a share of GDP throughout the postwar period. It would be unwise to draw conclusions about the borrowing/GDP ratio of nonfinancial business, because it is extremely volatile.

11. My tax data come from the U.S. Office of Management and Budget's historical Table 2.1 (available at tinyurl.com/l9prvq). See note 7 for sources of debt and

GDP data, and the appendix to Chapter 5 for sources of, and the methods I used to compute, rate-of-profit data.

12. For further discussion of the "potential labor force" concept, see note 4, above.

13. My potential labor force data come from column 2 of the "Annual Data" workbook of the CBO's "Key Assumptions in CBO's Projection of Potential Output" spreadsheet (available at tinyurl.com/yfqnp34). My actual labor force data come from Table A-1 of the "Household Data" section of the BLS's "Employment Situation Release" (available at bls.gov/cps/cpsatabs.htm). The percentage gap is the actual labor force minus the potential labor force, expressed as a percentage of the latter.

14. The duration data come from Table A-12 of the "Household Data" section of the BLS's "Employment Situation Release" (available at bls.gov/cps/cpsatabs. htm).

15. I computed hourly compensation figures by dividing total compensation (reported in the BEA's NIPA Table 1.10, line 2) by the number of hours worked by full- and part-time employees in domestic industries (reported in NIPA Tables 6.9 B–D, line 2). The GDP price index is reported in NIPA Table 1.14, line 1. The CPI-W series is available from the Department of Labor at www. bls.gov/cpi/.

16. The Census Bureau's Gini coefficient series currently starts with 1967. For 1967 and later years, I used the figures in the "Total" column of the U.S. Census Bureau's Table H-4 (available at tinyurl.com/243lpq5). For the 1947–1967 period, I used the "high quality" ("accept") figures reported in the World Bank's "Measuring Income Inequality Database" (available at tinyurl.com/5vr82z), which also came from the Census Bureau.

17. These computations are based on the data for "all races" in the Census Bureau's Table H-2 (available at tinyurl.com/243lpq5).

18. My figures for the "quantity" of nonresidential, nondefense structures of the federal government, and of state and local governments, come from the BEA's Fixed Asset Table 7.2A, lines 65 and 66, and Fixed Asset Table 7.2B, lines 74 and 75. Figure 25's "state & local + federal nondefense" series is the weighted average of the state and local quantity index and federal quantity index. The weights are the state and local share, and the federal share, of these structures, valued at their current costs; my data for these come from Fixed Asset Table 7.1A, lines 65 and 66, and Fixed Asset Table 7.1B, lines 74 and 75. Since we are concerned here with the physical quantity of structures, use of the current-cost figures is appropriate.

19. Figures for federal structures from 1997 to the present are omitted because they are not comparable to those of earlier years, owing to changes in the manner in which the data are classified.

5   FALLING RATES OF PROFIT AND ACCUMULATION

1. The rate of accumulation is the rate of growth of advanced capital: net investment as a percentage of advanced capital. I explain later in this chapter why the rate of accumulation is likely to track the rate of profit.

2. The term is mine; it should not be confused with "property-type income," a term once used by the BEA to refer to a similar but not identical concept that it now calls "net operating surplus."

3. The BEA figures come from NIPA Table 1.14, line 33, which reports after-tax profits before capital consumption and inventory valuation adjustments are made, as business accountants typically do. The S&P 500 figures are contained

in the "Divisors and Aggregates" worksheet of an Excel spreadsheet file published by Standard & Poor's, tinyurl.com/ynoqqe.

4. I downloaded these series ("Direct Investment Income Without Current-Cost Adjustment" and "U.S. Direct Investment Position Abroad on a Historical-Cost Basis") from the BEA's interactive "Balance of payments and Direct Investment position data" table, which is located at www.bea.gov/international/index. htm#omc.

5. The 20 countries, ranked by their average shares of total U.S. foreign direct investment and listed in descending order, are the United Kingdom, Canada, the Netherlands, Germany, Bermuda, Switzerland, Japan, France, Australia, Brazil, Mexico, Belgium, Italy, Ireland, UK Caribbean islands, Singapore, Hong Kong, Panama, Luxembourg, and Spain. The rate of profit trended upward only in Switzerland and Mexico, whose combined share of U.S. foreign direct investment was 8 percent of the total.

6. See the *OECD Glossary of Statistical Terms*, tinyurl.com/42mb5e4; the BEA seems not to provide a definition of its own.

7. Although I will provide estimates of inflation-adjusted rates of profit in this section, I also think that unadjusted, nominal rates are useful. As I explain in the appendix to this chapter, I do not think that any one rate of profit can act as an all-purpose measure of profitability.

8. In some cases, the relevant "cost" might be the *value* of this set of items, determined by the socially average amount of labor needed to produce them. Here, and in most cases, however, the relevant cost is the sum of value that the owners can *receive* for the items, that is, the labor-time equivalent of their money price. Marx utilizes the concept of inflation noted here in many places. Here are a few: "the same monetary expression of value—owing to the vicissitudes in the value of money itself—denotes different values [at different times]. The difficulty here lies in reducing the money prices to values" (Marx 1989b: 340). "[I]f a yard of linen has a value of 2s. and a price of 1s., the ... price is not ... the adequate monetary expression ... of its value. Nevertheless, it remains the *monetary expression* of its value—the *value expression* of the yard of linen—in so far as the labour contained in it is represented as general social labour, as *money*" (Marx 1994: 114, emphases in original). "If the price of gold is now halved or doubled, in the first case the same capital that was previously worth £100 is now worth £200 ... In the second case, the capital falls to a value of £50 ... In both cases, however ... [t]here would be no real change in the capital value in any case such as this, but simply a change in the monetary expression of the same value" (Marx 1991a: 236–7).

9. If the percentage growth rate of (nominal) net investment is greater than the percentage growth rate in the deflator (GDP price index or MELT), then it follows from the definitions of the adjusted rates of profit that the ratio of the adjusted rate of profit to the unadjusted rate tends toward

$$1 - \frac{growth \ rate \ of \ net \ investment}{growth \ rate \ of \ deflator}.$$

Thus, if the ratio of the growth rates is roughly constant, the ratio of the rates of profit will also tend to be roughly constant in the long run.

10. I implemented the spirit of the proposal even though I regard my original inflation-adjustment procedure as valid (see Kliman 2010a: 279).

11. Denote the index of fixed asset prices of year t as F_t, the GDP price index (or MELT) of year t as P_t, and an index of the physical depreciation, during year t, of fixed assets acquired k years earlier as D_{t-k}. If historical-cost depreciation figures are deflated by the price index of the year in which the associated investment was made, year $t-k$, then the inflation-adjusted depreciation, during year t, of fixed assets acquired in year $t-k$ is

$$\frac{F_{t-k}D_{t-k}}{P_{t-k}}.$$

If, instead, current-cost depreciation figures are deflated by the current year's GDP price index (or MELT), then the inflation-adjusted depreciation is

$$\frac{F_t D_t}{P_t}.$$

If the index of fixed asset prices changes by the same percentage that the GDP price index (or MELT) changes, then

$$\frac{F_{t-k}}{P_{t-k}} = \frac{F_t}{P_t},$$

and the two inflation-adjusted depreciation figures are therefore equal.

12. If the difference between historical- and current-cost valuation "does not have enormous empirical implications"—that is, if it is not the true source of the discrepancy between my empirical results and his—why does Husson not agree that the rate of profit failed to rebound in a sustained manner between the early 1980s and the latest economic crisis?

13. $rate\ of\ accumulation \equiv \left(\dfrac{net\ investment}{profit} \right)\left(\dfrac{profit}{advanced\ capital} \right)$

$\equiv \left(\dfrac{net\ investment}{profit} \right)(rate\ of\ profit).$

14. The rate of profit shown in Figure 5.8 is property income as a percentage of the historical cost of fixed assets; the rate of accumulation is net investment in fixed assets, valued at historical cost, as a percentage of the historical cost of fixed assets.

15. This conclusion does not depend on the fact that I valued depreciation at historical cost when computing profit and net investment. It also holds true, for all four measures of profit, when depreciation is valued at current cost.

16. These conclusions also hold true when depreciation is valued at current cost rather than at historical cost.

17. However, as I shall discuss in the next chapter, the current-cost (replacement-cost) "rate of profit" is *not* a legitimate measure of the rate of profit.

18. Although estimates of the absolute *amount* of moral depreciation would be very unreliable and difficult to produce, Chapter 7 will present profitability estimates that adjust for the apparent *increase* in moral depreciation that has taken place since the early 1980s.

19. I used the BEA's NIPA Table 1.13, line 2 (domestic business) and line 3 (corporate business) to compute this figure.

20. These figures are based on the BEA's Fixed Asset Table 6.1, line 2 (corporate), line 5 (noncorporate), line 8 (nonprofit institutions), and line 9 (households). The business sector's fixed assets are line 2 plus line 5, minus lines 8 and 9.

21. All computations in this paragraph and the next are based on data reported in Tables 722 and 727 of the *Statistical Abstract of the United States, 2009* (U.S. Department of Commerce 2009).

22. The case of partnerships in the "real estate and rental and leasing" industry is instructive. According to Table 727 of the *Statistical Abstract of the United States, 2009*, almost half of all partnerships were in this industry in 2005. Their average net income (minus loss)—*before* making any adjustment in order to estimate how much of their net income was actually property income—was $56,000 per partnership or $11,000 per partner.

6   THE CURRENT-COST "RATE OF PROFIT"

1. By "physicalists," I mean those who contend that, or deduce conclusions from models in which, physical quantities (input-output and physical wage coefficients) are the only proximate determinants of the rate of profit. When capital expenditures are revalued at their replacement cost, the "rate of profit" depends only on these physical quantities. See Kliman (2007, Chapters 5 and 7) for further discussion.

2. On the basis of his comments at the January 2010 *Historical Materialism* conference in New York City, I believe that Moseley would now repudiate the last sentence, but I have not seen anything in print to that effect.

3. Duménil and Costas Lapavitsas both seem to suggest that if a fall in the rate of profit was not a proximate cause of the latest crisis, it was not a cause at all. Lapavitsas (2010: 17–18) recently argued that "no significant decline in profit rates occurred on the approach to crisis … the crisis of 2007–9 has little in common with a crisis of profitability, such as 1973–5." These facts do not count as evidence against my view that the fall in the rate of profit was an underlying and indirect cause of the crisis and slump. But Lapavitsas then argued, "Things are not much better if it is claimed that the crisis resulted from underlying over-accumulation, but it was *postponed or delayed* through financial expansion … it is very strange political economy that treats overaccumulation crises as the normal state of the capitalist economy, except that they keep being postponed through various expedients. This is, indeed, a reversal of classical Marxism, for which restructuring is an inevitable response to overaccumulation, while crises are temporary and sharp upheavals that prepare the ground for the restoration of profitability" (2010: 18, emphasis added). Yet a declaration that something is "very strange" is no argument against it, and the issue here is not whether a theory conforms to Lapavitsas' notion of "classical Marxism" but whether it can account for the facts. In any case, his statement does not make sense. It "contrasts" the idea that the crisis *resulted* from underlying over-accumulation to the idea that crises *themselves* are temporary, sharp upheavals—as if these ideas somehow contradict one another. They do not.

4. In the discussion period that followed a presentation of mine at the January 2010 *Historical Materialism* conference in New York City, Duménil denied that he and Lévy cherry picked their data. An audio file that contains this exchange

is available at tinyurl.com/4y7ewfl. Duménil's comments on this issue begin approximately 6 1/2 minutes from the start of the fourth of the four files, "origins of the current crisis-PIV-QandA.WMA." Kliman (2010b) contains an edited transcript of the exchange and documentation of the claims I made during it.

5. This vision functioned as the "factual basis" of a widespread sense of hopelessness and impotence on the left and of resignation to the status quo, or mildly reformist alternatives to it. Now that the latest crisis has shown that the sustainability of the "neoliberal boom" was a myth, not a fact, it remains to be seen whether these attitudes will change, or whether a revised set of facts will be adduced in support of them.

6. Husson (2009) and Duménil have also recently argued in favor of the current-cost "rate of profit" on the grounds that the historical-cost rate of profit is affected by inflation, but current-cost valuation eliminates that effect. I will take up this issue later in this chapter. The audio file mentioned in note 4 contains Duménil's discussion of this matter, which immediately followed his comments on the cherry picking issue. I transcribed and critiqued his discussion of the inflation issue in Kliman (2010a: 247–9).

7. Data on the current cost of fixed assets comes from the BEA's Fixed Asset Table 6.1, line 2. The denominators of current-cost "rates of profit" typically use end-of-year figures; I followed this convention. See the appendix to Chapter 5 for sources of data on, and the methods I used to compute, current-cost measures of property income and before-tax profits.

8. The exchange, which I observed, took place on May 29, 2011 at the World Association for Political Economy conference, which was held at the University of Massachusetts at Amherst.

9. I chose the current cost of fixed assets at the end of 1928 as the initial value of the advanced capital.

10. I point this out because some critics of the TSSI have dismissed its critique of replacement-cost measurement of the rate of profit by arguing—incorrectly, as we see—that the issue has little empirical relevance.

11. The BEA publishes data for capital stocks in terms of current costs, but its concept of "capital stock" was not developed in order to measure profitability. The measures of net investment upon which it is based are intended to be "rough indicators of whether the corresponding capital stocks have been maintained intact" (Herman et. al. 2003: M–2).

12. Denote the amount invested as I, and the per-period revenue stream if the product's price remained constant as R. Then, applying the standard internal rate of return formula, we have

$$I = R\sum_{i=1}^{n}\left(\frac{1}{1+r^C}\right)^i \text{ and } I = R\sum_{i=1}^{n}\left(\frac{1+\dot{p}}{1+r^A}\right)^i.$$

If the number of periods n is infinite, then

$$R\sum_{i=1}^{n}\left(\frac{1}{1+r^C}\right)^i = R\left(\frac{1}{r^C}\right) \text{ and } R\sum_{i=1}^{n}\left(\frac{1+\dot{p}}{1+r^A}\right)^i = R\left(\frac{[1+\dot{p}]}{[1+r^A]-[1+\dot{p}]}\right).$$

Since the two right-hand-side expressions both equal I, they can be set equal to each other, and the relation given in the text is then easily derived.

13. We would obtain similar results if we assumed that what falls is the rate of inflation, but the computations would be more complex. As I noted in the last section, the disinflation of the 1980s accounts for why the current-cost "rate of profit" has risen although the historical-cost rate has fallen; both rates trended downward during the 1991–2007 period. The disinflation of the 1980s also explains why the current-cost rate has risen although the rate of accumulation has fallen.

14. The farmers could continue to produce, and even produce an increasing amount of corn each year—*if* they could persuade their bankers to extend them new loans. This is not very likely. As long as the farmers must pay a positive rate of interest, the ratio of their debt to their sales revenue will grow exponentially. It is also important to note that nothing is really different if the farmers are able to fund their own operations. Their books may not show that they owe interest to themselves, but if they continually extend zero-interest loans to themselves, they continually forego the interest that they could acquire by investing their money capital externally.

15. I obtained monthly earnings and price figures for the S&P 500 from Robert Shiller's "stock market data" spreadsheet file, which can be downloaded at www.econ.yale.edu/~shiller/data. To obtain annual earning-to-price ratios, I averaged the monthly earnings and price figures, and then took the ratio of these averages.

16. The physical quantity index of corporations' fixed assets is reported in the BEA's Fixed Asset Table 6.2, line 2. The GDP price index is reported in NIPA Table 1.1.4, line 1; I rescaled the reported figures, a procedure which leaves the rates of inflation unaffected. The appendix to Chapter 5 explains how I obtained a current-cost measure of property income, and note 7, above, explains how I computed the current-cost "rate of profit."

17. This inflation-adjusted rate values property income and net investment at current cost. In all other respects, it is the same as the inflation-adjusted property-income rate discussed in chapter 5. The average level of the latter rate between 1980 and 2006 was 10.3 percent less than its level in 1980. The appendix to Chapter 5 explains how I computed both rates.

7 WHY THE RATE OF PROFIT FELL

1. The GDP price index is reported in NIPA Table 1.1.4, line 1. The CPI-U series is available from the BLS at bls.gov/cpi/data.htm; I used the average annual figures. For sources of data on and methods used to compute the other variables, see the appendix to Chapter 5. Since the growth rates of real compensation and real net value added have been equal since 1970, it follows that real compensation per labor-hour and productivity (real net value added per labor-hour) have also risen at the same rate. Analyses that arrive at the contrary conclusion use one price index to compute real compensation but a different one to compute real net value added, resulting in an apples-to-oranges comparison (see Bosworth and Perry 1994, Feldstein 2008).

2. These figures are based on index numbers reported in Table 5 of the BLS's "Employment Cost Index Historical Listing: Continuous Occupational and Industry Series" (available at tinyurl.com/3ftgl73). The figures for private-industry workers in "professional and related" occupations, reported in the same table, indicate that their hourly compensation increased by 129 percent.

3. A graph in Duménil and Lévy (2011: 49) excludes wages of the top 5 percent and 10 percent of U.S. wage earners, and seemingly shows that compensation received by all other employees has fallen precipitously as a share of corporations' net value added since the early 1980s. But the adjustment procedure mixes apples and oranges. The unadjusted series pertains to total compensation, while the data used to adjust it exclude nonwage compensation (retirement and medical benefits), which is a disproportionately large share of less-well-paid workers' total compensation. In the U.S. in 2008, 12 percent of the median individual's income, but only 4 percent of the income of individuals in the top 10 percent, consisted of Medicare and private medical compensation (see Burkhauser and Simon 2010: 25, Table 1). Because of this difference, and because nonwage compensation has risen more quickly than wages, the adjustment procedure increasingly understates the compensation received by the bottom 90 percent of wage earners. It may be producing a spurious decline for other reasons as well, since BEA data are for compensation paid to individuals by corporations, while the data that Duménil and Lévy use to adjust the compensation figures, which come from Piketty and Saez, pertain to "tax units" rather than to individuals, and to wages as reported on personal tax returns. For further discussion of points made in the previous two sentences, see the first section of Chapter 8.

4. Although Husson says that I exclude managers' compensation from surplus-value, I actually exclude it from corporate profit, as noted above.

5. Constant-profit-share property income is thus net value added times the average ratio of property income to net value added between 1929 and 2007. The average ratio since 1947 is almost identical, so the choice of 1929 as the starting date has almost no effect on the results. See the appendix to Chapter 5 for further information on my rate-of-profit measures.

6. However, it does not help to account for the failure of the rate of profit to recover after 1982, because the profit share has been trendless since 1970.

7. "Nothing is more absurd, then, than to explain the fall in the rate of profit in terms of a rise in wage rates, even though this too may be an exceptional case" (Marx 1991a: 347).

8. To remove the changes in the MELT, I divided each year's figures for employee compensation by that year's MELT and used the MELT-adjusted series for the historical cost of fixed assets. For sources of data on and methods used to compute these variables, see the appendix to Chapter 5.

9. The fixed-asset data are reported in the BEA's Fixed Asset Table 6.2, line 2. The employment series is reported in NIPA Table 5.5A–D, line 3. I used figures for employment in all private industries because figures for employment in corporations are not available.

10. Further research is needed in order to account for the relative constancy of this gap. However, it is clear from the double-digit inflation of the 1970s and the subsequent disinflationary slump triggered by Federal Reserve policy that there are strict political limits to the rate of growth of money prices relative to values. Owners of assets will not sit idly by when their assets' command over labor, and goods and services, is rapidly being eroded by inflation.

11. This rate of profit is the annual change in the numerator of the overall CPS-MA rate of profit divided by the annual change in its denominator. The 10-year centered moving average is shown in the graph because the series is very volatile, but annual values of the CPS-MA rate of profit on new investments were used

to compute its average and trend. The series begins with 1948 rather than 1947 because 1946 was a transitional year of reconversion to peacetime production. In an economic sense, the post-World War II period began in 1947, so the first year for which there are post-reconversion changes is 1948.

12. The trendline value in 2000 was 2.1 percentage points below the trendline value in 1948. The *t*-value associated with the trend coefficient is –0.358. CPS-MA-NEW declined substantially after 2000, causing its average value since 1948 to fall from 10.2 percent in 2000 to 9.3 percent in 2007.

13. Note that the LTFRP does not imply that the rate of profit on new investments must fall in order for the overall rate of profit to fall. *In the numerical example that Marx* (1991a: 317) *provides at the start of his discussion of the LTFRP, the rate of profit on new investments is always zero, so it does not fall.* (Since surplus-value remains constant when more capital is advanced, the change in surplus-value—the numerator of the rate of profit on new investments—is zero.) But since the initial overall rate of profit is much greater than zero (66.7 percent), the four extra advances of capital cause it to fall (to 50 percent, 33.3 percent, 25 percent, and 20 percent).

14. As for the other two sources of decline in value—accidental damage and aging—I interpret Marx as having treated them like wear and tear rather than like a decline in value due to obsolescence. Although he does not explicitly discuss these factors as far as I know, he holds that products gain value to the extent that means of production used to produce them lose value because their use-value (physical utility) declines (Marx 1990a: 310–16), and this applies to aging, insofar as aging is distinguished from obsolescence, no less than it applies to wear and tear. In addition, he argues that since a certain "amount of waste is normal and inevitable under average conditions," the average amount of value lost to waste is transferred to products (Marx 1990a: 313). It is thus reasonable to infer that the average amount of value lost to accidental damage is likewise transferred to products, since it too is normal and inevitable under average conditions. In contrast, declines in value due to obsolescence cause the prior *average* expenditure on means of production to exceed the *average* expenditure that is now "normal and inevitable."

15. My data sources on and the procedures I used to compute historical-cost measures of fixed assets and depreciation are discussed in the appendix to Chapter 5.

16. These figures refer to the historical cost of *all* private-sector businesses' nonresidential fixed assets (reported in BEA Fixed Asset Table 2.3), not those of corporations alone. The BEA does not publish data on corporations' IPE&S assets. The figures for information processing equipment and software are on line 4. Total nonresidential fixed assets are the sum of nonresidential equipment and software (line 3) and nonresidential structures (line 37).

17. BEA depreciation figures are based on the estimated service lives of the various kinds of fixed assets rather than on depreciation figures reported in tax returns. The shorter the service life of an asset, the more rapidly it depreciates.

18. Taking BEA depreciation and fixed-asset data (both valued at historical cost) for the U.S. business sector in 1960 and 2009, and making various assumptions about the degree of moral depreciation, we can estimate how much of the rise in the rate of depreciation is due to increased moral depreciation, as in the following table. The results suggest that it is realistic to assume that all of the rise in the rate of depreciation is due to it.

	Moral depreciation (% of total depreciation)					
Non-IPE&S	10	40	10	40	10	40
IPE&S, 1960	40	55	45	60	50	65
IPE&S, 2009	70	70	80	80	90	90
% of change in rate of depreciation						
due to increased moral depreciation	103	86	118	102	133	117

19. The latter figure must be estimated because it is not reported by the BEA. Between 1937 and 1951, a period that preceded the information technology revolution, the rate of depreciation of corporations' fixed assets was on average equal to 94.96 percent of the rate of depreciation of all private-sector nonresidential fixed assets, and the relationship between the two rates was very stable during that period. I therefore multiplied the rate of depreciation of nonresidential private-sector non-IPE&S fixed assets by 0.9496 to obtain an estimate of what the rate of depreciation of corporations' fixed assets would have been if total depreciation had increased at the same rate as the depreciation of their non-IPE&S fixed assets. I then multiplied this rate by corporations' total fixed assets to obtain an estimate of the amount of depreciation that would have occurred.

8   THE UNDERCONSUMPTIONIST ALTERNATIVE

1. Their essay is reprinted as Chapter 6 of Foster and Magdoff (2009).
2. When discussing this matter in public talks, I have encountered three main objections. One is that the subjective utility of a dollar of health or retirement benefits is less than the subjective utility of a dollar of cash income. This may be true for some workers, but it is irrelevant here, where the issue is how national income is divided between working people and others. An extra dollar of income received by one group is a dollar less received by the other; this is so both when the income is received in the form of cash and when it is not. For the same reason, the subjective utility of benefits is also irrelevant to an analysis of the division of corporations' net value added into property income and employees' compensation. A second objection is that health benefits are not really the income of workers, since the money ultimately goes to health-care providers and insurers. This is like saying that cash income which workers spend on bread is not really their income, because it ultimately goes to grocery stores and bakeries. The final objection, lodged by Richard Wolff, is that recipients of retirement benefits and Medicare benefits are not workers, but *former* workers. This is like saying that recipients of cash wages are not workers because they receive their paychecks after the workweek is over. (In both cases, the recipients receive income in exchange for going to work, but only after they are finished working.) It is also like saying that the unemployed are not workers, but former workers, and that people who work eight hours a day, five days a week are only part-time workers because they don't work 24/7. For Wolff's objection and examples of the others, see the video of the first panel of the Economic Crisis & Left Responses conference at www.marxist-humanist-initiative.org/ccvideo. The conference was held in New York City on November 6, 2010.

3. The national income, compensation, and wage-and-salary figures are reported in lines 1–3, respectively, of NIPA Table 1.12. GDP is reported in NIPA Table 1.5, line 1. Net government social benefit data come from NIPA Table 2.1. I subtracted tax contributions for benefit programs (line 24) from the benefits (line 17) to obtain the net benefits. I counted all net government social benefits as income of working-class people because the data that would be needed to apportion the net benefits between them and others are not available. The overwhelming majority of the net benefits do accrue to working-class people; on average, about three-fourths of the net benefits consist of assistance to the poor and to low-income and disabled workers, and net retirement, disability, and veterans' benefits make up the majority of the remaining net benefits. Because my estimates overstate workers' income only slightly, it cannot plausibly be argued that their share of national income has declined to any significant extent since 1970.

4. Average hourly earnings (wages and salaries) of production and nonsupervisory (P&NS) workers are published in Table B-8 of the BLS's "Employment Situation" release (available at tinyurl.com/3lfvuwq). (The other pay data in Figures 8.2 and 8.3 are obtained from a different survey.) For the 1981–2005 period, my figures on P&NS workers' total compensation come from Table 3 of the BLS's "Employment Cost Index, Historical Listing, Current-dollar, 1975-2005" (available at tinyurl.com/67jqnqj). My pay data for all private-industry workers come from Table 5 (total compensation) and Table 9 (wages and salaries) of the BLS's "Employment Cost Index, Historical Listing, Continuous Occupational and Industry Series" (available at tinyurl.com/3ftgl73). To obtain annual Employment Cost Index numbers, I averaged the quarterly figures; in one instance, the first quarter's figure was not reported, so I averaged the middle two quarters' figures. To estimate P&NS workers' compensation in 1980 and from 2006 onward, I assumed that, in each of these years, the ratio of their total compensation to their wages and salaries increased at the same rate as the comparable ratio for all private-industry workers. It actually increased at a slightly faster rate between 1981 and 2005, so my assumption may lead to an *underestimate* of the growth of P&NS workers' compensation. The PCE index is reported in NIPA Table 1.1.4, line 2. The CPI-W index, published by the BLS, is available at www.bls.gov/cpi/; I averaged each year's monthly figures.

5. The quoted material comes from a "Frequently Asked Questions" page on the BLS's website, tinyurl.com/3avafeb.

6. The underlying average wage and salary data are for all tax units and the top 10 percent of tax units. They come from Tables B1 ("average wage" column) and B3 ("P90-100" average salary column) of Piketty and Saez's Excel spreadsheet file, available at elsa.berkeley.edu/~saez/TabFig2008.xls. Since the average wage of all tax units is equal to nine-tenths of the average wage of the bottom 90 percent plus one-tenth of the average salary of the top 10 percent, I was able to compute the average wage of the bottom 90 percent from these data.

7. The data are reported in Burkhauser, Larrimore, and Simon (2011: 37, Table 4, panel D). They use the CPI-U-RS series to adjust for inflation. The transfer payments considered in their study are cash social benefits provided by government, such as Social Security, unemployment insurance, and welfare benefits.

8. My analysis in this section is informed by those of Bleaney (1976), Dunayevskaya (1991), and Shaikh (1978).

9. For instance, former U.S. Secretary of Labor Robert B. Reich (2010) recently argued, "The rich spend a much smaller proportion of their incomes than the rest of us. So when they get a disproportionate share of total income, the economy is robbed of the demand it needs to keep growing and creating jobs." This supposed fact was the centerpiece of his essay's explanation of why the Great Recession occurred.

10. I have discussed the intended purposes of the schemes elsewhere (Kliman 2011); here I am dealing only with what the schemes themselves show.

11. "Any attempt to get away from this fundamental fact represents a flight from reality … [The existence of] reproduction schemes which apparently demonstrate the opposite does not change matters one whit: production is production for consumption" (Sweezy 1970: 172).

12. This analysis, under the pseudonym "Freddie Forest," first appeared in *New International*, April 1946 and May 1946.

13. Marx seems to be referring here to the sum of their personal consumption demand *and* their productive consumption demand (investment demand). Their personal consumption demand is *always* less than their accumulated profit, but a crisis would occur only if their investment demand were not great enough to offset this gap.

14. This is a 40 percent increase, more than double the percentage increase in the surplus that took place, according to Baran and Sweezy (1966: 24), in the U.S. between 1929 and 1963.

15. The process reduces to the following. Workers' share of income is $w_t = 0.65 + 0.1(0.9)^{t-1}$ and capitalist's share of income is $c_t = 0.15 + 0.05(0.9)^{t-1}$. $K_{t+1} = (1 + 0.15[1 - w_t - c_t])K_t$, $C_{Wt} = 0.15w_tK_t$, $C_{Ct} = 0.15c_tK_t$, $I_t = 0.15(1 - w_t - c_t)K_t$, $Q_{MAX\,t} = 0.15K_t$, and $K_0 > 0$. These relations satisfy the identity $K_{t+1} \equiv K_t + I_t$ as well as Baran and Sweezy's conditions—the surplus and the investment share of income continually rise while workers' and capitalists' personal consumption shares of income continually fall, the growth rate of the capital stock ($[K_{t+1} - K_t]/K_t$) and potential output continually rises, and the potential-output/capital ratio is constant. According to Baran and Sweezy, these conditions imply that actual output must fall short of potential output to an increasing extent. In fact, however, actual and potential output are always equal (in the example), since $Y_t \equiv C_{Wt} + C_{Ct} + I_t = 0.15w_tK_t + 0.15c_tK_t + 0.15(1 - w_t - c_t)K_t = 0.15K_t = Q_{MAX\,t}$.

16. Maddison's "Statistics on World Population, GDP and Per Capita GDP, 1–2008" are available at www.ggdc.net/maddison. The World Bank data come from its World Development Indicators & Global Development Finance databank, databank.worldbank.org/ddp/home.do.

17. The data are reported in NIPA Table 1.1.3, line 1 (GDP), line 2 (personal consumption), and line 9 (nonresidential fixed investment).

18. Let Q_A denote actual output, which is the same thing as income. Using the notation of Table 8.4, we can express the investment share of income as I/Q_A and the potential-output/capital ratio as Q_{MAX}/K. If $Q_A = Q_{MAX}$, then the growth rate of the capital stock, I/K, equals $(I/Q_A)(Q_{MAX}/K)$. And if $Q_A = Q_{MAX}$ and Q_{MAX}/K is constant, then, as we saw above, I/K is the economy's growth rate. It follows that an x percent rise in I/Q_A results in an x percent rise in the growth rate if Q_{MAX}/K is constant.

19. If we take into account the effect that declining investment will have on consumption and the resulting need for investment to fall even further in

order to restore "equilibrium," I estimate that real gross private domestic nonresidential investment would have to fall by 85 percent from the 2008 peak. (My estimate assumes that the percentage decline in consumption is 7.1 percent of the percentage decline in investment, which was the case in 2009.) Note by way of contrast that the fall between 1929 and 1933 was 71 percent. The difference is very significant, because these are gross investment figures; the percentage decline in real net investment would be far greater than in the Great Depression. My rough estimate is that, owing to the larger decline in gross investment, and the smaller size of net investment relative to gross investment in 2008 than in 1929, the percentage fall in real net investment—the physical destruction of capital—would have be close to double that of the early 1930s before "equilibrium" would be restored.

9   WHAT IS TO BE UNDONE?

1. The new Dodd-Frank financial reform law and policymakers often refer to "systemically important" firms. This phrase helps make clear that a firm can be too big to fail—even if it is not particularly big and its failure would not threaten the solvency of the firms with which it does business—if the government's failure to rescue it would endanger the "confidence" of investors in the financial system as a whole. Bear Stearns was not an especially large institution, nor was Lehman Brothers at the time of its collapse. According to the *Financial Times*, Bear Stearns was not among the world's largest 500 corporations (ranked by market capitalization) at the end of December 2007, and Lehman Brothers was not among them at the end of June 2008. See tinyurl.com/3goh85l and tinyurl.com/3oyq7wy.

2. In 2008 and 2009, 56 percent of Europe's bank assets were owned by its 1,000 largest banks, but only 13 percent of U.S. bank assets were owned by its 1,000 largest banks (IFSL Research 2010: 3, Chart 7).

3. Dunayevskaya commented that in his influential 1910 work *Finance Capital*, Hilferding (1981) "sees the new stage of capitalism in its financial razzle-dazzle appearance and becomes enamored of its capacity to 'unify' commercial, industrial, and financial interests[, rather] than [being] concretely aware of the greater contradictions and antagonisms of the new monopoly stage of capitalism ... What in truth emerges from a close study of Hilferding ... is that the new generation of Marxists following Engels's death ... *saw monopoly not as a fetter but as an organizing force of production*. So that the Second International, which had openly rejected Bernsteinism and gradualness, accepted Hilferdingism, which means tacit acceptance of the capacity of capital to gain a 'certain' stability, modify its anarchism as a 'constant' feature, and seeing in [the] new stage not a *transition* to a higher form, but something in itself already higher, although 'bad'" (Dunayevskaya 1951: 9291–2, emphases in original).

4. My data for manufacturing compensation come from pages 1 and 4 of the BLS's "International Comparisons of Hourly Compensation Costs in Manufacturing, 2008" (available at tinyurl.com/4vp4qrn). The export data come from the World Bank's World Development Indicators & Global Development Finance databank, databank.worldbank.org/ddp/home.do. The per capita GDP growth rate figures come from the United Nations, *Human Development Report 2009*; I downloaded them from hdrstats.undp.org/en/buildtables/.

5. I used World Bank and Central Intelligence Agency data to estimate labor productivity (value added, in terms of U.S. dollars, per employed worker) in the industrial sector in 2007. My estimates indicate that Chinese labor productivity was about 8.3 percent of the U.S. level. Taken together, this figure and the 4.2 percent relative hourly compensation figure suggest that unit labor costs (compensation per unit of output) in China were about half as great as in the U.S.

6. The growth rate data come from the World Bank, World Development Indicators & Global Development Finance databank, databank.worldbank.org/ddp/home.do.

7. Chang argues that the official figures underestimate the decline in China's growth rate: "Beijing's National Bureau of Statistics does not fully account for the output of the fast-growing service sector. That's why its estimate of 13.0 percent growth for 2007 is low by about two percentage points. Then, small businesses were the most vibrant part of the economy. Today, the failure to properly assess the output of small business is resulting in an *overestimation* of GDP because these enterprises, which tend to be more dependent on exports, are suffering more than the larger ones" (Chang 2010, emphasis in original). If we add two percentage points to China's 2007 growth rate and shave a bit off of its 2009 growth rate, we arrive at the conclusion that the impact of the crisis on China was comparable to its impact on Japan, Germany, and the United Kingdom.

8. Most of the information in this and the preceding paragraph comes from Wong, Liu, and Culpan (2010).

9. Although $700 billion in TARP funds were appropriated, not all of them were spent. In addition, loans made under TARP were typically paid back, and the government received profit from assets it purchased with TARP funds.

10. The Stiglitz Commission's final report states, "The fact that firms are always inventing ways of circumventing regulations means that governments have to view regulation as a dynamic process" (Commission of Experts 2009: 63)— that is, as a never-ending cat-and-mouse game in which the mouse continually manages to elude the cat. This is not a recommendation that inspires confidence in the effectiveness of regulation.

11. By "socialist economy," I mean a democratically run, communal economy in which people's ability to work is not a commodity and in which production and provision are oriented to the satisfaction of human beings' wants, not to the accumulation of ever-greater amounts of wealth-in-the-abstract ("value"). In order for economic activity to be reoriented in this manner, finance, money, exchange, and value would have to be eliminated.

12. Unfortunately, this perspective is publicly argued for and made the basis of practical politics much less commonly than it is believed.

13. Once Israel's runaway inflation ended in the mid-1980s, the kibbutzim faced an intractable debt crisis, which they dealt with largely by abandoning efforts to avoid market relations within the kibbutz (they produced for profit and used hired labor, often that of Arabs, long before that). "Today's kibbutz boasts differential salaries, shuttered dining halls, individual home ownership, private bank accounts and investment portfolios and, of course, richer and poorer kibbutzniks. Only about 80 kibbutzim, fewer than one-third, still preserve the old egalitarianism" (Goldberg 2010).

Bibliography

All URLs in the bibliography, endnotes, and text were last accessed on June 7, 2011.

ABC News 2009. "China's unemployed migrant workers could top 20 million," March 25. Available at tinyurl.com/c4hyc8.

Baker, Dean. 2008a. "Progressive Conditions for a Bailout." *Real-world Economics Review* 47, Oct. 3, pp. 243–49. Available at tinyurl.com/3fxfbb7.

—— 2008b. "Wall St Held a Gun to Our Heads," Sept. 29, guardian.co.uk. Available at tinyurl.com/4g7k4m.

Baran, Paul A. and Paul M. Sweezy. 1966. *Monopoly Capital: An Essay on the American Economic and Social Order.* New York: Monthly Review Press.

Beggs, Mike. 2009. Post to "lbo-talk" e-mail discussion list, Feb. 16. Available at tinyurl.com/3px6w9j.

Bernanke, Ben S. 2002. "Deflation: Making Sure 'It' Doesn't Happen Here," Nov. 21. Available at tinyurl.com/4fq2fu.

—— 2010. "Causes of the Recent Financial and Economic Crisis" (testimony before the Financial Crisis Inquiry Commission), Sept. 2. Available at tinyurl. com/3buvanz.

Bleaney, Michael F. 1976. *Underconsumption Theories: History and Critical Analysis.* New York: International Publishers.

Bosworth, Barry, and George L. Perry. 1994. "Productivity and Real Wages: Is there a Puzzle?" *Brookings Papers on Economic Activity*, 1994:1, 317–44.

Branigan, Tania. 2009. "Downturn in China Leaves 26 Million Out of Work," *The Guardian,* Feb. 2. Available at tinyurl.com/cplsb3.

Brenner, Robert. 1998. "The Economics of Global Turbulence," *New Left Review* 229, 1–265.

Bullard, James. 2010. "St. Louis Fed's Bullard: Fed is the Nation's 'Best Chance' for Avoiding Future Financial Crises," Feb. 23. Available at tinyurl.com/3bnu8qp.

Burkhauser, Richard V. 2011. "Presidential Address: Evaluating the Questions that Alternative Policy Success Measures Answer," *Journal of Policy Analysis and Management* 30:2, 205–15.

—— and Kosali I. Simon. 2010. "Measuring the Impact of Health Insurance on Levels and Trends in Inequality." National Bureau of Economic Research, Working Paper No. 15811, Mar.

——, Jeff Larrimore, and Kosali Simon. 2011. "A Second Opinion on the Economic Health of the American Middle Class." Ithaca, NY: Cornell University working paper.

Carchedi, Guglielmo. 2011. *Behind the Crisis: Marx's Dialectics of Value and Knowledge.* Leiden and Boston: Koninklijke Brill.

Celasun, Oya, and Geoffrey Keim. 2010. "The U.S. Federal Debt Outlook: Reading the Tea Leaves." IMF Working Paper WP/10/62. Washington, DC: International Monetary Fund.

Chang, Gordon G. 2010. "China's Economy To Reach $123 Trillion?," *Forbes.com*, Jan. 8. Available at tinyurl.com/yanpgtz.

China Labour Bulletin. 2010. "The Strike that Ignited China's Summer of Worker Protests," Sept. 15. www.clb.org.hk/en/node/100875.

Clarke, Simon. 1988. *Keynesianism, Monetarism and the Crisis of the State.* Aldershot, UK: Edward Elgar.

Commission of Experts of the President of the United Nations General Assembly [Stiglitz Commission]. 2009. *Report of the Commission of Experts of the President of the United Nations General Assembly on Reforms of the International Monetary and Financial System,* Sept. 21. Available at tinyurl.com/yjos2rt.

Congressional Budget Office. 2001. "CBO's Method for Estimating Potential Output: An Update," Aug. Available at tinyurl.com/3r7w2h6.

Curry, Timothy and Lynn Shibut. 2000. "The Cost of the Savings and Loan Crisis: Truth and Consequences," *FDIC Banking Review* 13:2, 26–35.

Desai, Radhika. 2010. "Consumption Demand in Marx and in the Current Crisis," *Research in Political Economy* 26 [*The National Question and the Question of Crisis*], 101–43.

—— and Alan Freeman. 2011. "Value and Crisis Theory in the 'Great Recession'," *World Review of Political Economy* 2:1, 35–47.

Domar, Evsey D. 1957. *Essays in the Theory of Economic Growth.* New York: Oxford University Press.

Duménil, Gérard and Dominique Lévy. 2004. *Capital Resurgent: Roots of the Neoliberal Revolution.* Cambridge, MA: Harvard University Press.

—— 2005. "The Profit Rate: Where and How Much Did it Fall? Did it Recover? (USA 1948–1997)." Available at gesd.free.fr/dle2002f.pdf.

—— 2011. *The Crisis of Neoliberalism.* Cambridge, MA: Harvard University Press.

Dunayevskaya, Raya. 1951. [Letter to C.L.R. James.] In *The Raya Dunayevskaya Collection,* 9291–8, Detroit, MI: Wayne State University Archives of Labor and Urban Affairs, Walter P. Reuther Library.

—— 1978. "Dialectics: The Algebra of Revolution." Available at tinyurl.com/3sazge5.

—— 1991. *Rosa Luxemburg, Women's Liberation, and Marx's Philosophy of Revolution,* 2nd ed. Urbana, IL and Chicago: University of Illinois Press.

—— 2000. *Marxism and Freedom: From 1776 until today,* 6th edn. Amherst, NY: Humanity Books.

Egoavil, Michael. 2009. "Fictitious Capital and Credit Schemes," *With Sober Senses.* Available at www.marxist-humanist-initiative.org/?p=1319.

Fackler, Martin and Steve Lohr. 2010. "U.S. Hears Echo of Japan's Woes," *New York Times,* Oct. 30. Available at tinyurl.com/3w94onv.

Farjoun, Emmanuel and Moshé Machover. 1983. *Laws of Chaos.* London: Verso.

Federal Deposit Insurance Corporation, Division of Research and Statistics. 1997. *History of the Eighties—Lessons for the Future,* vol. 1. Available at www.fdic.gov/bank/historical/history/vol1.html.

Federal Reserve Bank of San Francisco. 2007. *The Subprime Mortgage Market: National and Twelfth District Developments* (2007 Annual Report). Available at tinyurl.com/634qdxa.

Feldstein, Martin S. 2008. "Did Wages Reflect Growth in Productivity?" National Bureau of Economic Research, Working Paper No. 13953, Apr.

Fisher, Irving. 1933. "The Debt-Deflation Theory of Great Depressions," *Econometrica,* 1:4, 337–57.

Fogel, Robert W. 2007. "Capitalism and Democracy in 2040: Forecasts and Speculations," National Bureau of Economic Research, Working Paper No. 13184, June.

—— 2010. "$123,000,000,000,000: China's Estimated Economy by the Year 2040. Be warned," *Foreign Policy,* Jan.–Feb. Available at tinyurl.com/ycplbe6.

Foster, John Bellamy and Fred Magdoff. 2008. "Financial Implosion and Stagnation: Back to the Real Economy," *Monthly Review* 60:7, Dec., 1–29. Available at tinyurl.com/2evjc9f.

—— 2009. *The Great Financial Crisis: Causes and consequences.* New York: Monthly Review Press.

Francis, David R. 2007. "Supply-siders Take Some Lumps," *Christian Science Monitor,* Oct. 1. Available at tinyurl.com/5wdy4dq.

Freeman, Alan. 2009. "What Makes the US Profit Rate Fall?" Available at tinyurl.com/y9pfjgl.

Friedman, Milton. 1999. "Mr. Market" [Interview with Friedman], *HooverDigest.* Available at tinyurl.com/3zmqryt. Reprinted from *Barron's,* Aug. 24, 1998.

Fry, Richard and D'Vera Cohn. 2010. "Women, Men and the New Economics of Marriage." Pew Research Center. Available at tinyurl.com/3mxxan4.

Fullarton, John. 1845. *On the Regulation of Currencies,* 2nd edn. London: John Murray.

Gerschenkron, Alexander. 1962. *Economic Backwardness in Historical Perspective: A Book of Essays.* Cambridge, MA: Belknap Press of Harvard University Press.

Geske, Michael J., Valerie A. Ramey, and Matthew D. Shapiro. 2004. "Why Do Computers Depreciate?" Available at tinyurl.com/3cbt3jh.

Gjerstad, Steven and Vernon L. Smith. 2009. "Monetary Policy, Credit Extension, and Housing Bubbles," *Critical Review* 21:2–3, 269–300.

Goldberg, J.J. 2010. "What Actually Undermined the Kibbutz," *Jewish Daily Forward,* Apr. 16. Available at www.forward.com/articles/127122.

Greenspan, Alan. 1996. "The Challenge of Central Banking in a Democratic Society," Dec. 5. Available at tinyurl.com/3sbvpgc.

—— 2000. "Technology and the Economy," Jan. 13. Available at tinyurl.com/a23za.

—— 2009. "The Fed Didn't Cause the Housing Bubble," *Wall Street Journal,* Mar. 11. Available at tinyurl.com/bz5aqc.

Hahnel, Robin. 2010a. "The Economic Crisis and the Left," *ZNet,* Mar. 16. Available at tinyurl.com/638c84l.

—— 2010b. Re: Internal Contradictions [blog comment], *ZNet,* Mar. 17, 21:39 p.m. Available at tinyurl.com/638c84l.

Harman, Chris. 2007. "Theorising Neoliberalism," *International Socialism Journal* no. 117. Available at www.isj.org.uk/?id=399.

—— 2009. *Zombie Capitalism: Global Crisis and the Relevance of Marx.* London: Bookmarks.

Harvey, David. 2010. *The Enigma of Capital and the Crises of Capitalism.* Oxford: Oxford University Press.

Henwood, Doug. 1994. "After Non-collapse," *Left Business Observer* no. 63, May. Available at tinyurl.com/67upgxa.

Herman, Shelby W. et al. 2003. *Fixed Assets and Consumer Durable Goods in the United States,* U.S. Department of Commerce, Bureau of Economic Analysis, Washington, DC: U.S. Government Printing Office. Available at www.bea.gov/national/pdf/Fixed_Assets_1925_97.pdf.

Herszenhorn, David M., Carl Hulse, and Sheryl Gay Stolberg. 2008. "Talks Implode During a Day of Chaos; Fate of Bailout Plan Remains Unresolved," *New York Times,* Sept. 26. Available at tinyurl.com/3oqnvu.

Hilferding, Rudolf. 1981. *Finance Capital: A Study of the Latest Phase of Capitalist Development.* London: Routledge & Kegan Paul.

Holloway, John. 2002. *Change the World Without Taking Power: The Meaning of Revolution Today*. London: Pluto Press.

Hoover, Herbert. 1952. *The Memoirs of Herbert Hoover*, Vol. 3: *The Great Depression, 1929–1941*. New York: Macmillan.

Husson, Michel. 2008. "A Systemic Crisis, Both Global and Long-Lasting," Workers' Liberty website, July 24. Available at tinyurl.com/6bk2c29.

—— 2009. "Les Coûts Historiques d'Andrew Kliman." Nouveau Parti Anticapitaliste website, Dec. 27. Available at tinyurl.com/3d5bkqg. Also available at hussonet. free.fr/histokli.pdf.

—— 2010. "The Debate on the Rate of Profit," *International Viewpoint Online*, no. 426, July. Available at tinyurl.com/6ffkafd.

IFSL Research. 2010. *Banking 2010*. Available at tinyurl.com/6ztbhkp.

Izzo, Phil. 2010. "Economists Split Over Financial Overhaul," *Wall Street Journal* blog, July 15. Available at tinyurl.com/6g6cfsb.

Jablecki, Juliusz and Mateusz Machaj. 2009. "The Regulated Meltdown of 2008," *Critical Review* 21:2–3, 301–28.

Jaclard, Anne. 2010. "You Can't Change the Mode of Production with a Political Agenda," *With Sober Senses*, Aug. 20. Available at www.marxist-humanist-initiative.org/?p=444.

James, C.L.R. and Grace C. Lee. 2006. *Facing Reality*. Chicago, IL: Charles H. Kerr.

Katz, Arnold J. and Shelby W. Herman. 1997. "Improved Estimates of Fixed Reproducible Tangible Wealth, 1929–95," *Survey of Current Business*, 69–92. May.

Kliman, Andrew. 1999. "Debt, Economic Crisis, and the Tendential Fall in the Profit Rate." Available at akliman.squarespace.com/crisis-intervention.

—— 2003. "Value Production and Economic Crisis: A Temporal Analysis," in Richard Westra and Alan Zuege (eds), *Value and the World Economy Today*. London and New York: Palgrave Macmillan, 119–36.

—— 2007. *Reclaiming Marx's "Capital": A Refutation of the Myth of Inconsistency*. Lanham, MD: Lexington Books.

—— 2009. "'The Destruction of Capital' and the Current Economic Crisis," *Socialism and Democracy* 23:2, 47–54.

—— 2010a. "Masters of Words: A Reply to Michel Husson on the Character of the Latest Economic Crisis," *Marxism 21* 7:2, 239–81.

—— 2010b. "Showdown at the HM Corral: On Duménil and Lévy's cherry picking of the data," Feb. 19. Available at akliman.squarespace.com/crisis-intervention (Ethics section).

—— 2011. "The Reproduction Schemes as an Unbalanced Growth Model," *Critique of Political Economy* 1, 33–61.

Kolo, Vincent. 2009. "Chinese Regime Braced for 'Mass Conflicts' in 2009," *Chinaworker*, Jan. 8. chinaworker.info/en/content/news/606/.

Krugman, Paul. 2008. *Frontline* television interview, Nov. 14. Edited transcript available at tinyurl.com/d9pcb6.

—— and Robin Wells. 2010. "The Slump Goes On. Why?," *New York Review of Books*, Sept. 30. Available at tinyurl.com/429uz6p.

Laibman, David. 1999. "Okishio and His Critics: Historical Cost Versus Replacement Cost," *Research in Political Economy* 17, 207–27.

Lapavitsas, Costas. 2010. "Financialisation and Capitalist Accumulation: Structural Accounts of the Crisis of 2007–9," Feb. Research on Money and Finance Discussion Paper, School of Oriental and African Studies, University of London.

Lenin, V.I. 1971. *The State and Revolution*. In Lenin, V. I., *Selected Works: One-volume edition*, pp. 264–351. New York: International Publishers.

Lockrow, Michael. 2009. "Bubble Mania Beginning?," Asia Risk Return blog, Nov. 12. Available at tinyurl.com/3un9gb2.

Luxemburg, Rosa. 1964. *The Accumulation of Capital*. New York: Monthly Review Press.

Mandel, Ernest. 1991. Introduction. In Marx, Karl, *Capital: A Critique of Political Economy*, Vol. III, pp. 1–90. London: Penguin.

Marx, Karl. 1973. *Grundrisse: Foundations of the Critique of Political Economy*. London: Penguin.

—— 1989a. "Critique of the Gotha Programme," in Marx, Karl, *Karl Marx, Frederick Engels: Collected Works*, Vol. 24, pp. 75–99. New York: International Publishers.

—— 1989b. *Karl Marx, Frederick Engels: Collected Works*, Vol. 32. New York: International Publishers.

—— 1989c. "Marginal Notes on Adolph Wagner's *Lehrbuch der Politischen Oekonomie* [Notes on Wagner]," in Marx, Karl, *Karl Marx, Frederick Engels: Collected Works*, Vol. 24, pp. 531–59. New York: International Publishers.

—— 1990a. *Capital: A Critique of Political Economy*, Vol. I. London: Penguin.

—— 1990b. "Results of the Immediate Process of Production," in Marx, Karl, *Capital: A Critique of Political Economy*, Vol. I., pp. 948–1084. London: Penguin.

—— 1991a. *Capital: A Critique of Political Economy*, Vol. III. London: Penguin.

—— 1991b. *Karl Marx, Frederick Engels: Collected Works*, Vol. 33. New York: International Publishers.

—— 1994. *Karl Marx, Frederick Engels: Collected Works*, Vol. 34. New York: International Publishers.

Mattick, Paul [Jr.]. 2011. *Business as Usual: The Economic Crisis and the Failure of Capitalism*. London: Reaktion Books.

McNally, David. 2011. *Global Slump: The Economics and Politics of Crisis and Resistance*. Oakland: PM Press.

The MIT Dictionary of Modern Economics, 4th edn. 1992, David W. Pearce (ed.) Cambridge, MA: The MIT Press.

Morgenson, Gretchen. 2010a. "Count on Sequels to TARP," *New York Times*, Oct. 3. Available at tinyurl.com/3p5e2pk.

—— 2010b. "Strong Enough for Tough Stains?," *New York Times*, June 27. Available at tinyurl.com/3xmwr9f.

Moseley, Fred. 2008. "Some Notes on the Crunch and the Crisis," *International Socialism* No. 119. Available at tinyurl.com/3sh5lf5.

—— 2009. "The U.S. Economic Crisis: Causes and Solutions," *International Socialist Review* 64, March–April. Available at tinyurl.com/yzkey8s.

Nakajima, Chizu. 2010. "Monday View: Greed's the Sole Cause of Every Financial Crisis," *Daily Mail (Mail Online)*, June 20. Available at tinyurl.com/5ujpoe9.

National Council on Public Works Improvement. 1988. *Fragile Foundations: A Report on America's Public Works*, Feb., np. Available at tinyurl.com/6yhouoo.

New York Times. 2007. "Citi Chief on Buyouts: 'We're Still Dancing'," July 10. Available at tinyurl.com/66dtljx.

Office of Financial Stability, United States Department of the Treasury. 2010. *Troubled Asset Relief Program: Two Year Retrospective*, Oct. Available at tinyurl.com/4yvokyd.

Okishio, Nobuo. 1961. "Technical Changes and the Rate of Profit," *Kobe University Economic Review* 7, 85–99.

Onishi, Hiroshi. 2011. "The Ongoing World Crisis as Already Explained by *Capital* in 1868 and Imperialism in 1917," *World Review of Political Economy* 2:1, 26–34.

Piketty, Thomas, and Emmanuel Saez. 2003. "Income Inequality in the United States, 1913–1998," *Quarterly Journal of Economics*, 118:1, 1–39.

Posner, Richard A. 2009. *A Failure of Capitalism: The Crisis of '08 and the Descent Into Depression*. Cambridge, MA: Harvard University Press.

Potts, Nick. 2009. "Back to C19th Business as Usual: A Surprise?" Presented at conference of the Association for Heterodox Economics, Kingston (London), July.

—— 2011. "Marx and the Crisis," *Capital & Class* [forthcoming].

Ramirez, Steven. 2010. "Dodd-Frank I: Section 121 and Prudential Divestitures," Corporate Justice blog, July 20. Available at tinyurl.com/3c75whz.

Rasmussen Reports. 2009. "Just 53% Say Capitalism Better Than Socialism," Apr. 9. Available at tinyurl.com/ylcedqy.

Reich, Robert B. 2010. "How to End the Great Recession," *New York Times*, Sept. 2. Available at tinyurl.com/26cra4p.

Reinhart, Carmen M. and Kenneth S. Rogoff. 2008. "Banking Crises: An Equal Opportunity Menace." NBER Working Paper No. 14587, Dec.

—— 2009. *This Time is Different: Eight Centuries of Financial Folly*. Princeton, NJ and Oxford: Princeton University Press.

Resnick, Stephen and Wolff, Richard. 2010. "The Economic Crisis: A Marxian Interpretation," *Rethinking Marxism* 22:2, 170–86. Available at tinyurl.com/3k65m24.

Roberts, Michael. 2009. *The Great Recession: Profit Cycles, Economic Crisis. A Marxist View*. London: Lulu Enterprises.

Rosengren, Eric S. 2008. "The Impact of Financial Institutions and Financial Markets on the Real Economy: Implications of a 'Liquidity Lock'," Oct. 9. Available at tinyurl.com/432yo9j.

Rostow, W.W. 1960. *The Stages of Economic Growth: A Non-Communist Manifesto*. Cambridge: Cambridge University Press.

Schmidt-Hebbel, Klaus, Luis Serven, and Andrés Solimano. 1994. "Saving, Investment, and Growth in Developing Countries: An Overview." Policy Research Working Paper No. 1382, World Bank, Nov.

Schumpeter, Joseph A. *History of Economic Analysis*. New York: Oxford University Press.

——1976. *Capitalism, Socialism and Democracy*. New York: Harper & Row.

Shaikh, Anwar. 1978. "An Introduction to the History of Crisis Theories," in *U.S. Capitalism in Crisis*. New York: URPE.

—— 1999. [Post on "long wave recovery"], Progressive Economists News List, Feb. 5. Available at tinyurl.com/3emqgcy.

Shiller, Robert J. 2008. "The Fed Gets a New Job Description," *New York Times*, Apr. 6. Available at tinyurl.com/5nup49.

Silverstein, Ken. 2010. "Six Questions for Richard Posner on Capitalism and Crisis," *Harper's Magazine* (web content), Mar. 17. Available at tinyurl.com/6a8qh4n.

Skapinker, Michael. 2008. "The Market No Longer Has All the Answers," *Financial Times (ft.com)*, Mar. 24. Available at tinyurl.com/45ypvcg.

Socialist Voice. 2008. "The Economic Crisis: Greed is the Cause," *Socialist Voice*, July. Available at tinyurl.com/6cv5vw9.

Stiglitz, Joseph. 2008. "How to Prevent the Next Wall Street Crisis," *CNN.com*, Sept. 17. Available at tinyurl.com/5vdvs7b.

—— 2009. "The Anatomy of a Murder: Who Killed America's Economy?," *Critical Review* 21:2–3, 329–39.

Stockhammer, Engelbert. 2009. "The Finance-dominated Accumulation Regime, Income Distribution and the Present Crisis," Apr. Department of Economics

Working Paper No. 127, Vienna University of Economics & Business Administration.

Sweezy, Paul M. 1970. *The Theory of Capitalist Development: Principles of Marxian Political Economy*. New York: Modern Reader Paperbacks.

—— 1995. "Economic Reminiscences, *Monthly Review* 47:1, 1–11, May.

Taylor, John B. 2009. "Economic Policy and the Financial Crisis: An Empirical Analysis of What Went Wrong," *Critical Review* 21:2–3, 341–64.

Tevlin, Stacey and Karl Whelan. 2003. "Explaining the Investment Boom of the 1990s," *Journal of Money, Credit and Banking*, 35:1, Feb., 1–22.

U.S. Department of Commerce, Bureau of Economic Analysis. 2003. *Fixed Assets and Consumer Durable Goods in the United States, 1925–99*. Washington, DC: U.S. Government Printing Office. Available at bea.gov/national/pdf/Fixed_Assets_1925_97.pdf.

—— 2008. BEA Depreciation Estimates. Available at bea.gov/national/FA2004/Tablecandtext.pdf.

U.S. Department of Commerce. 2009. *Statistical Abstract of the United States, 2009: The National Data Book*. Available at tinyurl.com/5rmo4sg.

U.S. Department of Labor, Office of the Secretary. 2005. Submission for OMB Review: Comment Request, Apr. 8. Available at tinyurl.com/6bwrgt5.

U.S. Senate Committee on Foreign Relations (Subcommittee on Foreign Relations). 1977. *International Debt, the Banks, and U.S. Foreign Policy*, 95th Cong., 1st session.

Vey, P. 2009. "These new regulations will fundamentally change the way we get around them" (cartoon), *The New Yorker*, Mar. 9. Available at tinyurl.com/6ekbdl9.

Wallinson, Peter. 2010. "The Dodd-Frank Act: Creative Destruction, Destroyed," *Wall Street Journal* (online), Aug. 31. Available at tinyurl.com/5uhjjzz.

Weeks, John. 2011. *Capital, Exploitation and Economic Crisis*. London: Routledge.

Weiner, Edward. 1999. *Urban Transportation Planning in the United States: An Historical Overview*, revised and expanded edn. Westport, CT: Praeger.

White, Lawrence H. 2010. "The Roaring Twenties and the Austrian Business Cycle Theory" (Chapter 3 of *The Clash of Economic Ideas*), June. Working paper no. 10-29, Mercatus Center, George Mason University.

Wolff, Rick. 2008a. "Capitalism's Crisis through a Marxian Lens," *MRZine*, Dec. 14. Available at mrzine.monthlyreview.org/2008/wolff141208.html.

Wolff, Richard. 2008b. "Capitalist Crisis, Marx's Shadow," *MRZine*, Sept. 26. Available at mrzine.monthlyreview.org/2008/wolff260908.html.

—— 2010. "Taking Over the Enterprise," Jan. 10. Available at tinyurl.com/5ro2r9x.

Wong, Stephanie, John Liu, and Tim Culpan. 2010. "IPhone Workers Say 'Meaningless' Life Sparks Suicides," Bloomberg News, June 2. Available at tinyurl.com/28dok36.

Ye, Juliet, and Andrew Batson. 2009. "Calculating China's Unemployment Rate," *Wall Street Journal* blog, Apr. 2. Available at tinyurl.com/3qvumzs.

Zinn, Howard. 2008. "Spend the Bailout Money on the Middle Class," *The Nation*, Oct. 27, 4–5.

Index

accelerating growth, 168, 171, 173–4, 175–6, 179–80

accumulation of capital, *see* investment

actual-potential labor force gap, *see* labor–market conditions

AIG, 35, 181, 184

alternative to capitalism, 203–6

Asian currency crisis, *see* East Asian currency crisis

Asian Tigers, 176, 186

austerity measures, 183, 203–4

bailouts, 182–3, 194, *see also individual entries*

Baker, Dean, 36–38

Bank of America, 35

banking crises, 57–9, *see also* savings and loan crisis

Baran, Paul, 12, 151, 162, 167–75, 178–80, 224n14, 224n15

Bear Stearns, 181–3, 184, 225n1

Beggs, Mike, 103

benefits, government-provided, 223n3

Bernanke, Ben, 40–1, 44–46, 182, 196–7, 202, 209n7

Bleaney, Michael, 223n8

book value, 109

Bosworth, Barry, 155–6, 219n1

Branigan, Tania, 189

Brenner, Robert, 9–10, 15, 208n1 (chap. 1), 208n2 (chap. 2)

Bretton Woods system, 58–9, 73, 191

bubbles, 210n2, *see also* dot-com bubble, home-price bubble

Bullard, James, 184

Burkhauser, Richard, 159–60, 220n3, 223n7

Bush, George W., 34, 183

capital-gains tax, on home resales, 29

capitalism, 1

  alternative to, 203–6

  capitalists as personifications of, 196

  collapse of, 4, 26, 181, 183, 198–9, 210n14

  instability of, 26–7, 196–7, 183, 184–5, 202–3, 225n3

  internal contradictions, 26–7, 106

  and owners' interests, 181–3, 185

  public opinion regarding, 203

  and working people's interests, 198, 200–2, 226n11

  see also capitalist production; state-capitalism

capitalist production, 1–2, 6–7, 51, 124

  contradictory nature, 26–7

  and cost-cutting, 184, 205–6

  goal of, 20–1, 183, 210n16, 226n11

  see also value

Carchedi, Guglielmo, 7–8

Carroll, Lewis, 108

causality, 1, 96–97

  indirect, 16, 217n3

Celasun, Oya, 24

centralization of capital, 184

Chang, Gordon, 197, 226n7

cherry picking, of data, 67, 104–5, 110, 178, 217n4

China, 199, 204

  compensation of employees, 186–7, 188, 226n5

  economic growth, 51–3, 186–8, 226n7

  exchange-rate policy, 189

  repression of workers, 188, 190

  and savings glut hypothesis, 44, 45

  unemployment, 189

  working conditions, 190

China Labour Bulletin, 190

Chrysler, 181

circulating capital, 80–2

Clarke, Simon, 201, 212n2

class struggle, 3, 24, 190, 200–2, 203–4

clearinghouses, derivatives, 194

Cohn, D'Vera, 159

collapse, *see under* capitalism